DESIGN
DUET

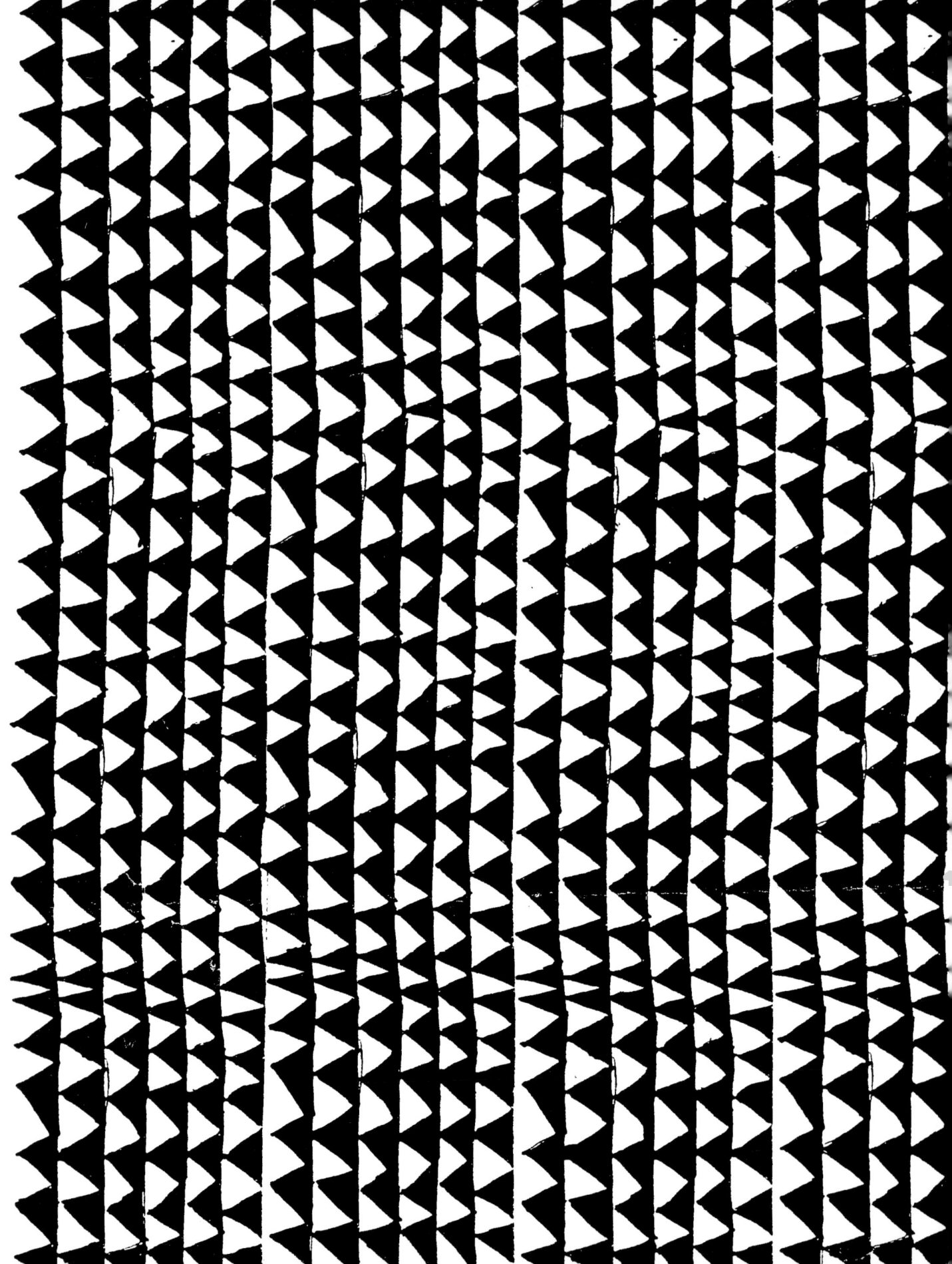

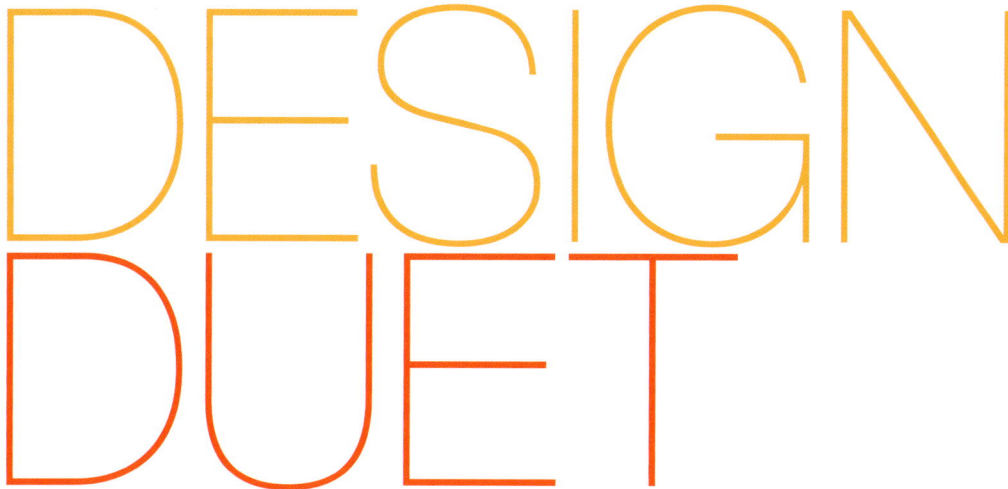

DESIGN DUET

Robert Keith Black and J. Ormond Sanderson, Jr.

Texts by Tom Patterson and Roger Manley
Photographs by John Mark Hall

NC STATE UNIVERSITY

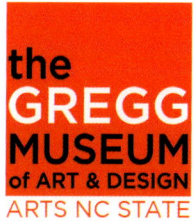
the GREGG MUSEUM of ART & DESIGN ARTS NC STATE

Published on the occasion of the exhibition
*Design Duet: the creative lives of Robert Keith Black
and J. Ormond Sanderson Jr.*
March 15–September 9, 2018

ISBN 978-0-9831217-9-4

Designed and typeset by Amy Ruth Buchanan,
3rd sister design, Durham, North Carolina.
Printed in the USA through Four Colour Print Group,
Louisville, Kentucky
All photographs by John Mark Hall unless
otherwise credited.

gregg.arts.ncsu.edu
(+1) 919.515.7902

———

(*front cover*) Robert Black, *Mystique #4*, 2010, acrylic on
canvas, 60" x 60".

(*end sheets and frontispiece*) Black and white patterns on
previous pages are examples of the raw materials Robert Black
uses to create the acrylic over paper on canvas collage paintings presented throughout this catalogue. Black, or his partner,
Ormond Sanderson, first draw patterns with ink on paper,
then photocopy them repeatedly before cutting them into tiny
squares that can be applied to canvases or other surfaces like
mosaics and painted over with transparent washes.

(*opposite*) Examples of stained glass Robert Black made while
in graduate school at the University of Georgia at Athens. Glass
objects on the table are from India.

(*pg. vi, opposite epigraph*) Ormond Sanderson, *Waltz*, ca. 1960,
enamel inside copper bowl, 7" diameter.

(*pg. vi, opposite table of contents*) Robert Black, *Divided Bowl*
with *Zodiac Disks*, mid-1970s, stoneware, 18" diameter. Detail,
with olive shells. *Photo by Roger Manley.*

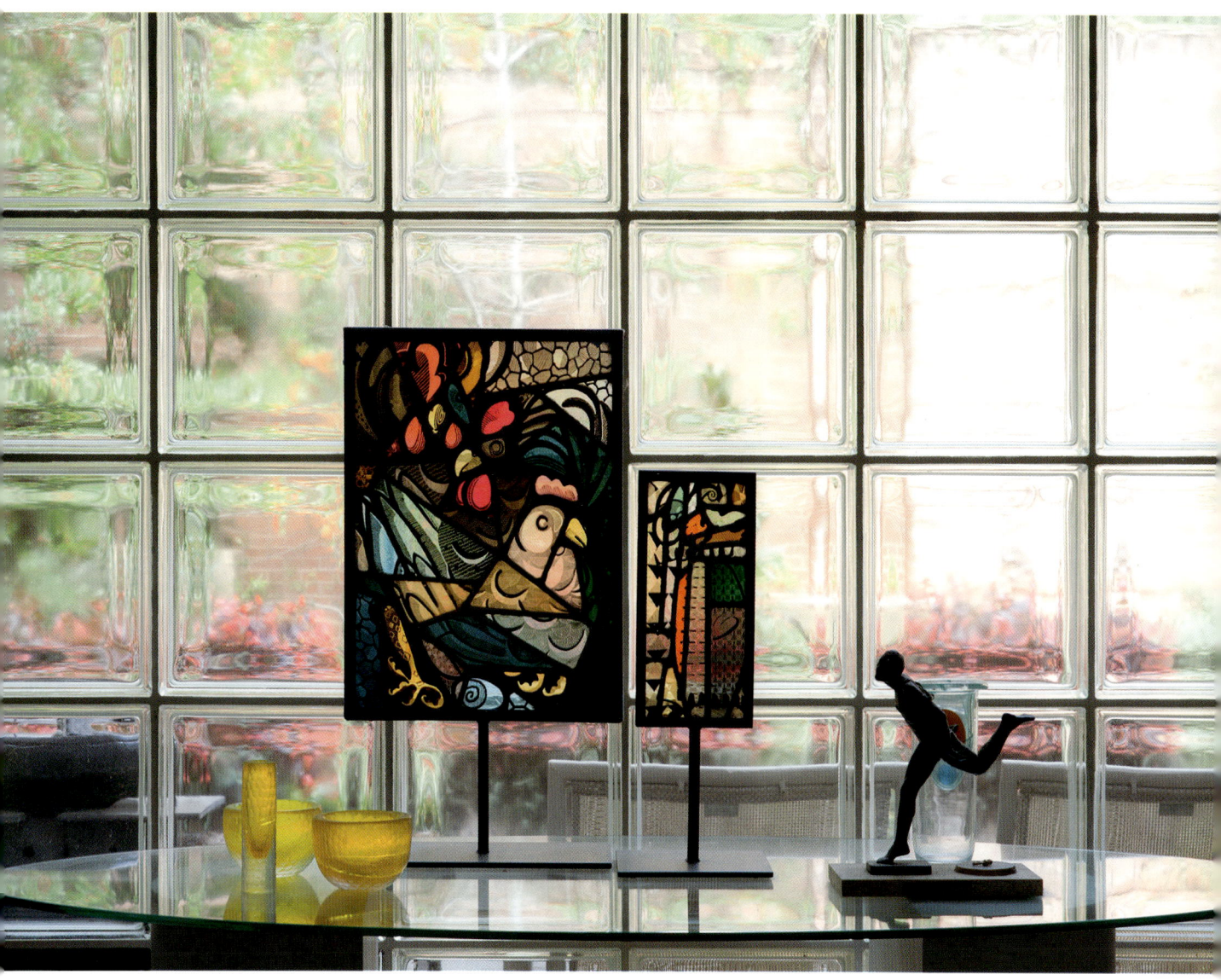

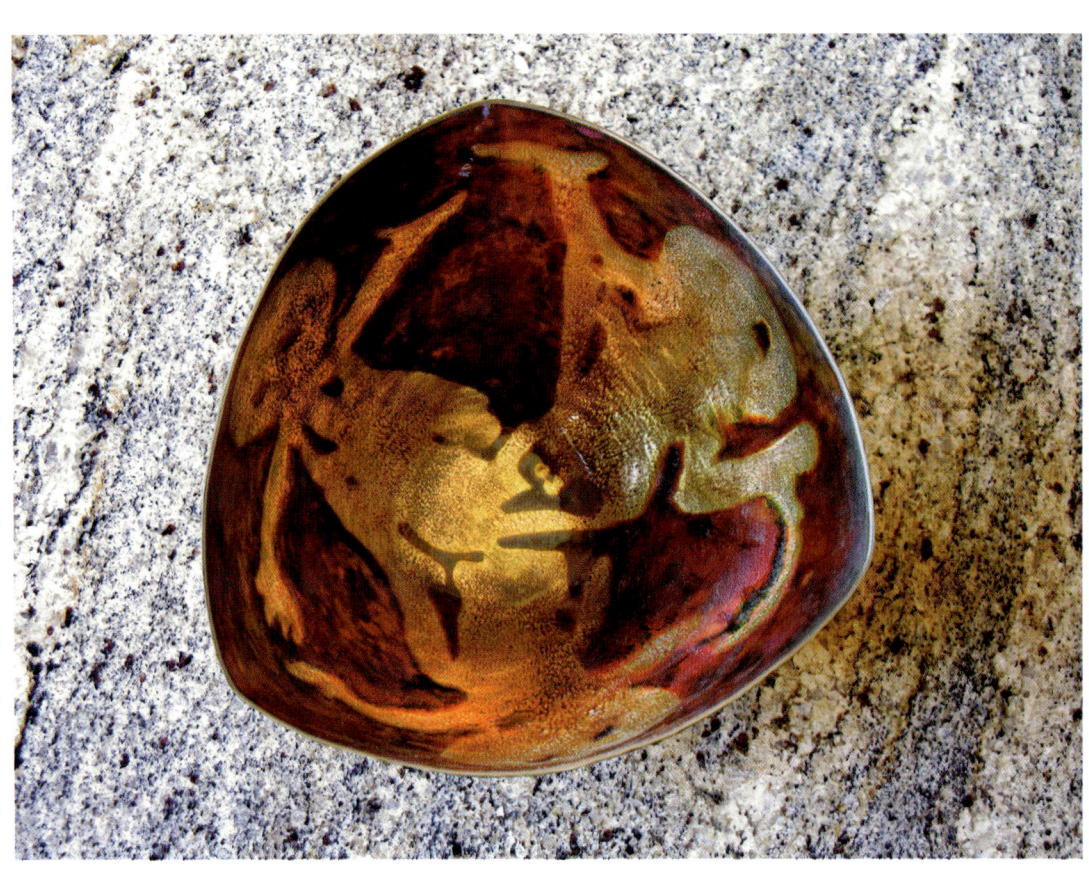

In my dreams I heard a voice:
—Habīb, would you like this onion
Or just a slice of it?
At this I fell into great disquiet
This enigmatic question
Was the question of my life!
Did I prefer the part to the whole
Or the whole to the part
No, I wanted both
The part of the whole as well as the whole
And that this choice would involve no contradiction.

—Gunnar Ekelöf

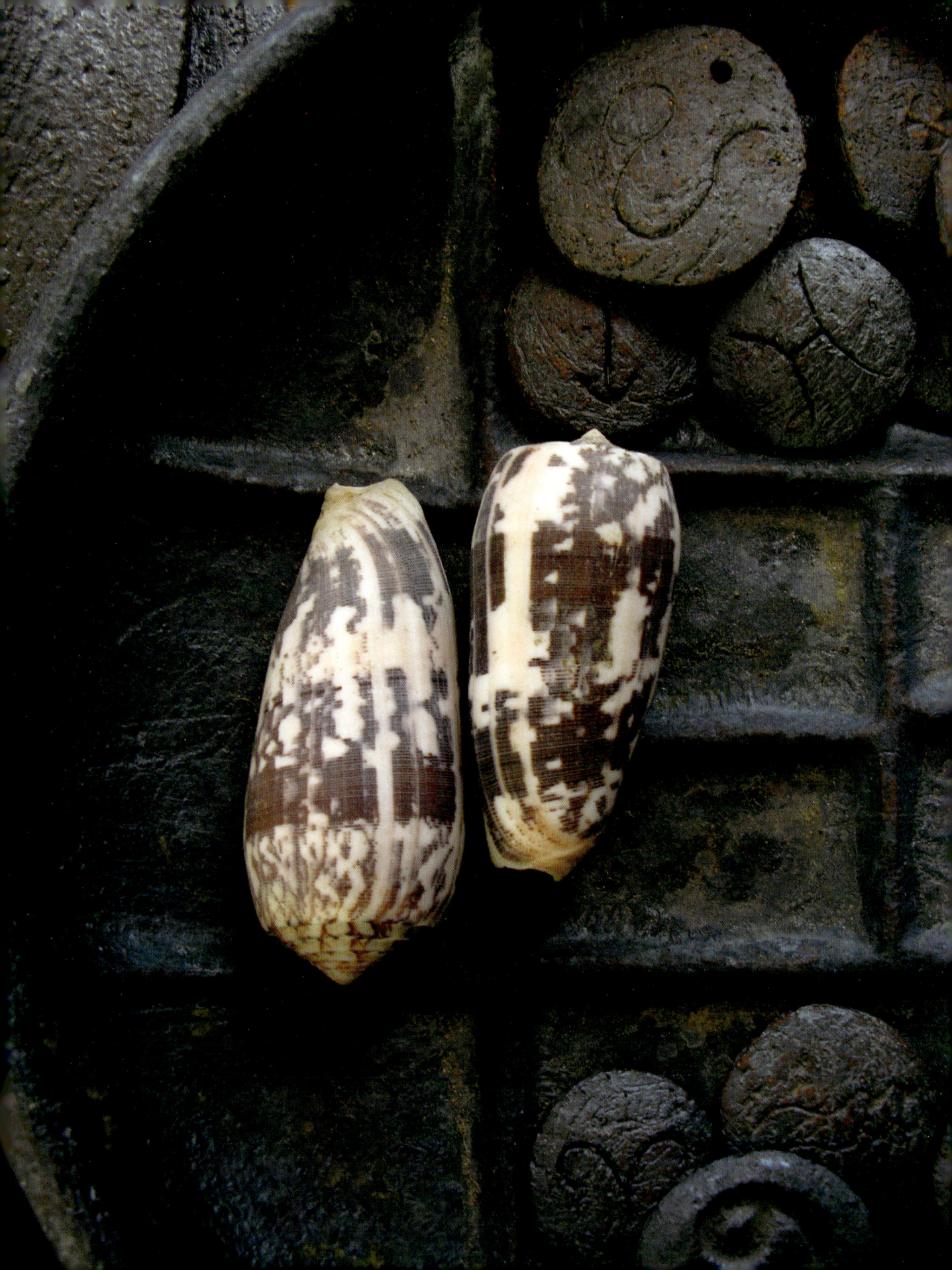

Contents

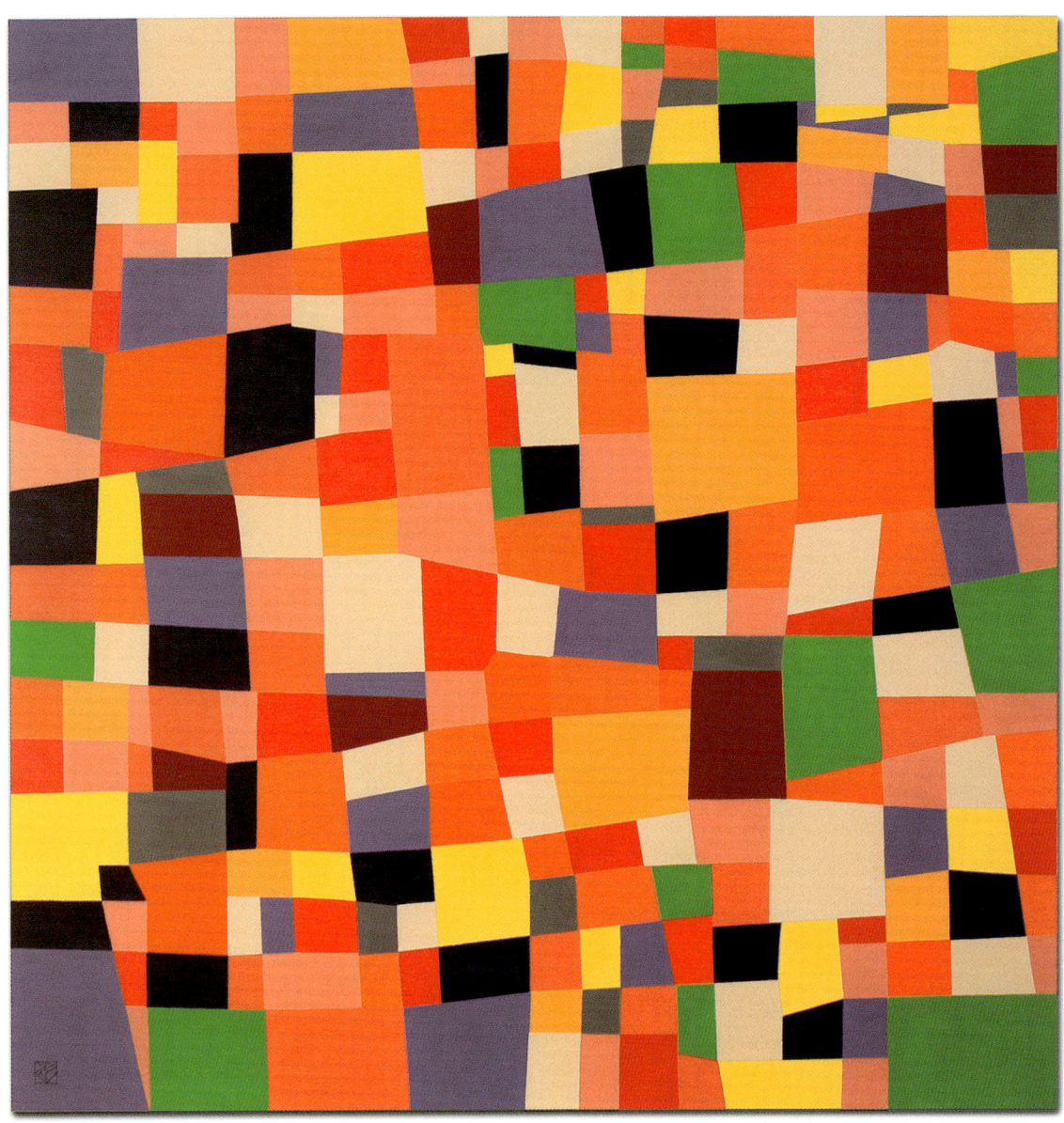

Robert Black, *Mystique* #1, 2010, acrylic on canvas, 60" x 60".

ROGER MANLEY

Tao Factor

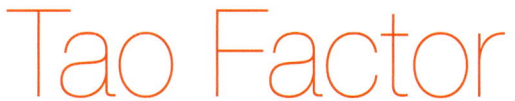

Block the openings, shut the doors, and all your life you will not run dry.
—Lao Tzu[1]

The art of mastering life is the prerequisite for all further forms of expression, whether they are paintings, sculptures, tragedies, or musical compositions.
—Paul Klee[2]

"I start with a line, and then it goes here, and then across to here, and then back again, see?" he said. As the tall, mustachioed man standing near the completed painting traced the lines with his finger, its underlying structure, which had been obscured by the dazzling colors bounded by the lines, suddenly became obvious.

He turned to another piece. This time, the lines were more regular and intricate, but the same range of colors and confident angles with which the lines intersected or caromed off one another made it a ready companion. One could imagine both of them hung as a diptych. If there were space enough on the wall, the next painting completed could join them just as easily, like another sibling in an extended family. The shelves of ceramics surrounding us were all "of a piece" as well, clustered into groups of heads or seated figures, anthropomorphic animals with rudimentary human faces, polyhedral pots or pots with swirling bas-

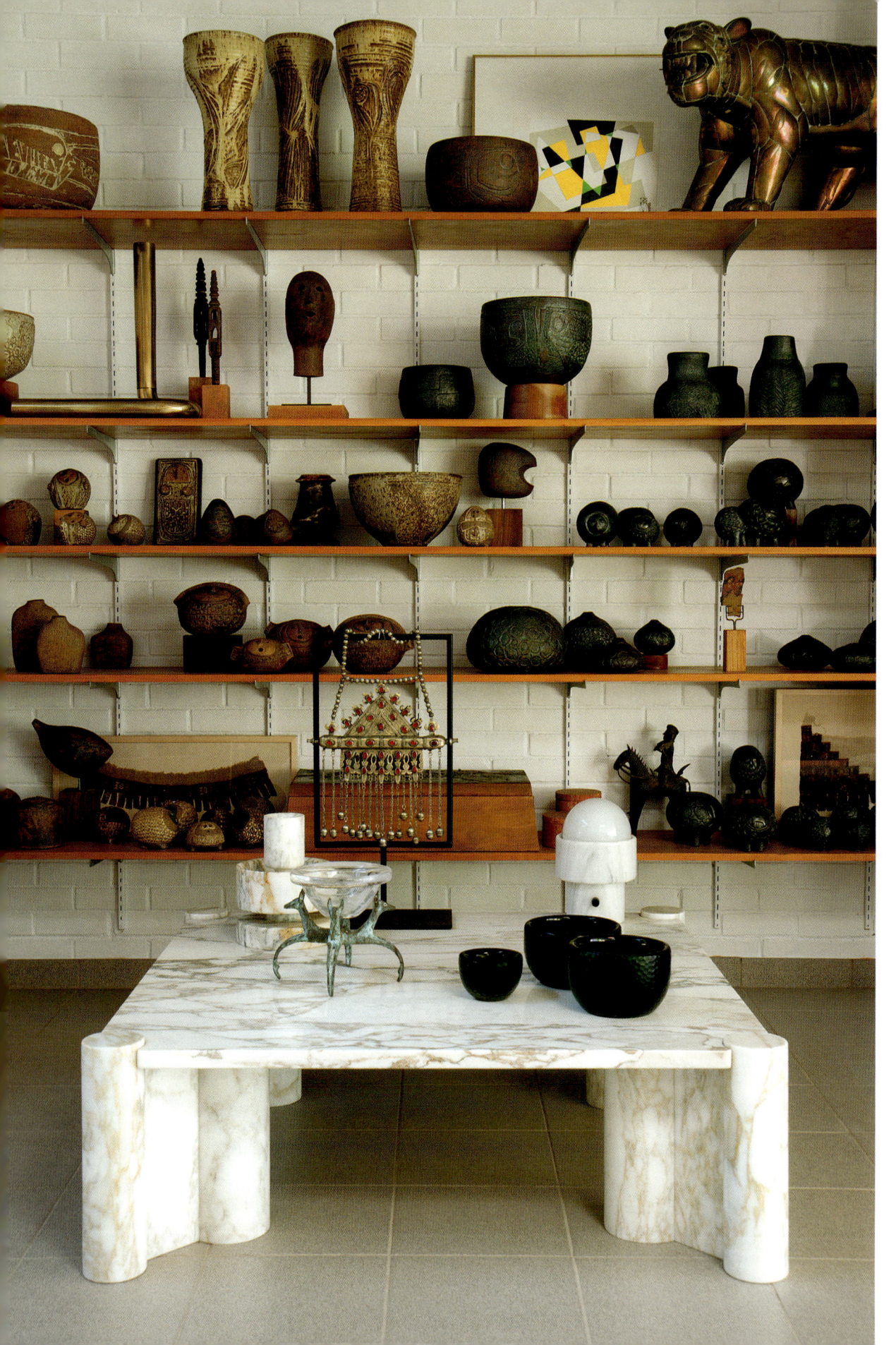

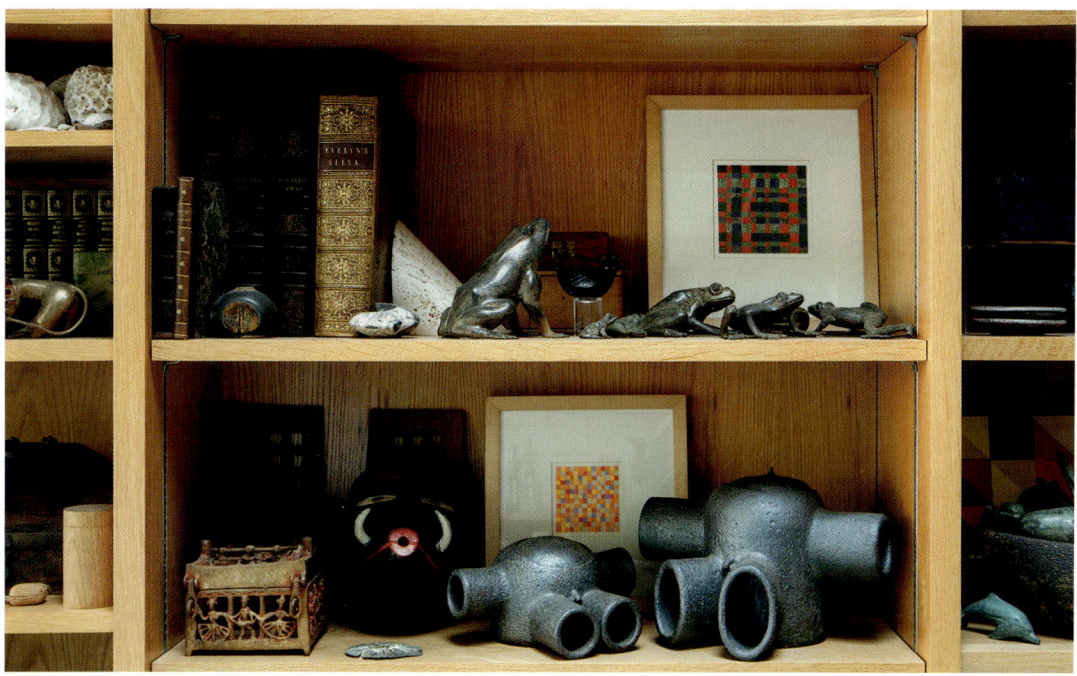

relief designs, by turns highly textured or with iridescent metallic surfaces, each seeming to belong among its nearest neighbors. Frogs and toads or tiny containers covered with collaged paper mosaics punctuated the expanded still life arrangements offered on every shelf.

Robert Black has been steadily making art for more than seventy years, and although now in his late 80s, he is still busy in his studio. Due to sheer persistence and force of habit, the process of making art has become as natural to him as breathing. For Black, to be alive is to make art, and because there is almost never a gap from one day to the next, each new piece naturally streams from the one just completed, and in turn opens the way to the next that will follow. One has the impression that if all his works could be photographed in exact chronological sequence and assembled together like frames in an imaginary movie, what would emerge would be a smoothly morphing progression of childhood drawings becoming abstractions, and abstractions slowly taking on solidity to become richly sculptural bas-reliefs and then free-standing sculptures. Next, the sculptures would become more fluid and transition into ceramics, then become clay vessels turning into heads, and heads into figures, both human and animal. At some point in the same movie about his creative process, the building-up of clay to make ceramics would morph into the building up of paper pieces into

Two of Robert Black's *Playtime* sculptures sit next to a Mexican mask and brass box from India. Frogs are a favorite creature for the couple and are found throughout the house.

———

(*opposite*) "Jumbo" marble table by Gae Aulenti (1964) in front of shelves of Robert Black's stoneware. Above is a brass jaguar by Mexican artist Sergio Bustamante.

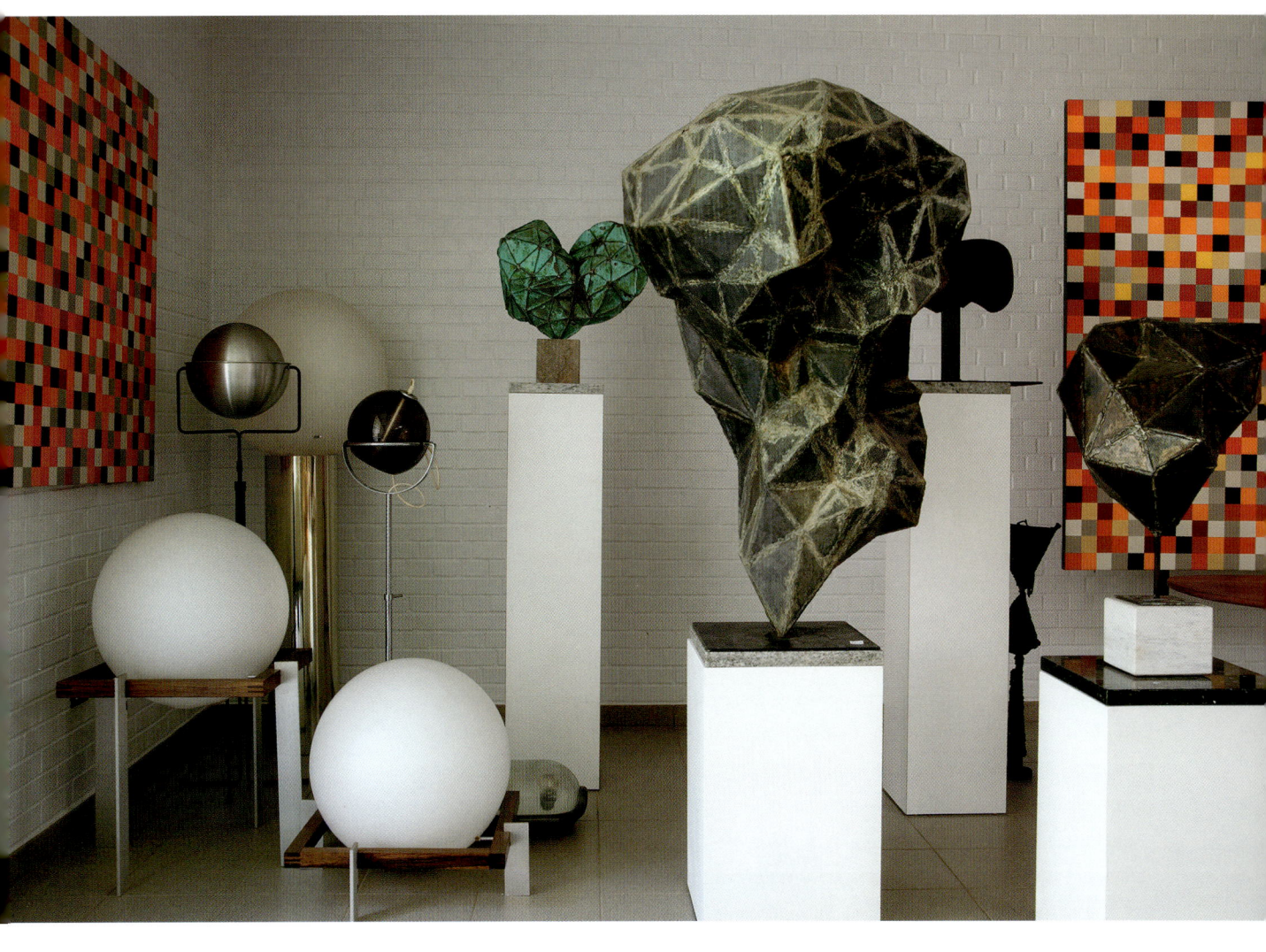

Black's massive sculpture, *Cumulus,* looms at center; to the right is *Mantra,* while behind it is the more rounded *Equilibrium*. All are brazed and patinated copper, created in 1982. Round white lamps are from Habitat. Two paintings from Black's *Exuberance* series hang behind them.

collages, then the collages would resolve into patterns and spread across canvasses, and so on, until finally coming back around to painting and back to the human face, as Black extended each new branch of his creative tree.

Though a film like that might be able to suggest such a flow, the kind of sampling of a lifelong output at dispersed intervals required to put together an overview exhibition makes such connections harder to detect. It's not easy at first to discern the links between lidded ceramic pots with monochromatic surfaces as dark and textured as meteorites, and intricately-assembled collage-paintings in bright primary colors made years later—yet they do exist.

"Drawing is the art of taking a line for a walk," said Bauhaus sage Paul Klee.[3] With that in mind, it becomes possible to see Black's work as not only taking his lines for strolls around their flat surfaces, but eventually sending them leaping off their flat canvas or paper surfaces to become angular metal sculptures or faceted pots, now not merely walking, but dancing in space. Like any human dance, the best parts happen when individuals meet. The intersections where Black's lines meet, whether on the brazed and patinated copper sculptures that resemble the clusters of mineral crystal specimens strategically parked around his studio, or on the large paintings that line the house's long central hallway, create multiple competing focal points that draw one's attention, first one place and then another, and thus generate enough energy to sustain repeated encounters with his work.[4] This is a principle that architects and great capital city planners have long understood: streets radiating from obelisks, statues, arches or grand buildings present multiple opportunities to approach these focal landmarks from a variety of angles and a yield a variety of experiences, though each possible experience and effect is entirely designed and completely intentional.

Creating stunning visual experiences is something that Black's lifetime partner, Ormond Sanderson, has mastered. Earlier in his equally long and just as dedicated artistic career he pursued music, and then took on the exacting medium of vitreous enamels, and then stained and sandblasted glass. But his creative energy for most of the past few decades has been concentrated on orchestrating the seasonal performances of thousands of perennials in the extensive interior courtyards and exterior landscaping surrounding the couple's house, as well as on the curating and staging of the incredibly varied collection of modernist furniture, ethnographic artifacts, mineral specimens, fossils, designer pieces, and decorative objects that accompanies the artworks displayed indoors.

While the bulk of the art objects that they created and now display throughout the house may be Black's, the ensemble, as a whole, largely reflects Sanderson's meticulous eye, and the harmonious effects it offers are no less of an

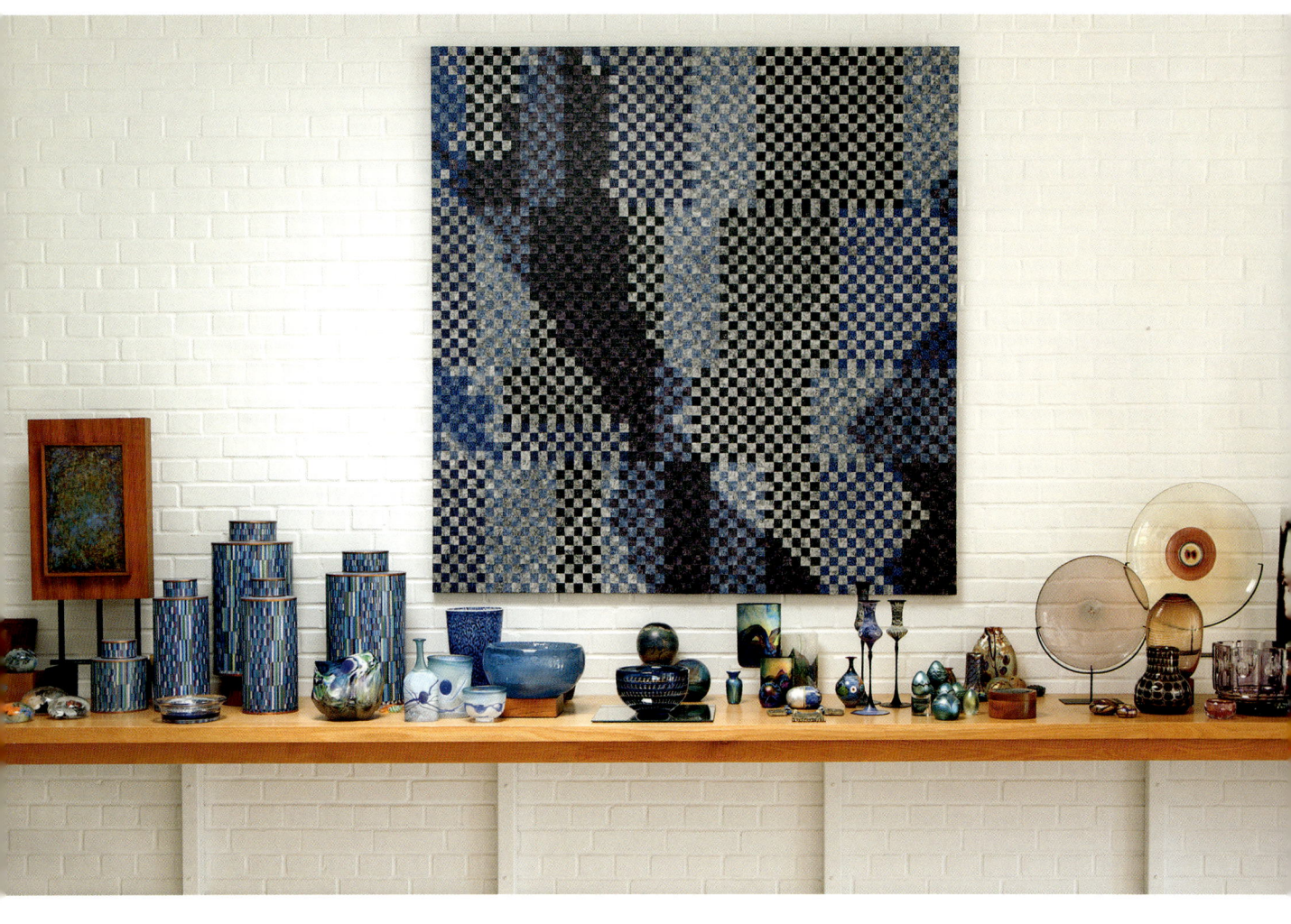

Black's painting, *Blue Ridge,* hangs above a shelf arrayed with glassware from Venini, Orrefors, Kosta Boda, and Orient and Flume. To the left are cloisonné canisters by Parisienne artist Fabienne Jouvin and enameled panels by Ormond Sanderson.

accomplishment. Although Black certainly played a major role—the design of the house was mostly his—Sanderson is primarily responsible for creating a series of environments within it that amplifies the art they've both made. Suddenly realizing that all the pieces on a particular table—an African mask, several Murano jars, Bohemian glass goblets, and iridescent eggs—have a lively texture of dots in common, calls attention to the densely dotted surface of the painting hanging above them. In another room, a Robert Black painting presenting a checkerboard pattern of variegated blues seems to flow off the canvas and into surrounding space because all of the objects that Sanderson positioned immediately around it share a similar palette, including a pair of enamels he made that easily hold their own with Black's painting.

For the visitor, recognizing the interplay between each artwork on the wall and its neighboring objects turns every encounter into a game of discovery. Every part of the house and garden offers a different tableau, perfected over a matter of years but far from static. Because the glass brick walls found throughout the house render it open to the constantly changing effects of exterior light, because the exterior landscape's vegetation constantly changes in response to seasonal climates, and because the materials that comprise so much of the interior décor are of transparent glass or light-reflecting metal, the effects achieved in each display never remain the same for long. Revisiting the same shelf at hourly intervals reveals new discoveries every time.

Tom Patterson's essay in the following pages outlines the circumstances that brought these two artists together, and portrays the journey that led them to create the private, but intensely satisfying setting they now share. At one point, he describes the house, which Black and Sanderson transformed from an abandoned rural school, as being like a temple. The description is completely apt, for a temple is a place where one goes to escape the common world of ordinary, humdrum existence. Their entryway gate, the curving drive beyond it, and the first set of exterior doors that lead to a large, enclosed courtyard presaging the interior of the house, together function as a kind of "spiritual airlock" that suddenly makes the surrounding central North Carolina countryside of soybean fields, convenience stores, and pickup-dominated roads seem utterly far away.[5]

A temple is also a place one enters in order to feel the spiritual presence of something larger than the ordinary world. In this case, that presence is evoked by beauty in all its forms. Living nature (plants, animals, the weather), natural forms (fossils, minerals), fine design, architecture, art, craft, staging, presentation, and the beautiful utility of tools are all facets of the same spirit of celebrating beauty in the secluded world that Black and Sanderson have created together. If one shares a meal or sits down to a conversation with these men, other senses besides the visual are engaged as well, and no less exquisitely.

Unfortunately, although they invite in friends and visitors from time to time and take obvious pleasure in walking them through each room and noting their astonished responses, only the two of them will ever know the vast majority of the enchantments their private world encompasses. In an attempt to convey even the vaguest sense of it, a large number of the images in this book are devoted to showing their art and collections in their context. Photographer John Mark Hall has lent his considerable compositional eye and camera skills to sharing some of the discoveries he made over the course of several days of shooting, but since these were made in only one season, they can only represent a page or two torn from the whole annual performance at best. Meanwhile, any exhibition held anywhere other than the house itself could scarcely do more than hint at the effects they've achieved.

Even so, it would have been a shame not at least to *try* to bring their art to a larger audience, for the vessels and enamels, collages, paintings, and sculptures included in the *Design Duet* exhibition still afford plenty of delights on their own. We are indebted to the two artists for lending these objects to the Gregg Museum—and temporarily diminishing their own environment—in order to allow more of the rest of us to see what they've accomplished.

While we are extremely grateful for the more than generous support they gave to the museum during its recent transformation and reopening, we would have wanted to do this exhibition anyway, even if they hadn't given anything at all, because they offer such a fine chance for the Gregg to advance one of its key educational goals, which is to encourage students to be more fearless in their pursuit of a worthwhile life. Along with encouraging awareness of *everything*— the weak as well as the strong, the spaces between things as well as the things themselves—Chinese philosopher Lao Tzu's ancient guide, the *Tao Te Ching*, stresses the importance of not becoming overly attached to a static present or remaining fixed on a single purpose, but instead keeping oneself open to potentiality and possibility.[6] Robert Black and Ormond Sanderson have proved, by their living example, that adapting themselves to evolving situations—transforming from musicians and artists to teachers, then to shop owners, then businessmen, architects, builders, landlords, collectors, and back to artists—need not come at the expense of living creatively or productively, nor mean sacrificing graciousness or dignity. If visitors to the exhibition or readers of this publication take to heart any portion of that, after seeing what these two men have done, then this presentation will have done its job.

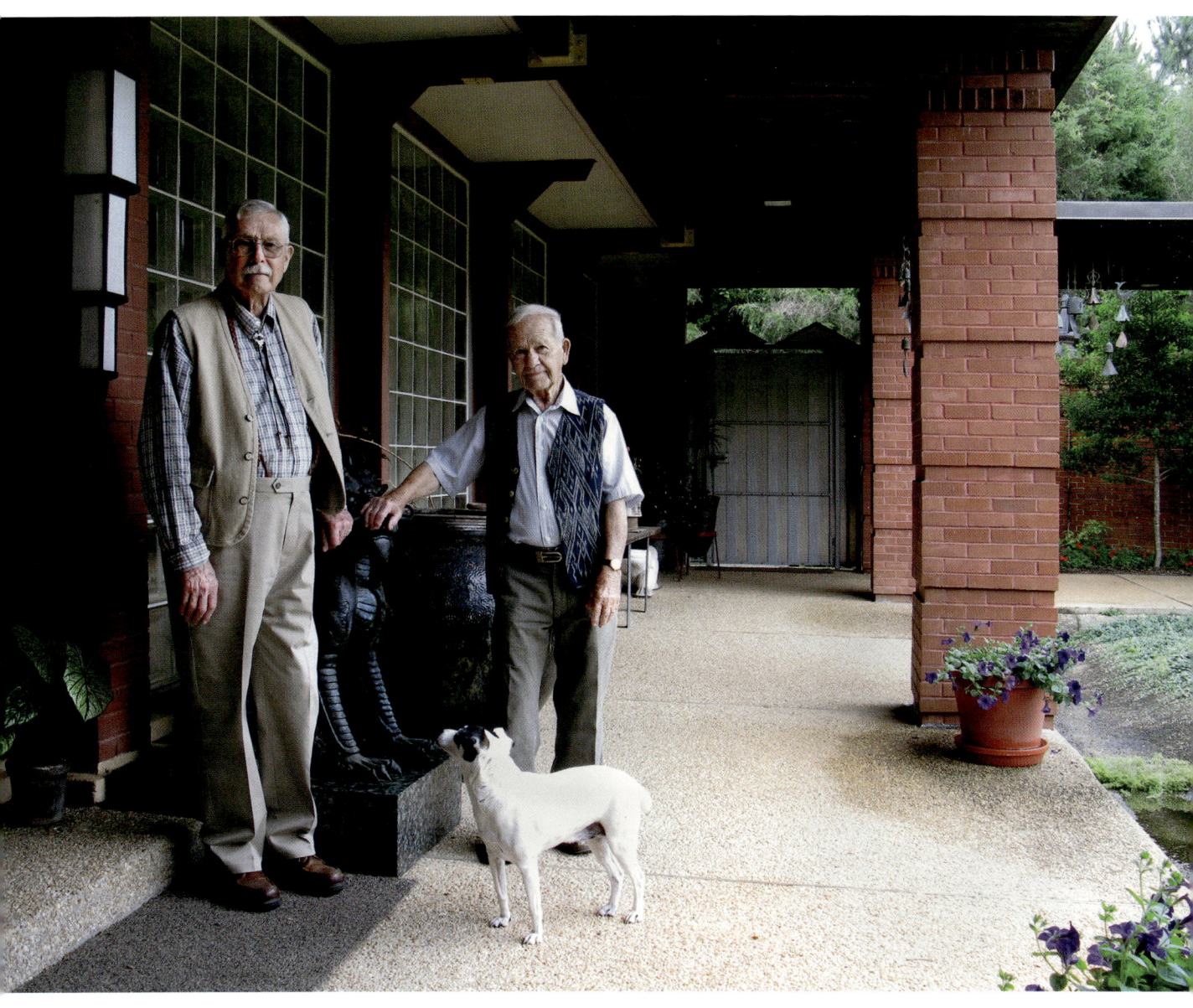

Black and Sanderson in the large courtyard with their Jack Russell Terrier, Bunky, 2017.
Photo by Roger Manley.

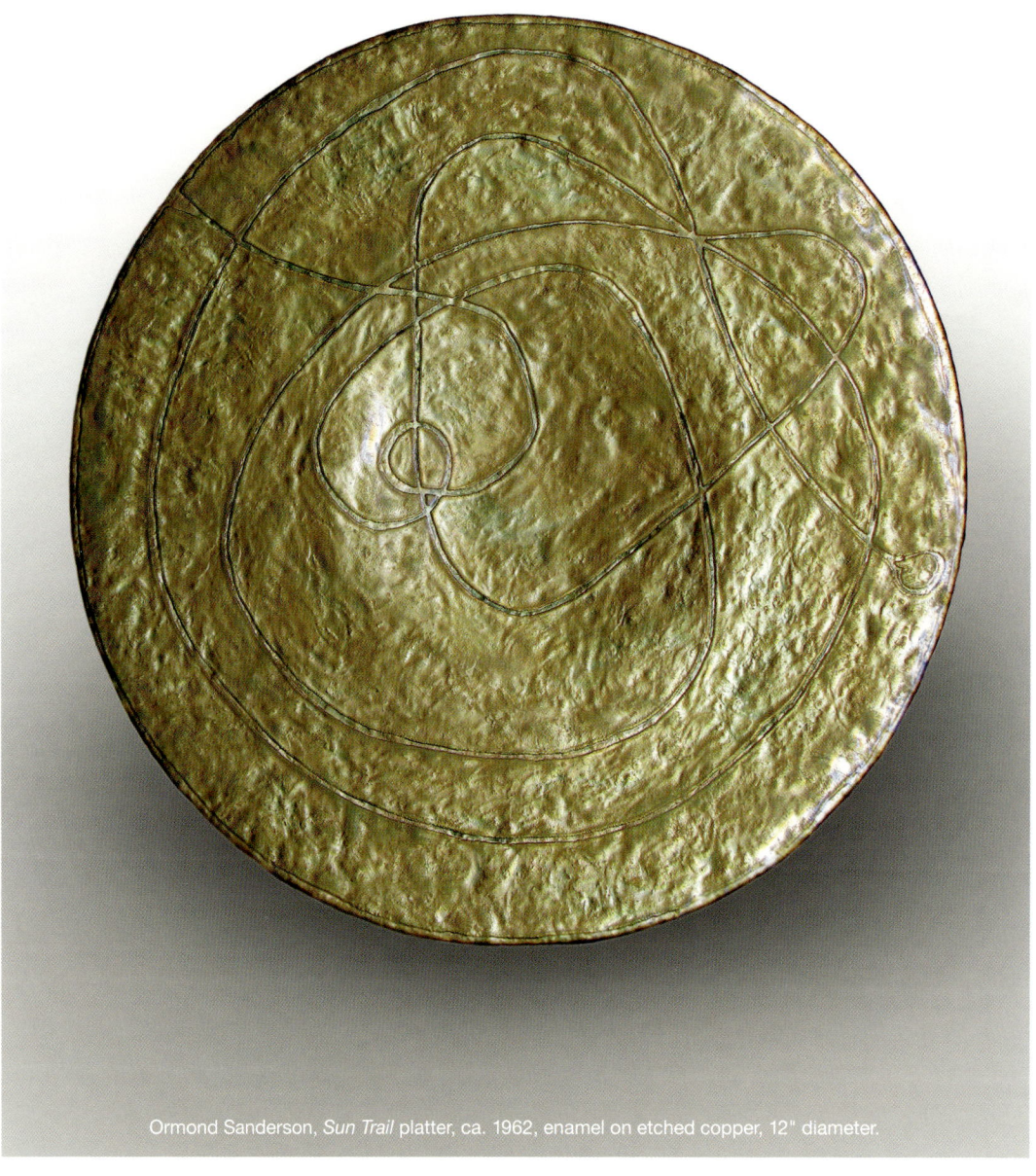

Ormond Sanderson, *Sun Trail* platter, ca. 1962, enamel on etched copper, 12" diameter.

TOM PATTERSON

A Synergy of Two

The Sixty-Year Creative Partnership of Robert Black and Ormond Sanderson

"You don't know what you're getting into until you do it."

—Ormond Sanderson

Collaboration has proved to be a creatively invigorating mode of working for many artists. Musicians join forces in bands or orchestras, dancers form troupes, and actors work as ensembles. Films and stage performances draw on the collaborative efforts of artists from multiple disciplines. The results of such joint endeavors inevitably reflect the principle of synergy, which holds that interaction of any two or more agents yields an effect greater than the sum of their parts.

Such collaborative ventures are routine in the performing arts but rarer in the literary and visual arts. The latter forms are composition-focused and typically require extended periods of introspection and solitary effort, often leaving little time and energy for close-up professional exchanges and cooperative ventures with others in the same field. Two artists who have successfully managed such a collaboration over the long haul are Robert Black and Ormond Sanderson. For sixty years, they've lived and worked together as artists, designers, and collectors, not to mention life partners. Over much of that period they were also successful purveyors of art, craft, and designer furnishings. Each has independently pursued his own art practice, but they've also devoted much of their energy to their overlapping, cooperative roles as business owners, store managers, and buyer-curators.

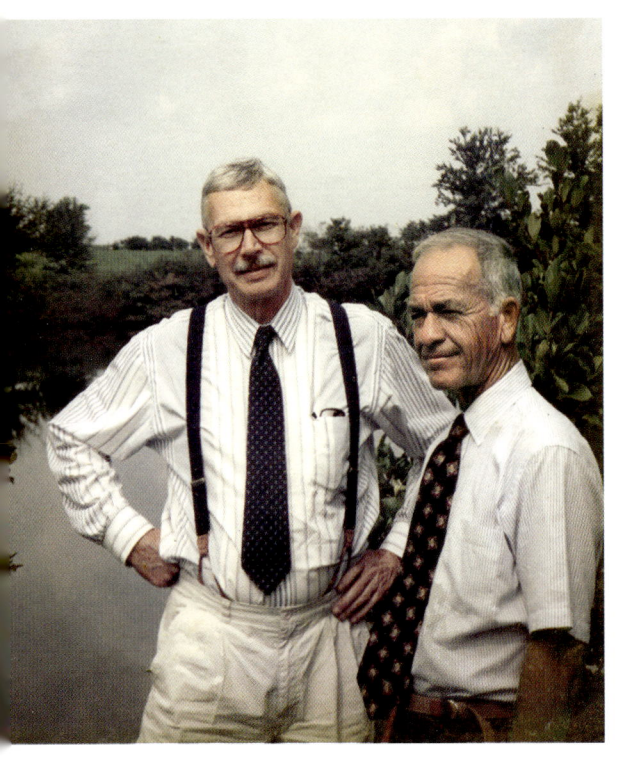

Black and Sanderson
in Gaffney, SC, 1994.

Black and Sanderson started their professional lives as college instructors, but soon after meeting each other they gave up formal teaching. Instead, they opted to pursue their respective art practices alongside one another and support themselves by commercially representing other artists, craftsmen, and designers. After leaving their teaching jobs at a small college in eastern North Carolina in the late 1950s, they launched a creative business venture they named Strawvalley, after the physical features of its location overlooking a valley overgrown with broom straw, on what was then still a largely rural road connecting Durham and Chapel Hill. That's where they made their home for the next four decades as their creative visions took shape and matured.[1]

In establishing themselves as artists and art-focused businessmen, Sanderson and Black positioned themselves early on as dealers of North Carolina pottery and other traditional crafts from the surrounding region. They also taught themselves about the latest developments in other specialty fields involving aesthetically pleasing, utilitarian objects. They pored over art and design periodicals and visited commercial outlets in several countries for cutting-edge interior-design items. Relying on their shared spirit of adventure, their strong visual instincts, and their youthful energy (they were in their thirties when they went into business), they carved out and nurtured a fruitful niche for themselves in a fast-growing area.

Origins and early career developments

Ormond Sanderson—full name, Jesse Ormond Sanderson Jr.—grew up in Raleigh and Durham, North Carolina, during the Great Depression, the son and elder offspring of a schoolteacher. From a humble start, teaching children on western North Carolina's Cherokee Indian Reservation, his father eventually ascended to become superintendent of Raleigh's public schools. With his father away on the Reservation much of the time during his earliest years, young Ormond grew especially close to his mother, whom he remembers as a competent organizer and engaging hostess interested in fashion, jewelry, and social functions. She consistently supported his personal enthusiasms.

Childhood experiences in the southern outdoors stimulated his early interest in wild nature, which would later find expression in his work as a visual artist and craftsman. Also influential in this regard were his memories of iridescent goldfish swimming in a pool in Duke University's gardens, where he went for walks during extended visits to his maternal grandmother's large house near the campus. His growing curiosity about the wider world, meanwhile, was stimulated by his conversations with foreign students at Duke who rented rooms in his grandmother's house. He also recalls making sketches of famous buildings like the Taj Mahal during those years.

Sanderson's first passion, however, was not visual art but music. Even as a child he demonstrated a prodigious talent for the piano, which he studied privately at two local colleges, Peace and Meredith, while attending public schools in Raleigh. His parents strongly encouraged these endeavors, buying a Steinway concert grand for him to practice on at home. His devotion to playing it and perfecting his technique was almost monastic. Sharply focused and introverted during this period of his life, he stayed home to practice when he wasn't putting in his requisite hours at school. After graduating from high school, he spent a summer in Chautauqua, New York, studying with Bach scholar James Friskin, before enrolling at the University of Michigan's school of music in Ann Arbor, where he eventually earned bachelor's and master's degrees in piano performance. He was subsequently drafted into the Third Army, and stationed at Fort Jackson, South Carolina, where he was assigned to play glockenspiel in the resident band while other draftees he had begun to know were sent off to fight in the Korean War. More than a few returned with frost-bitten feet and fingers, and Sanderson recalls feeling emotionally shaken after seeing them suffer—an experience that reinforced his determination to pursue a peaceful, creative path in his own life.

After concluding his obligatory military service, he returned to civilian life and to Ann Arbor, where he entered the PhD program in music. When he belatedly realized that the program emphasized theory over performance—his forte— he abandoned the idea of pursuing a doctoral degree and returned to the South. Moving back in with his parents, he resumed his efforts at the Steinway grand. Before long, his parents had the piano relocated to a lower level of the house and the end farthest from their bedroom, so that his late-night practice sessions wouldn't interfere with their sleep. He remained in Raleigh for nearly a year, and except for a few public recitals at Meredith and Peace colleges, he remained privately immersed in his work at the Steinway until another small, southern college out of state offered him his first full-time job in his field. An Army friend from Mississippi had informed him of an opening for a piano instructor at Blue

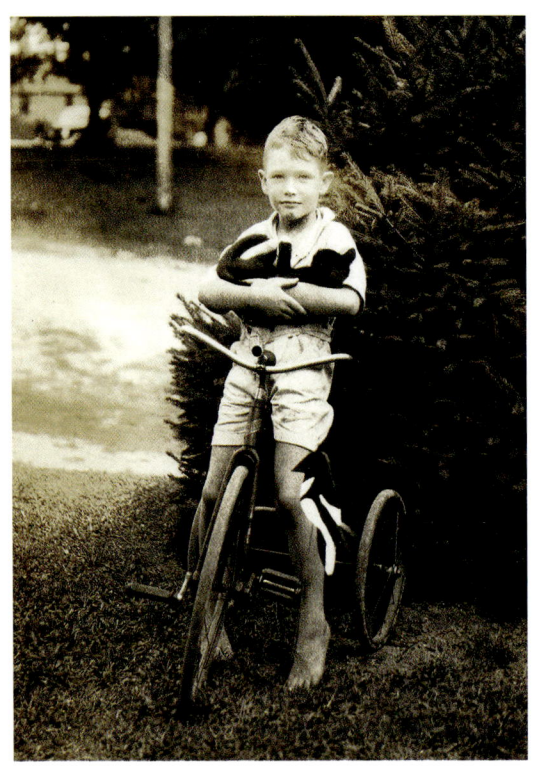

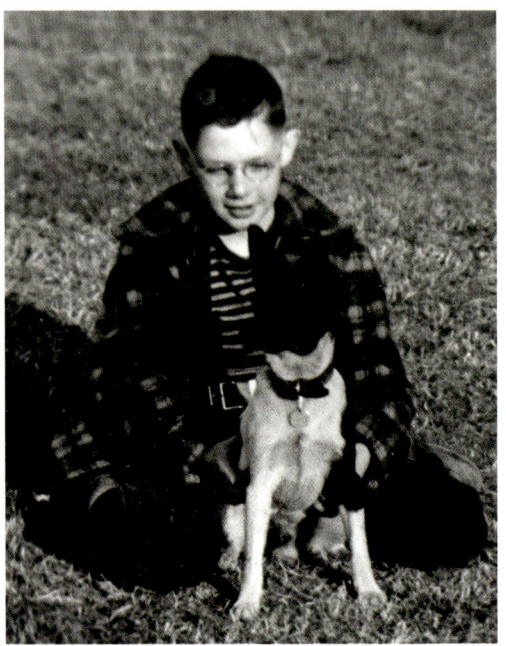

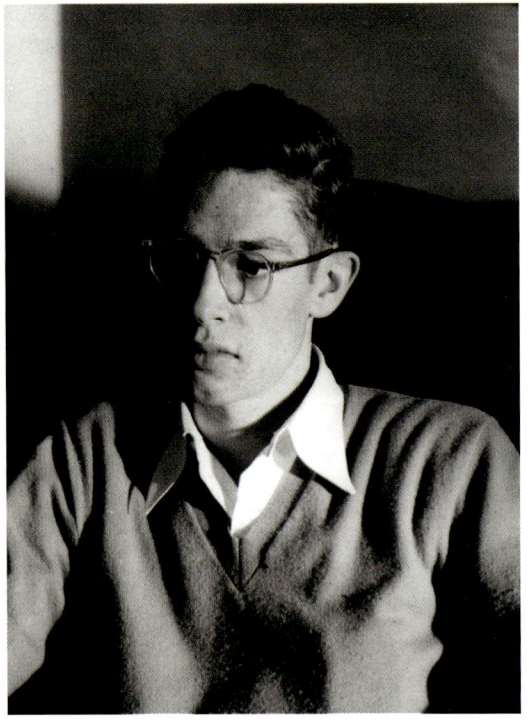

(*clockwise from upper left*) Robert with kitten, 1935. Robert and Jitter, 1938. Robert as an 18-year-old student at Parsons, 1948.

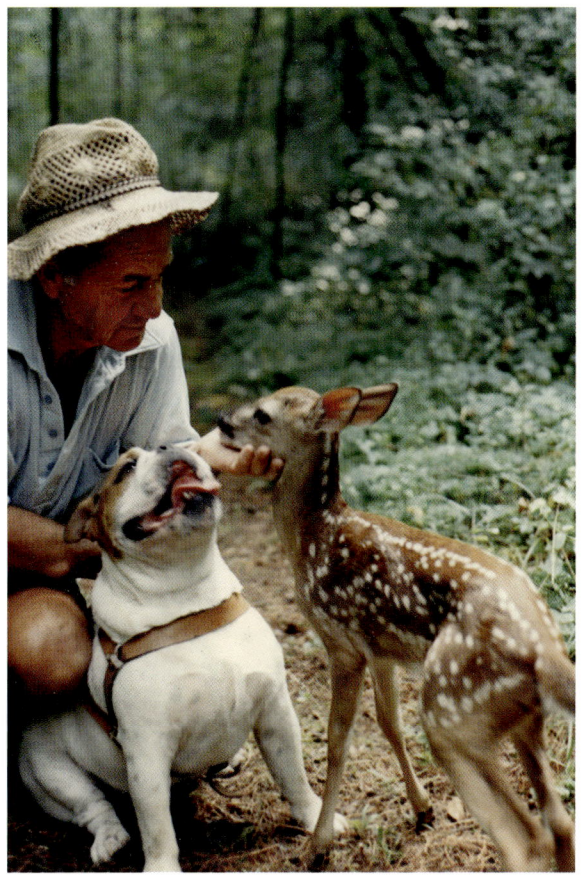

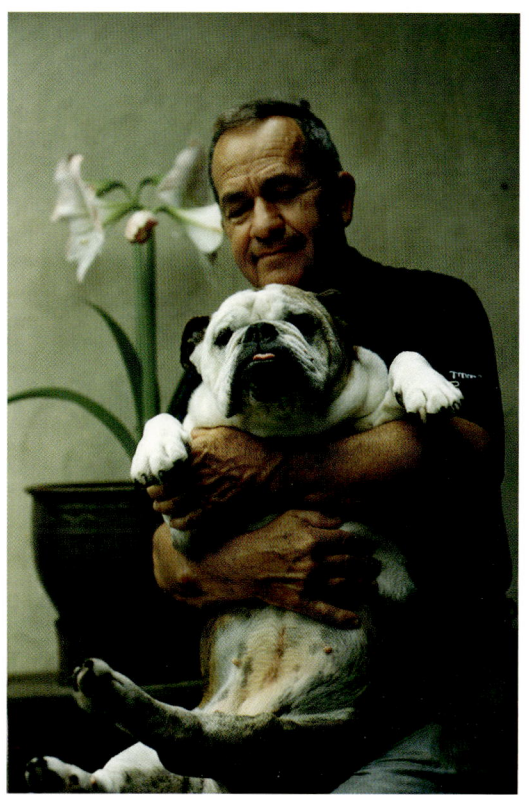

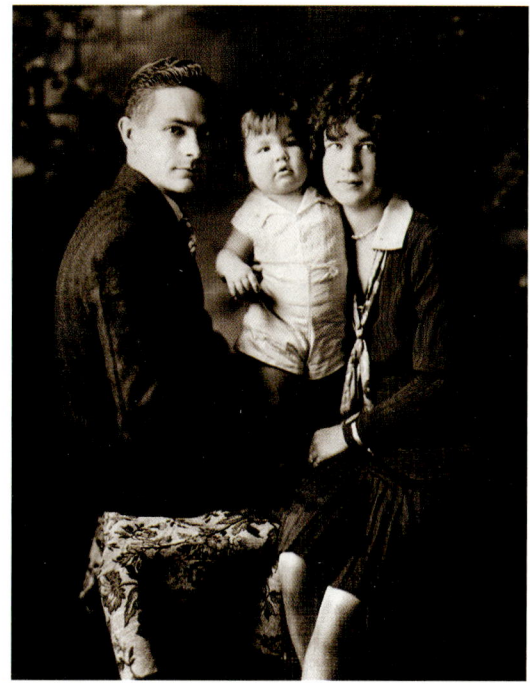

(*clockwise from upper left*) Ormond with Bumble and fawn, 1990. Ormond with Rosacoke, 1989. Ormond and his parents, 1929.

Mountain College, a four-year women's school affiliated with the Baptist Church located in the northeast part of that state, near Tupelo.

"As far as I was concerned, Blue Mountain, Mississippi, was another planet," Sanderson recalls. He drove his white Jaguar coupe there to audition for the job in 1954, and the college hired him. But the position quickly fell short of his hopes. His performances were limited to accompanying the school's operatic productions, and his piano students lacked discipline and dedication. Unwilling to prolong an uninspiring, non-challenging job for which he felt temperamentally unsuited, he declined to return for a second academic year. Once again, he returned home to Raleigh and the consolation of his Steinway grand. This time, he spent more than a year and a half at his parents' house—long enough for all three of them to grow impatient with the arrangement. Finally, a family friend who taught at Atlantic Christian College in Wilson, almost an hour east of Raleigh, informed Sanderson's father that the college was seeking a piano instructor. With his father's encouragement, Sanderson applied for the position and was promptly hired. This set the stage for his first encounter with Robert Black, a new recruit to Atlantic Christian's art faculty.[2]

* * *

Ten months younger than Sanderson, Robert Keith Black was the second child and only son of a chemistry professor and his wife. Born in Raleigh, he grew up in the nearby town of Wake Forest, where his father chaired the chemistry department at Wake Forest College, a small, Baptist-affiliated school.[3] During his childhood and youth, Black was introverted and indifferent to sports, unlike most boys his age. His enthusiasms were aesthetic, specifically art and classical music. Even as a boy, he took an active interest in visual art. He enjoyed drawing—landscapes and buildings were favored subjects—and he attended private art classes. During his teens, he gravitated toward abstraction, reacting against teachers who favored straightforward portraiture and other realistic subject matter. Black's musical interests were more passive than Sanderson's. He enjoyed listening to classical music and studied the piano, but only long enough to convince himself that he lacked sufficient talent to ever play well. After finishing high school, he entered the hometown college where his dad taught. Because Wake Forest College offered no art classes, he majored in biology, which at least involved the useful exercise of drawing specimens in sharp detail.

After graduating, Black left the small-town South for New York City and the Parsons School of Design. Parsons was the first school in the United States to offer programs in advertising and the design fields—fashion, interior, and graphic design. Black remembers choosing the school "in desperation" after his experience at a college with no art classes, and at a time when he knew nothing about other art schools in and around New York. Having focused on drawing and painting, he arrived at Parsons with no special interest in design. The instructors introduced him to New York's art museums, where his classes met to make renderings of exhibited works. They also took him and other students to galleries, leading interior design stores, and historic private homes with exemplary decor. Parsons students were schooled in furniture design and room design, with intensive training in procedures and techniques for drawing furnished rooms. Details and proportions were emphasized. The latter studies pointed Black in the direction of architecture, which would become a lifelong passion.

His art studies were interrupted by the draft and two relatively uneventful years of obligatory service in the Army. Stationed at Fort Gordon, Georgia, he spent his time filing enlistment records and working in information and education services. The G.I. Bill then paid his way through graduate school at the University of Georgia in Athens. He chose to go there largely on the strength of his interest in the paintings of Lamar Dodd, the department's founding chairman. The graduate program's emphasis on technique and art practice rather than teaching also appealed to him. After completing the program, however, he found that the most reliable jobs for newly certified masters of fine art were in education, so he accepted a teaching position at Texas Wesleyan College in Fort Worth. Although the college was primarily a training ground for teachers, Black was its only art instructor. "It was just an absolute desert as far as any interest in art," he recalls. Convinced that Texas Wesleyan offered no viable future for him, he left at the end of his second academic year.

From Fort Worth, Black returned to his native North Carolina and found work in the fall of 1957 teaching art at Atlantic Christian College, where Ormond Sanderson had just joined the college's faculty as well. By pure coincidence, they both moved into the same building, the Varita Courts apartments in downtown Wilson, where Black's unit happened to be directly above Sanderson's. Their first meeting was brought about by Black's dog, a rambunctious Doberman pinscher named Fricka, who bounded freely around his apartment playing with a rubber ball. The sound of her paws pounding on the floor reverberated deafeningly in Sanderson's rooms below, prompting him to come up and investigate. Almost immediately after Sanderson knocked on Black's door and introduced himself in the process lodging his complaint, they recognized each other as kindred spirits on a number of levels.

Aside from their mutual aesthetic interests and complementary strengths in music and art, they were also, as far as they knew, the only gay men teaching

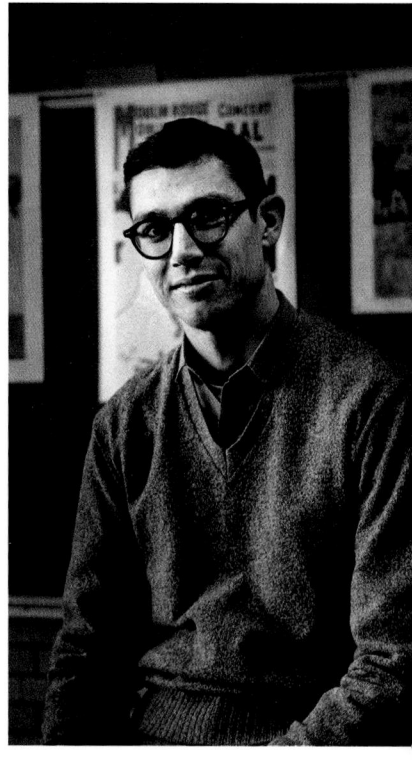

Robert Black as art teacher at Atlantic Christian College, 1958.

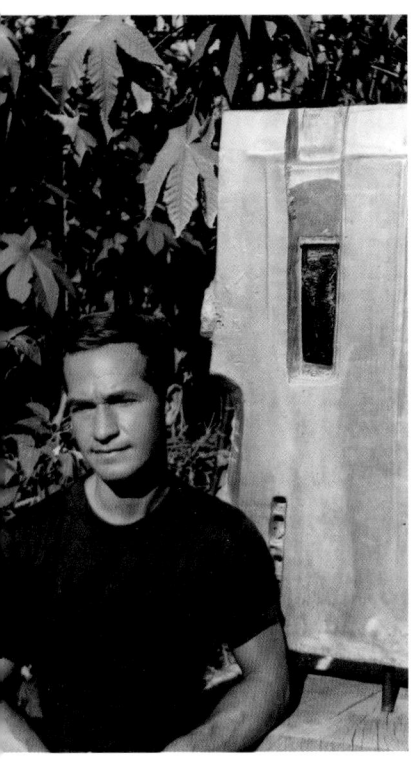

Ormond Sanderson,
late 1960s.

at Atlantic Christian. The distinction was hardly a minor issue in an era when homosexuality was still criminalized and considered deviant by the standards of straight, "mainstream" society. Although socially conditioned to accept such prejudicial attitudes without question, both Sanderson and Black had already been exposed to more progressive views on sexual identity by the time they met. Black's art-school experience in New York had introduced him to a world where being gay was not only accepted but commonplace. Sanderson, meanwhile, had encountered a more liberal, intellectually open-minded community at the University of Michigan, where gay students weren't stigmatized as much as they were in the South. Both had also known a few gay fellow soldiers during their years of military service, but neither had been involved in a serious relationship before their paths crossed in Wilson.

Soon after discovering they were upstairs-downstairs neighbors, Sanderson and Black decided to give up their separate apartments in order to split the rent on a slightly larger unit in the same building. They've been inseparable ever since.

To enliven the spartan quarters they now shared, Black painted a wall of their main room with a boldly colored geometric-abstract mural influenced by the works of designer Alexander Girard. Unfortunately, when their landlady eventually found out about the mural, she was horrified. She demanded that Black immediately paint over it, and return the wall to its original dull gray.

Pleased as they were to have met each other, Sanderson and Black were both dissatisfied with their jobs, and commiserated over what they perceived as a lack of creative ambition on the part of their students. They had both come to realize they weren't teachers by nature, and began discussing what they might do to align their careers more closely with their most fundamental interests.

"If you're a teacher, you have to give everything to your students," says Black. "I saw that in my father when I took a class with him once. But I realized I wasn't interested in giving everything to my students. I wanted to save some for myself."

"We discussed what we could do, as far as art was concerned, that would be more creative and educational than teaching, and that might provide inspiration for other people," Sanderson recalls.

In fact, Sanderson had already begun rethinking his entire career path. After devoting his life to becoming a concert pianist, he had gradually come to realize that he faced an insurmountable physical obstacle. His hands were too small to enable him to approach the virtuosic performing abilities of celebrated contemporaries such as Glenn Gould or Van Cliburn. Teaching had been his father's field, but he had never been enthusiastic about it, and he had only taken teaching jobs to support himself. Meanwhile, his new relationship with Black and the proximity it gave him to Black's creative practice had reinvigorated his childhood interest in drawing and making images. Inspired, he took a leap of faith, choosing to walk away from the piano and take up the tools and materials of a visual artist and craftsman.

Offering each other mutual encouragement, he and Black made a mutual leap out of academia. After completing the academic year and fulfilling their teaching duties at Atlantic Christian in the late spring of 1958, they left the college, their gloomy, gray-walled apartment, and the town of Wilson behind to embark on a new, ambitious, and seemingly dicey venture out in the "real world."

Strawvalley

They'd begun firming up their exit plan in November, after a visit to an old farm site that had been in Sanderson's family since his maternal grandfather, Thomas Lipscombe Russell, bought it during the Great Depression. Sanderson's uncle Woodard "Woody" Russell was the absentee owner at the time of their visit, when they inspected the property and its existing structures—a vacant farmhouse, a two-room cabin, a barn, and a former blacksmith's shop, all built in the early twentieth century. Of special interest to Sanderson and Black, the farm overlooked the two-lane road connecting Chapel Hill and Durham, known as the Durham-Chapel Hill Boulevard (later widened and four-laned to become Highway 15-501). The entire Russell farm encompassed about two hundred acres that had been split roughly in half by the Boulevard's construction in the early 1950s. To accommodate the right-of-way, the house and outbuildings had been moved from their original locations. When they first inspected the property, the farmhouse sat on a hillside, easily visible to passing traffic. There were only a few businesses on the road, among them a motel and a Howard Johnson's restaurant. The house had limited electricity and no insulation or indoor plumbing; water came from a hand-pumped outdoor well. Both the house and outbuildings were in dilapidated condition, but the two young college instructors figured they could make some improvements and turn the property to their own purposes.

Their parents didn't know what to make of this seemingly abrupt change in their plans. "Both of us went through college and grad school, and prepared ourselves to be teachers," Black recalled. "And then, for our parents to see us give that up all of a sudden—they were baffled."

"It was a traumatic shock for my parents," adds Sanderson, "because I was walking away from my teaching job and from my plans for being a concert pianist." While they were glad he had met Black, they were concerned about this bold career move. Nonetheless, they agreed to buy and give their son the lot on which the house and outbuildings were located, about three quarters of an acre in all. Black's parents, meanwhile, helped him purchase an adjoining lot of the same size.

Their initial plan was to move into the house, transform the cabin into a crafts shop, and convert the blacksmith's shop into a studio where they could make their own art. They arranged to cut back their teaching schedules to half-time for the 1958 spring semester, so they could work on their new project in their spare time. To finance this start-up phase of their venture, Sanderson sold his two most prized material possessions—his Jaguar and his Steinway grand piano—while Black cashed in an insurance policy and some war bonds he owned. Their enthusiasm and industriousness enabled them to open for business later that same summer.

To stock their new shop at the outset, they traveled to Seagrove, North Carolina—a regional center of traditional pottery-making about ninety miles southwest—where they bought wares from J.B. Cole, Jugtown, and other venerable pottery production workshops.

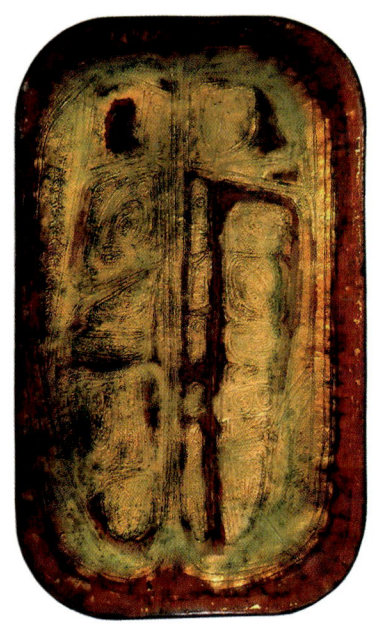

Ormond Sanderson, *Duet* tray, ca. 1963, vitreous enamel on etched copper, 10½" x 6¼".

Meanwhile, they enlisted an engineer from NC State to help them build a small electric kiln for firing their own work. Black, who had previously focused on painting, had begun to develop his own strain of contemporary pottery, with clear references to utilitarian forms but intended strictly for contemplative and decorative purposes. Sanderson, meanwhile, eagerly plunged into an exploration of other visual art mediums. Having given up his piano studies and rigorous practice routine, he began experimenting with the ancient craft of vitreous enamel, which involves heating powdered glass until it flows and then hardens to become a glossy, semi-transparent coating on a metal base, often with multiple layers of different colors applied in sequential firings. Though typically employed by jewelers, metalsmiths, and, since the nineteenth century, home-appliance manufacturers, Sanderson used the enameling process to create two-dimensional, biomorphic abstractions—somewhat akin to abstract-expressionist paintings—and to augment two- and three-dimensional, mixed-media pieces that took advantage of the reflective, iridescent qualities of the medium. He taught himself the craft by trial and error, informed by his related research. His untutored, independent approach enabled him to develop his own technique and style, which distinguished his work from that of other enamel artists of the time. His skills developed rapidly enough that when the 1964–65 New York

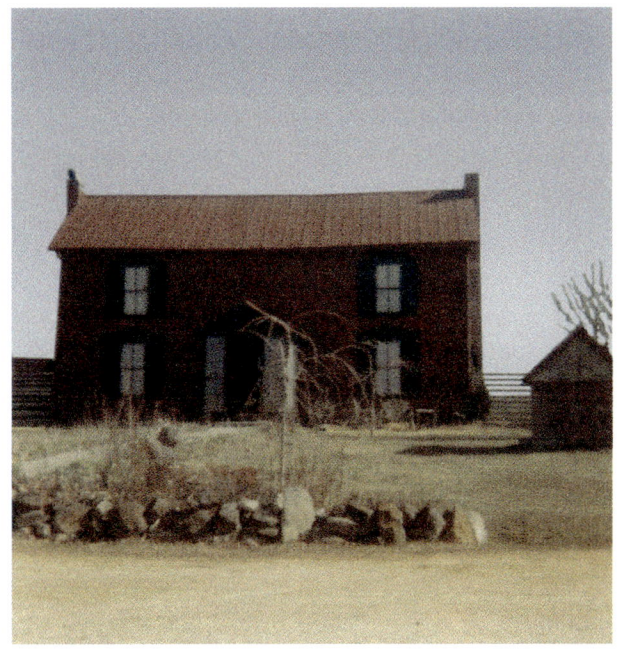

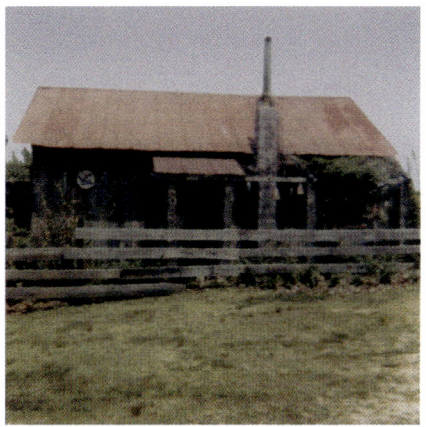

(*clockwise from above*) Strawvalley farmhouse, former blacksmith shop (which served as Black's and Sanderson's studio), and the old cabin they used as a sales gallery, 1960.

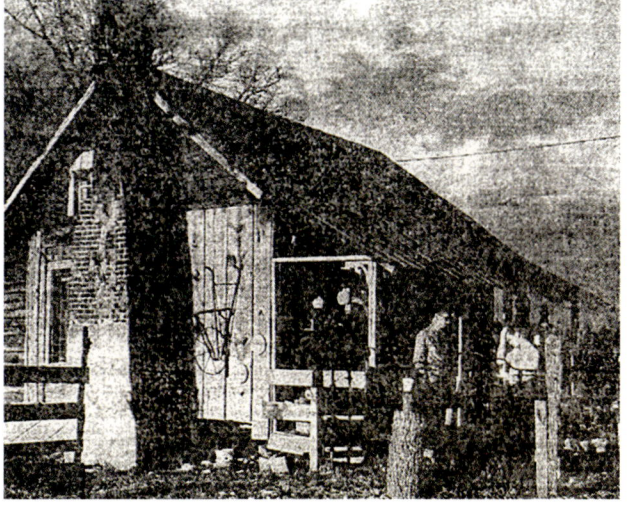

World's Fair opened, major examples of his work were selected for exhibition in the American Pavilion. In the late 1960s, he broadened his approach after participating in a ten-day workshop taught by Peter Ostuni, a New York painter who had created several public murals in vitreous enamel.

Material and moral support from both their parents helped Black and Sanderson establish themselves commercially. Sanderson's parents, still living in nearby Raleigh, regularly brought them food and supplies as they accommodated themselves to their new home and worked to improve it. The cabin proved difficult to heat, so after the first winter they moved the store into the ground floor of the farmhouse, while they consolidated their living quarters upstairs. To make the place more visible to passing traffic, they painted the house's exterior red and installed a large sign over the porch, which they enclosed in 1960 in order to expand their retail space.

Not long after vacating the cabin, they were approached by Gypsy Hollingsworth, a local collector of Appalachian antiques and artifacts, who decided the cabin would make a good home for a large, nineteenth-century loom she owned. She gave it to them outright, and they re-assembled it in the cabin, nearly filling its largest room. When they gave local weaver Rita Kunkle permission to operate the loom, she re-strung it and began using it to weave fabric for pillows she sold in their shop. Other weavers soon began dropping by to see this rare creative instrument in operation, and before long, some of them also began weaving tapestries and pillows to sell there.

Sanderson and Black took turns minding the store and working in their studios. Reflecting on their business strategy during those years, Black recalls, "A lot of our inspiration came from knowing and talking with people in the arts and crafts field. We went to the crafts fairs in Asheville and met the craftsmen there and bought things from them. We realized there was a lot of interest in folk crafts, and we wanted to have something that local people here would respond to. We thought people would be more interested in crafts than in fine art, especially in a location like ours, where there were a lot of out-of-state travelers who might want to take something home. There were people traveling up and down the highway between New York and Florida, and a lot of people who would drive up from Atlanta. So we directed our store more toward crafts, because we thought they would be more salable."

Their instincts proved to be on target, but it took several years for the strategy to pay off. While business was slow through most of the 1960s, they persevered, chatting up customers to encourage sales, reinvesting any proceeds, and living as frugally as possible. For a few years, they continued to specialize in re-

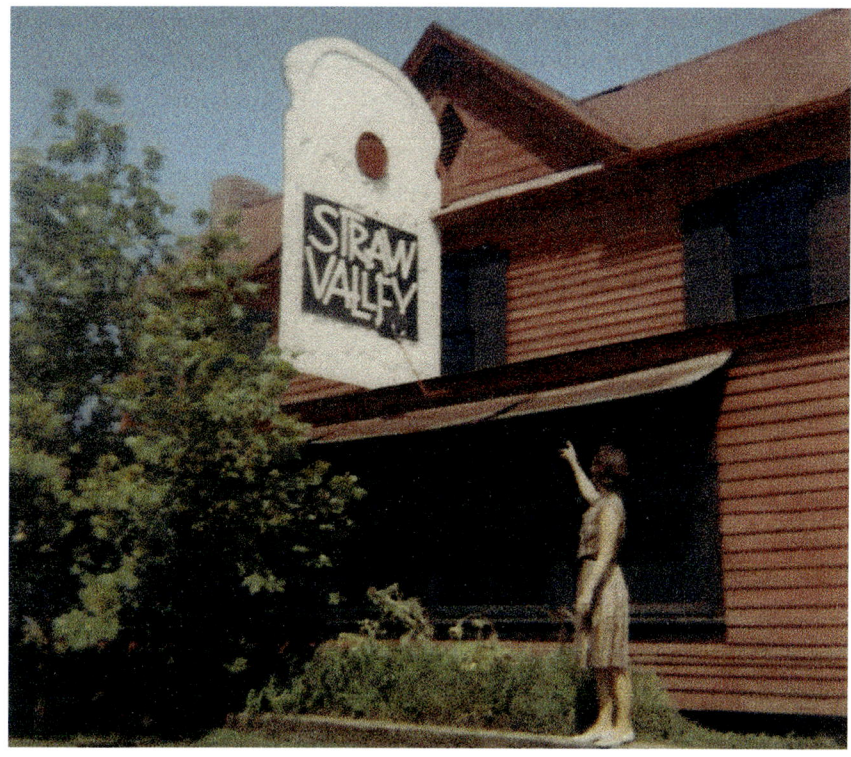

Patricia Burch was Strawvalley's first hired salesperson. Early 1960s.

gional pottery, then added a selection of cookware to their inventory. They never stopped making improvements, doing most of the hardest work themselves. In 1963, they dismantled, moved, and rebuilt the barn. In keeping with the property's former life as a working farm, they acquired a small menagerie of farm animals—chickens, sheep, geese, Guinea hens, and peacocks, along with dogs, cats, pigeons, and a ram. These animals constituted a "veritable petting zoo," as Black tells it, requiring a lot of attention but helping to attract new customers.

Aesthetically discerning residents of the surrounding area soon discovered Strawvalley, and began bringing friends along with them to shop there. "There was nothing artistic around Durham and Raleigh in those days," Sanderson remembers, "so they sought us out to be associated with something artistic." Their local clientele included Mary Semans, the influential philanthropist and arts patron, and writer Reynolds Price, then teaching at Duke University. Faculty members at other area colleges and universities—including NC State and UNC-Chapel Hill—began visiting the shop as well, often after their spouses discovered it. Duke's famous rice-diet program was headquartered nearby, and Strawvalley attracted a number of its clients, including show-business celebrities such as comedian Buddy Hackett and singer Nelson Eddy.

Increased business enabled them to hire a few part-time clerks, freeing up time to make additional improvements and pursue their own creative work. Most of their employees were women whose husbands worked at one or another of the area universities, either as professors or in other capacities.

Modern expansions

Although their initial commercial focus was on selling southern crafts, Sanderson and Black had also become admirers of contemporary international design. During his student years at Parsons, Black had been introduced to New York design showrooms such as Georg Jensen, Knoll, and Bonnier's. He returned to the city with Sanderson to revisit these venues and peruse furniture, lighting fixtures, and other interior-design items in styles now collectively known as "mid-century modern." Their interest in contemporary design was further informed by European architecture and design magazines, such as *Md Moebel Interior Design* (Germany), *Domus* (Italy), and *Mobilia* (Denmark). These periodicals also had an impact on their artistic practices, according to Black, who says, "They inspired me to do things I otherwise wouldn't have done."

His most ambitious such endeavor was taking up architecture. "I was fascinated with architecture," he remembers, "and we promoted our business to architects. We wanted to encourage them to buy quality furniture from us for their buildings." By this time, central North Carolina had begun experiencing a building boom, largely resulting from the University of North Carolina's decision to establish a School of Architecture and Landscape Design at NC State in 1946,[4] and the opening of Research Triangle Park in 1959, which brought to the area dozens of companies specializing in information technology, health and pharmaceutical sciences, textile chemistry, business analytics, biotechnology, and environmental sciences. These led in turn to all the suburbs, banks, hotels, schools, restaurants, and shopping centers that sprang up to service them.[5] Black and Sanderson hoped the influx of highly educated people new to the region might result in new customers for their wares.

Consulting closely with Sanderson, Black designed a modern, single-story house with two art studios that they gradually achieved by modifying and then adding to what was originally the old blacksmith's shop behind the farmhouse. This redesign and renovation took place in stages between the late 1950s and the late 1960s. The building incorporated a shed roof design and simple post-and-beam construction, widely popular in the post-World-War-II era. It was also influenced by concurrent architectural projects with rusticated or industrial com-

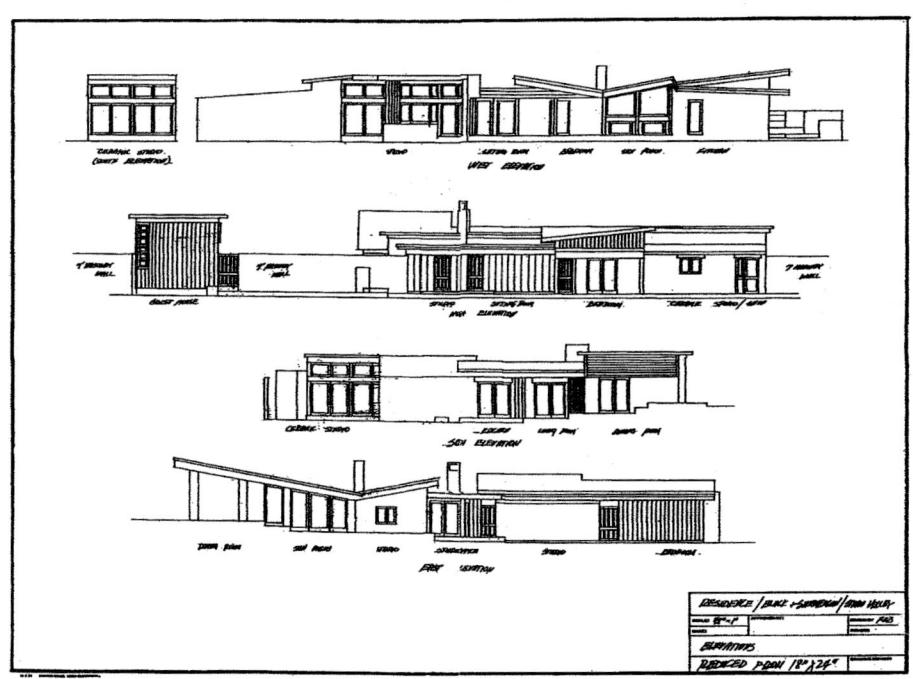

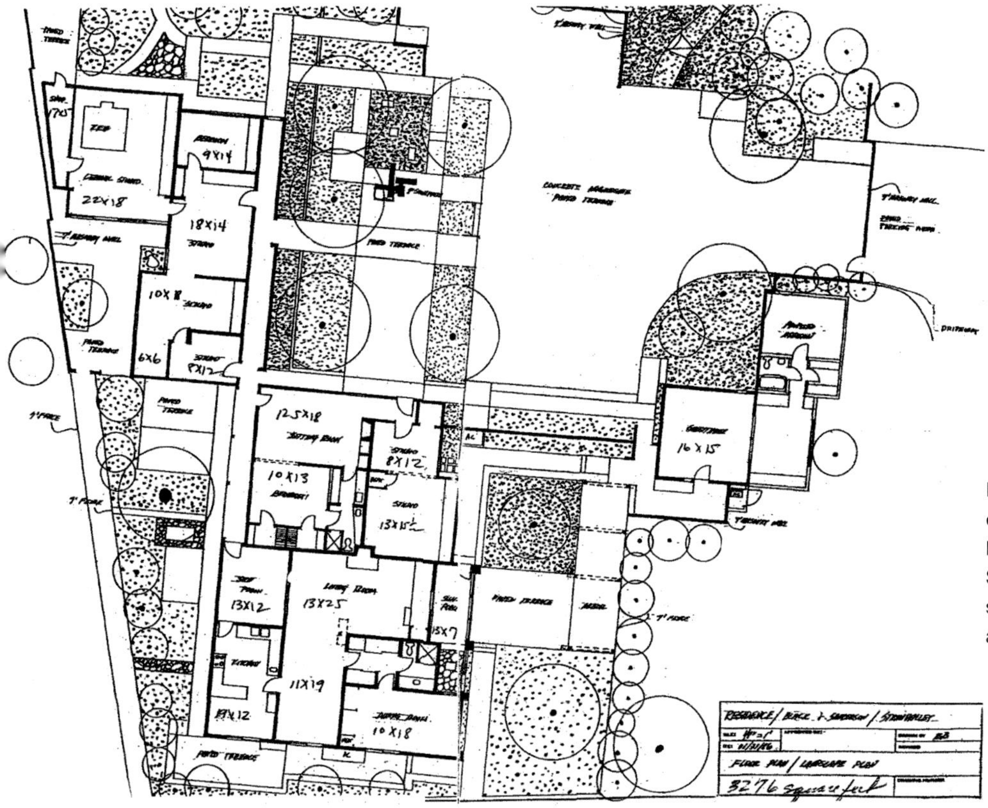

Robert Black's plan and elevations for a new building that reimagined Strawvalley's old blacksmith shop expanded as a modernist house.

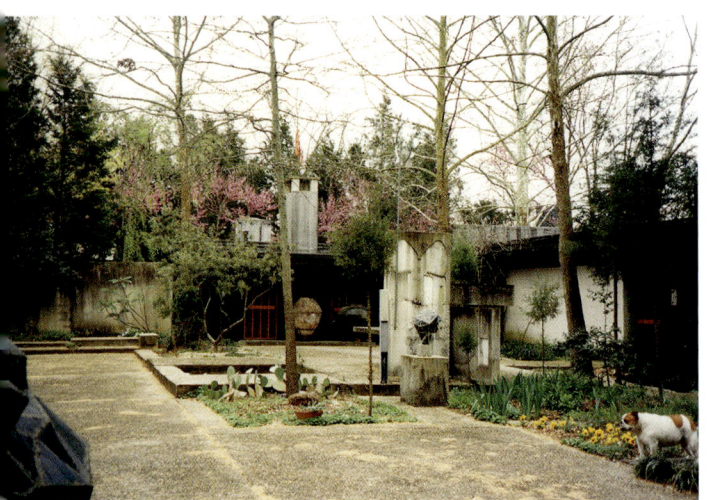 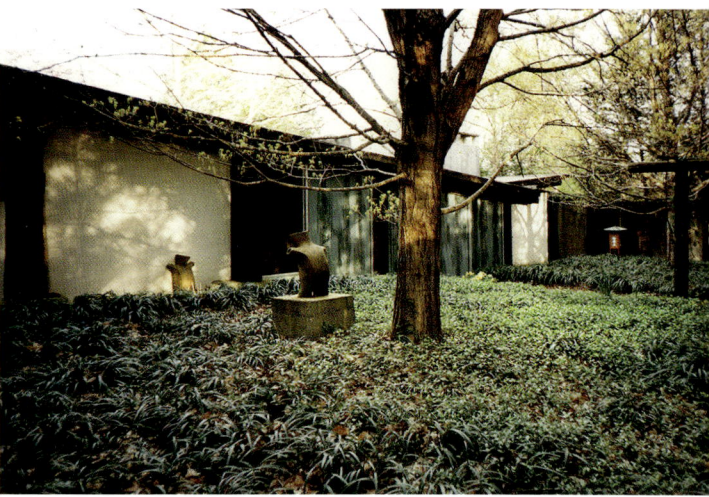

By 1975, Sanderson's landscaping around their house at Strawvalley had begun to mature. Glass interior walls facing private courtyards would be employed again three decades later, when they transformed an abandoned school into a new home.

ponents, including the Charles and Ray Eames House in Los Angeles; the Sea Ranch in Sonoma County, California; and a couple of Raleigh homes built by faculty members at NC State's School of Design. "I designed as the building grew, and designed it to complement what was there," Black recalls. "Money was very tight, and the design was influenced by what we needed and could afford and could build ourselves." While they worked on their house, they salvaged windows, hinges, and other components from older Durham homes that were being razed, and Black incorporated them into the design. Twelve-inch floor tiles left over from the construction of the new North Carolina State Legislative Building in Raleigh were salvaged and used in the new kitchen as well as the living and dining rooms.[6]

After completing the house project, they began considering the prospect of relocating their business. Rather than making further repairs to the old farmhouse—which had termite damage and other problems—they decided to raze it and build a new retail facility. They weren't satisfied with plans produced by local architects for this new structure, so Black put his pottery production on hold while he designed a new, modern showroom that "reflected the direction we wanted to project." They hired a local construction crew to build it, but cut their costs by doing much of the finish work themselves. They then chose a straightforward, easily remembered name for the new facility: Design Gallery. In keeping with the building's modern architecture, they expanded their inventory well beyond the selection of regional crafts for which they had become known. For Design Gallery's grand opening in 1969, they stocked it with new merchandise, including contemporary lighting fixtures, Scandinavian accessories, and furnishings by major designers such as Harry Bertoia, Marcel Breuer, Mies van der Rohe, and Eero Saarninen. Sanderson and Black designed wooden boxes and sets of angular metal candle stands, commissioned regional craft artists to fabricate them, and featured them alongside pieces by internationally recognized designers in their new sales displays.

Like growing numbers of their contemporaries during those years, they were particularly drawn to the clean-lined aesthetic and simple functionality of design objects from northern Europe. At the time, modern furniture from Finland, Sweden, and especially Denmark, mass-produced from inexpensive materials, was affordable in addition to its aesthetic appeal. It had already gained popularity in much of the country by the time Sanderson and Black opened their new showroom, but it wasn't yet widely appreciated in the South, according to Black, who recalls having to educate their clients about the finer attributes of Scandinavian design. They prominently featured examples at Design Gallery throughout the early 1970s, until rapidly escalating prices eventually forced them to scale back that component of their inventory. Meanwhile, they continued to offer other modern furnishings, fixtures, and decorative items.

It was also during this period that Sanderson developed an interest in contemporary decorative glassware, which they began collecting and selling. An installation of Venini glass in their showroom was destroyed around 1976 when an errant deer crashed through a display window, apparently disoriented by the shiny array of reflective surfaces. The insurance payment that compensated them for the loss was sufficient to help finance a trip to Venice—an international center of handmade glasswork—during which they sought out special examples by masters of the medium.

Design Gallery attracted many new visitors and clients, including architects, regional artists, and students from NC State's School of Design. It also brought them an unsolicited client in the form of local entrepreneur Ray Goad, who commissioned them to design a new restaurant for a nearby shopping center. Their design for the three-room establishment, known as RJ's, featured sandblasted-glass exterior doors, an ornamental fountain, vibrantly colored murals and wall coverings, designer furniture, a Plexiglas sculpture, a wood-paneled tap room, and distinctive lighting fixtures including globe bulbs and paper lanterns designed by Isamu Noguchi. They augmented these built-in components with objects from the Design Gallery inventory, displayed in custom-designed glass cases.

Around the same time they opened Design Gallery, Sanderson and Black were approached by architects Arthur Cogswell and Werner Hausler, who were

RJ's restaurant with Isamu Noguchi lanterns, 1971. Sanderson and Black occupy a table near the fountain.

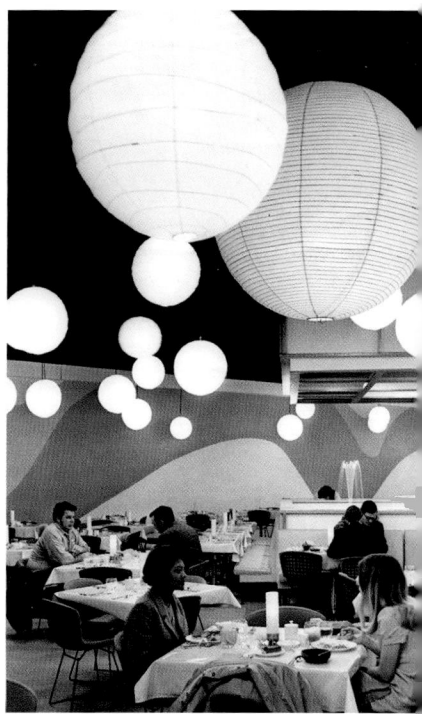

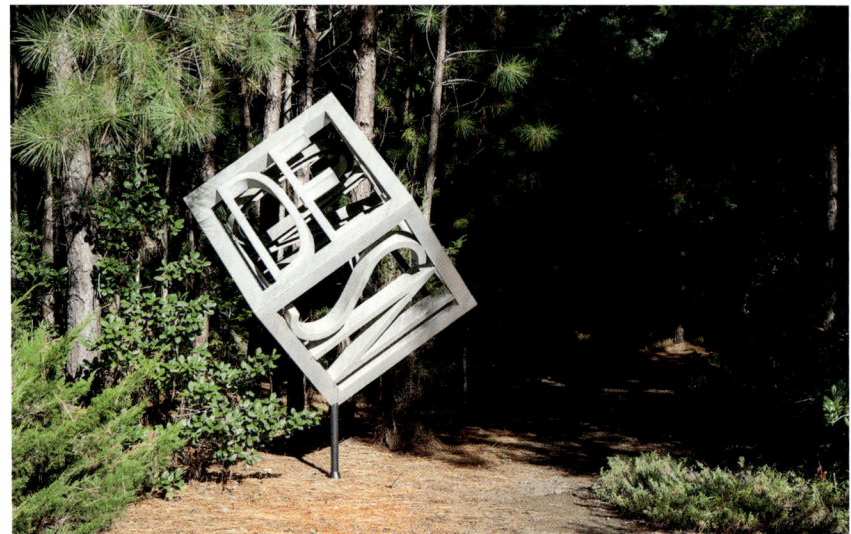

Stainless steel sign that Robert Black created for Design Gallery, 1969, seen here in its current location next to their home.

interested in constructing a pair of two-story buildings on the land immediately west of the Design Gallery, to house their firm's offices and provide additional spaces for office and retail tenants. The four men agreed to a joint venture in which the architects would design the buildings and supervise their construction, while Sanderson and Black would provide the finances.

In 1972, Sanderson and Black bought the ninety undeveloped acres adjoining their property on its north side, which were still owned by Sanderson's uncle. During the same year, the new Cogswell/Hausler complex opened under the name Strawvalley—one word. Marketed as "an ecological concept,"[7] it attracted tenants that included an interior designer, a Scandinavian fabrics store, a frame shop, a needlepoint shop, and a women's clothing store, as well as a psychiatrist's office and a health-and-fitness club. After buying Sanderson's and Black's share of their development in 1973, the architects lost the property in foreclosure proceedings the following year. The two buildings were later sold to a tenant who co-owned the resident health-and-fitness club.

Having relinquished their share of that development, Sanderson and Black enlarged Design Gallery to add additional rental spaces for craft and design-oriented businesses. The first addition attracted two of the Strawvalley complex's former tenants—the Anna Darden women's clothing store, and the frame shop, which later became Somerhill Gallery. After it opened in 1976, Sanderson and Black added another space to house a local crafts shop, the Craft House of Durham, which connected Design Gallery with the other new addition to create a rectangular complex.

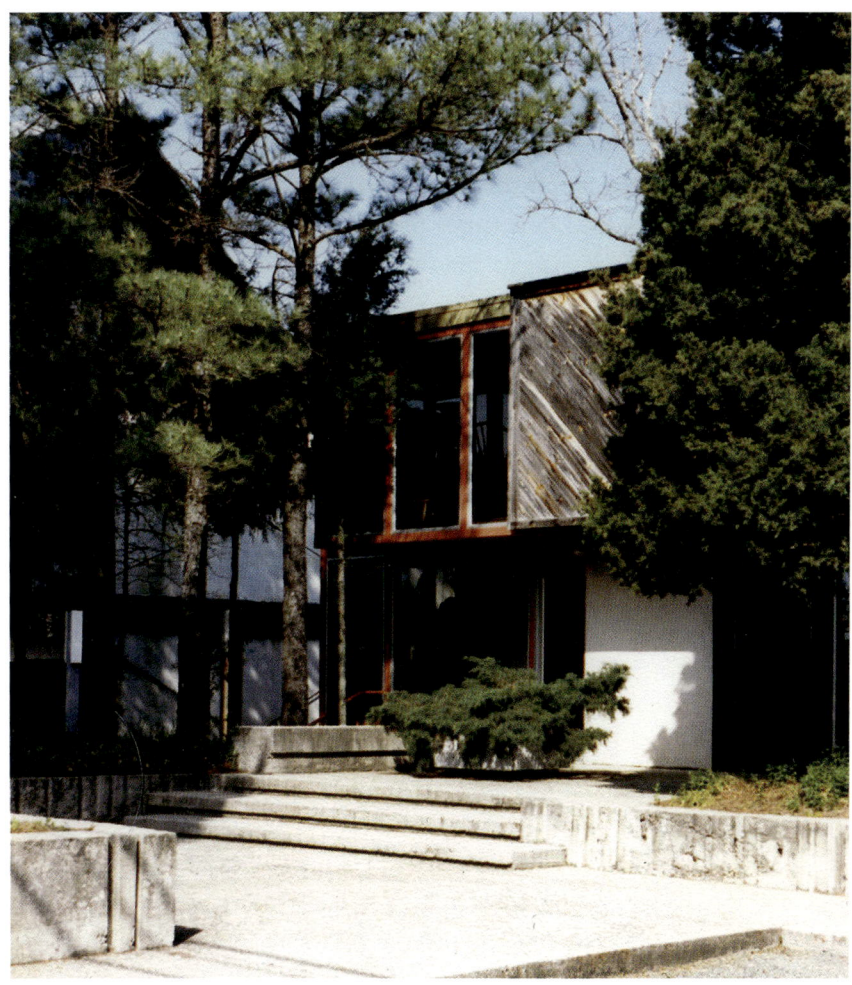

SABL Gallery opened in 1982.

In 1981, they sold Design Gallery to local designer Milton van Hoy and built SABL Gallery, combining the first two letters of their last names and pronouncing it "sable." Following Black's design, the building featured a tubular steel frame and a glass facade that opened onto a deck where they hung a collection of bronze wind bells by visionary architect Paolo Soleri. Completed in 1982, their new gallery was a forum for their own work and a variety of indigenous art, artifacts, and exotica, including painted Peruvian pottery, East Indian cast brass objects, and rare fossils. The new paintings Black exhibited there signaled his return to the medium after years of focusing on ceramics and architecture. Related works he showed were derived from hand-drawn, hand-colored papers that he printed in multiples, cut into pieces, and strategically glued to cover large, stretched canvases.

Meanwhile, Sanderson had begun experimenting with etching the metal surfaces of his enameled pieces, often with striking results, as evidenced by examples he showed at SABL and later retained for their collection. Although creatively satisfying, this medium proved to be problematical, not only due to the time-consuming steps involved and the meticulous attention it demanded, but largely because it released toxic fumes produced by the nitric and hydrofluoric acids used in the etching process. Working in his unventilated studio, he began experiencing lung problems and eventually had to abandon the activity.

He then switched to working with a technique that involved sandblasting clear glass surfaces, analogous to the practice of etching metal. After covering a glass surface with duct tape, he would cut and peel away parts of it to create geometric-abstract designs. When sandblasted, the impact would frost all the unprotected areas of glass while the taped areas remained pristinely clear when the protecting tape was peeled away. Sanderson used the technique to create windows and doors for their own residence as well as commissions, including an administration-building snack bar at Wake Forest University in Winston-Salem.

Although this was a period of renewed creative fertility, it was marred by several major business setbacks. When Interstate 40 was constructed in the early 1980s, it claimed ten acres on the west side of their property, while the onramps and concurrent widening of Durham-Chapel Hill Boulevard claimed another acre of frontage, effectively cutting their business off any from direct access to that main thoroughfare as well. The commercial impact was immediate and devastating. Their neighboring shops soon vacated, and the spaces failed to attract new tenants. Instead of leaving the abandoned storefronts completely empty, Black used them to display some of his paintings. But they could read the handwriting on the wall. It was time to begin seeking a buyer for their property and making plans to leave.

The end is a new beginning

As soon as Interstate 40 opened in 1984, Sanderson and Black were besieged by realtors eager to put the property under contract. They proceeded cautiously, turning down a number of potential buyers over the next five years. Negotiations with various parties continued until 1989, when they accepted a purchase offer from Homart Development Company, a Chicago-based subsidiary of Sears. The transaction involved the same ninety acres they had bought from Sanderson's uncle in 1972. Excluded from the sale were their residence and the stores, which they kept. Before the sale could be completed, they had to overcome opposition from competing business interests as well as environmental groups that advocated leaving the site undeveloped. They also had to meet the stringent requirements of Durham city government officials. Black points out that the sale and the buyer's plans for the site never won full approval from the city planning board.

"It took a lot of wrangling to get approval from the city council," he recalls. "It was an exhausting process."

After the sale finally went through in 1994, Sanderson and Black used part of the proceeds to make real-estate investments outside the area, buying twenty-year, triple-net leases on a Food Lion grocery store in Greensboro, North Carolina, and a Walgreens franchise in Hendersonville, Tennessee.[8]

The land they sold behind the Strawvalley site was promptly developed as New Hope Commons, an open-air shopping center with more than 470,000 square feet of retail space and major franchises such as Walmart, Best Buy, Barnes & Noble, and Old Navy. Anticipating the invasive impact on their home, Sanderson and Black had already begun looking for a new place to live when New Hope Commons opened in 1995. Seeking another opportunity to modify a suitable, pre-existing building or group of buildings, as they had done at Strawvalley, they surveyed available real estate in the Research Triangle, in and around Charlottesville, Virginia, and as far afield as Santa Fe, New Mexico. None of the properties they inspected met their requirements until sometime in 1998, when they answered a newspaper advertisement for the Anderson School, a decommissioned public-school complex in a rural area about an hour's drive northwest of Durham.

They promptly investigated and discovered a sprawling, one-story brick building, most of which dated from the 1950s. Named for the unincorporated community that surrounded it, the school had served area students from first grade through high school since the Great Depression, when the first school building was erected on the property, until it had closed in the late 1980s. Measuring some 12,000 square feet, the structure presented attractive options for renovation. It also had ample space for storage and display of their collection of objects and their own work, including Black's largest paintings. The mostly wooded property encompassed about fifteen acres and also included a small, one-story house previously reserved for the school's principal. It took them only a few weeks to decide on buying it.

"If we hadn't bought it, it would have probably been demolished and made into a trailer park," Sanderson said.

As they had done forty years earlier with the farmhouse and outbuildings at Strawvalley, they took possession of an abandoned structure on undeveloped

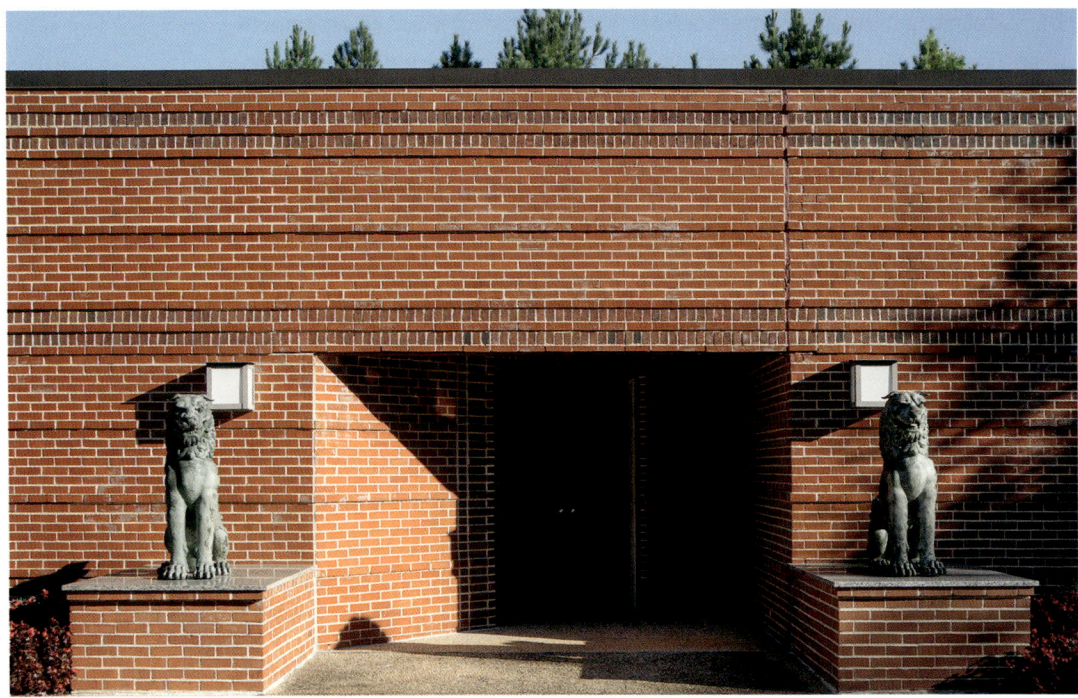

Entrance to Oak Court, built 1999-2003.

land and proceeded to transform it into a showplace for art, craft, and design. This time, though, there was no financial pressure to make it a commercial venture, so there had been no good reason to locate themselves in a heavily trafficked area or maintain a public profile. Their new property would be strictly residential and completely private—a secluded refuge for their own enjoyment and that of their friends and invited guests. They would eventually find other ways to share their collection with a broader public.

Their renovation of the site was extensive. They created two courtyards—a narrow one along the north side and a larger one with two levels on the south side, where they located the main entrance to the compound. The courtyards, glass brick, and large windows with which they replaced several walls opened the building to the outdoors, enabling the sun to illuminate much of the interior space during daylight hours. These open features were inspired by the designs of modern Mexican architects, especially Luis Barragán and his disciple, Ricardo Legoretta, whose buildings Sanderson and Black had admired during a trip to Mexico in the 1970s. These architects also influenced Black's decision to incorporate two features in the interest of privacy that were highly unusual in rural North Carolina—a solid brick perimeter wall that completely enclosed the building and courtyards, and a raised earthen berm surrounding the building's wooded sides. The idea for the horizontal raised-brick bands ornamenting the enclosure wall were among Sanderson's contributions to the design. Leaving the building's original flat roof intact, they installed a new pitched roof structure on top of it, with openings for the two original skylights. They also added two belvederes along the new roof's peak, to create interior height and let in additional light. Towering over the whole structure is the school's original chimney, which they left intact.

In some cases, plans were changed while the renovation was in progress. Black's original design for the building's atrium, for example, included a cast-concrete wall with cast-concrete columns to support the roof. He had been intrigued with the architectural potential of cast concrete ever since being introduced to the work of Le Corbusier (Charles-Édouard Jeanneret), a Swiss-French planner and modernist pioneer who often used concrete in his designs. During a West Coast visit, Black and Sanderson had been impressed with the enormous, cylindrical concrete columns supporting the ramp to the lobby of San Francisco's airport. Although these features inspired Black's idea for the wall and atrium columns, he reluctantly abandoned the idea after learning that the contractor they'd hired had no experience with cast concrete and hesitated to make his first attempt with this project. In the end, Black decided brick construction would serve as a better alternative for both the wall and the columns. The courtyards and other additions, including a garage and the expansion of several rooms, increased the overall footprint of the home to about 14,000 square feet.

Black summarizes his goal for the redesign plan in straightforward terms: to transform what had long been a no-frills institutional structure into a "pleasing building design." The room that had once served as the school's science lab became a high-ceilinged sitting room with a colonial-modernist theme, while the opaque brick walls of what had one been social studies and home economics classrooms were replaced with glass-brick expanses that made them light and airy. As for the surrounding acreage, Black explains, "The landscaping followed the same pattern of fitting the design to the existing terrain and using native plants." Oak trees that had towered over the property for decades inspired Sanderson's suggestion that they name their new home Oak Court.

Although already in their seventies by this point, Sanderson and Black still did much of the intensive labor themselves. "We spent a lot of time making finishing touches on the new building and moving things from Durham," Black recalls. "We had lots of things we didn't want to let the movers move, and we brought those up in our car. For a while, we were driving up here and back every day. It took about three years to do the renovations and move everything.

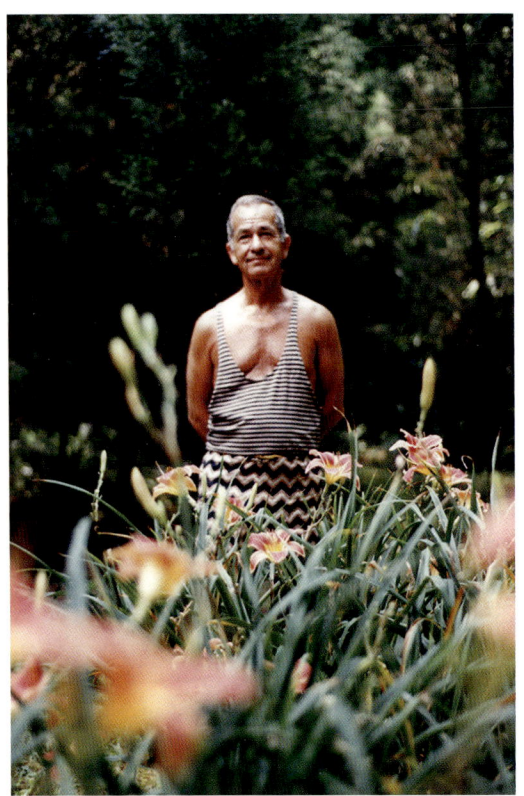

Ormond Sanderson among his daylilies.

Then we came up here to live around 2003, and we worked on the landscaping. The builder had scraped all of the vegetation away from the building to build the berms around it, so we began buying shrubs and trees and planting them around the building. We did all of the landscaping work, I guess because we had always done it ourselves before, at Strawvalley."

Sanderson was largely responsible for the landscape design. He planted Eleagnus around the perimeter of the property, and retained some of the pre-existing vegetation, including the large oaks that had suggested the compound's name. He also planted a couple of exotic trees that he and Black have yet to identify (in the meantime Sanderson calls them "Chinese firs") and that he had propagated by planting and nurturing seeds. Other trees and shrubs he introduced to the property's landscape include magnolia, Japanese cedar (Cryptomeria), Leland cypress, crape myrtles, camellias, quince, acuba, cross vine, yellow jasmine, weeping Japanese cherry, Foster's holly, Burford holly, various junipers, azaleas, trifoliate oranges, mimosa, osmunda, euonymus, nandena, mahonia shrubs, ajuga, and hellebores. Inside the surrounding wall he planted liriope, vinca, and an expanse of yellow-flowering sedum acre as ground cover in the main south courtyard. He and Black brought a number of these plants with them from Strawvalley, where they had originally cultivated them. Also from Strawvalley was a collection of lillies and daylilies Sanderson had started years earlier, and which they now planted in the upper garden at Oak Court.

In 2004, the two artists began turning their attention indoors to their studios, the other rooms in their new home, and the eclectic array of artworks and other objects they had brought with them after forty years of collecting and dealing in fine art, crafts, and design. In 2007, they finally sold the stores and their distinctive former residence at Strawvalley, followed in 2011 by the last lot they owned there, at the intersection of I-40 and Durham-Chapel Hill Boulevard. They remained absentee landlords and managers of properties elsewhere until very recently, when they finally sold the Walgreens and Food Lion that were their last remaining commercial real-estate holdings.

Artists first

Although they've worn different hats and developed different sets of skills to accommodate their other interests, Black and Sanderson have always considered themselves artists first and foremost. While they've been each other's primary audience, always ready to offer encouragement and suggestions, each has developed his art in his own way and according to his own needs.

Black began as a painter and eventually came full-circle back to painting, after years of working in a variety of two- and three-dimensional mediums. There were a few fallow periods, when his art necessarily took a back seat to other priorities, but he has remained remarkably prolific over the long run, while his work has evolved along several different lines. His earliest surviving pieces from his graduate-school days at the University of Georgia include a few landscape-related compositions, abstracted still-lifes, and paintings in an abstract-expressionist vein. He also made several stained-glass panels during that period, featuring lively jigsaw-like figural compositions. Except for the glasswork, he continued pursuing these varied directions in his art through his relatively brief period of college-level teaching.

The first big shift in Black's creative trajectory came around the beginning of the 1960s, when he and Sanderson were beginning to establish themselves at Strawvalley. Their survey of the regional craft scene, ostensibly for items to sell in their new shop, paralleled and influenced Black's shift to pottery, which he pursued for most of that decade. While many of his ceramic pieces are vessel forms that can serve utilitarian purposes—as flower vases, for example—others are more purely sculptural. In any case, Black has said he considers all of them sculptures. Some of the non-functional pieces are overtly figural, such as his series of stylized, open mouthed heads. Another series of small, hollow pieces was created in collaboration with Sanderson, who incised the wet clay forms with whimsical animal imagery before they were fired.

Black's creative output went into a temporary lull during the 1970s, when he and Sanderson were consumed with the responsibilities of operating Design Gallery and managing the adjacent rental spaces. The paintings and collage-paintings Black began to make toward the end of that decade signaled a reactivation of his creative drive and a fresh approach to geometric abstraction. After they sold the gallery in 1981, he inaugurated a new body of three-dimensional work in the form of of abstract sculptures made from copper sheets cut into irregular triangles crimped along the edges and welded together. He cites visionary architect Buckminster Fuller's geodesic domes as influences on this series, which he continued to develop until the late 1980s. Amorphous and organic-looking, these pieces are reminiscent of wasp or hornet nests, and the dark patinas they've taken on with exposure to the elements suggest heavy smoke stains.

The demands of managing and selling the Strawvalley property and moving to Caswell County severely limited Black's studio time through the 1990s and into the new millennium. Once he and Sanderson were settled at Oak Court, with their spacious, sunlit studio in good order, he returned to working on canvas in the geometric-abstract mode he had been exploring when business obligations sidelined him. Many of these works are fairly large, measuring four feet or more in either dimension, and their surfaces are heavily worked—a fact that becomes especially evident on close inspection of the cut-paper paintings, as he calls them. From a few feet away they look like they're composed of multiple interlocking, boldly painted geometric shapes. But up close, it's obvious they're made from paper cut into hundreds, or even thousands, of tiny squares, each painstakingly glued to the canvas like tiles in a mosaic. Black's works in this vein, which he continues to explore, represent his distinctive contribution to a broadly defined modernist tradition extending from the Bauhaus through Color Field painting to Neo Geo and other strains of postmodern geometric abstraction. He has recently adapted the bold palette characteristic of these works to the creation of surprisingly straightforward, cartoonish portraits of imaginary subjects. Although he has made only a few of them so far, these whimsical figurative works reflect his enduringly experimental approach and his unflagging enthusiasm for "trying something new," a phrase he uses often in discussing his art's development.

Sanderson's work as a visual artist has developed along more idiosyncratic lines, with little reference to the kind of structured, academic art training his partner received. His only formal education in visual art was a class he took at the University of Michigan, in which faculty artist Erik Kamroski introduced him to basic techniques for working in stained glass and vitreous enamel. Kamroski also taught him about the formal relationship between music and art. Although Sanderson continued to focus his energy on piano performance through the 1950s, he retained a measure of inspiration from Kamroski's example. When he made the shift from music to art, he quickly gravitated to the mediums he had studied with Kamroski. Although he made some stained glass works, it was vitreous enamel that compelled his sustained interest. Once he had begun devoting serious attention to that medium, he followed his own instincts, experimenting freely rather than trying to imitate any of his forerunners. He auto-

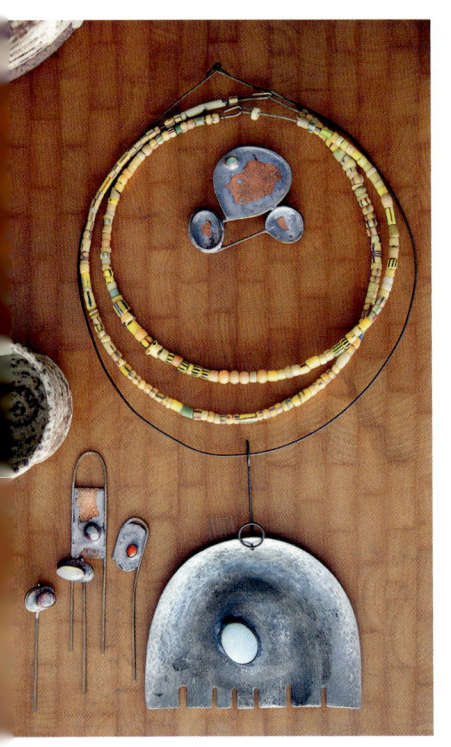

Sanderson necklaces and pins, 1965. Enamel and patination on pewter, with opals, carnelians, and trade beads.

matically gravitated to imagery based in the natural world, which had fascinated him since childhood. His intricately drawn, imaginatively abstracted flora and fauna became a hallmark of his enamel work, as did the unpredictable effects of oxidization on his metal surfaces—effects he welcomed, unlike most of his counterparts who worked with this medium. Both he and Black are convinced it was these unusual features of his work that attracted serious interest early on. Though he eventually abandoned vitreous enamel and shifted his creative focus to cast concrete and etched glass, he also created his own abstract sculptures in clay and worked in collaboration with Black on the previously mentioned series of intimately scaled sculptures, augmenting Black's ceramics with incised imagery of his own design.

While Black primarily pursued art in the studio, Sanderson applied his singular visual sensibilities to other areas of their lives. Chief among these have been gardening and landscaping—at both Strawvalley and Oak Court—and his interior-design efforts. From Sanderson's perspective, there's not much artistic difference between making enamel-coated plaques or etched-glass doors, and creating a pleasing composition of shrubs or a satisfying arrangement of furnishings. It's all equally creative.

At home at work

During their first three decades together, Sanderson and Black had made themselves accessible to a broad, aesthetically attuned public at a unique, high-profile venue on a major regional thoroughfare. But by now those days are almost thirty years gone. Finding this relentlessly creative duo today requires a trip some distance away from the busy thoroughfare where they had spent so much of their lives, into a quiet, lightly traveled section of southern Caswell County, North Carolina. An asphalt driveway turns off the nearby country road and leads through a dense, diversified forest to an unmarked parking area that faces an elegantly imposing brick façade. Flanking two unmarked, heavy, green-painted wooden doors is a pair of life-size bronze lions from China, standing guard on brick pedestals. A first encounter suggests that a kind of spiritual fortress or mysterious grand temple awaits beyond the doors. And it is indeed a temple, but one constructed to serve a shared but singular vision of beauty, fine art, and clean design.

The green doors open into a sunlit courtyard surrounded by a broad walkway, distributed along which one finds an array of striking objects that include massive, ancient Chinese and Mediterranean ceramic vessels, a larger-than-life bronze sculpture of Zeus or Poseidon, and a similarly outsized bust of a shaven-headed Estonian military officer, displayed on an industrial wooden cart. Hundreds of Paolo Soleri's bronze and clay wind bells hang suspended near the edge of the roof to chime with any breezes wafting through the courtyard, where lush ground-cover plants share the open space with one of Black's angularly abstract, sheet-copper sculptures and an installation of weather-sculpted stones reminiscent of a Zen temple's rock garden. Across the courtyard, two pairs of sliding glass doors open into a realm of mostly spacious, sunlit rooms showcasing museum-quality modern furnishings, designer glassware, textiles, lighting fixtures, and other special objects, all tastefully arranged to encourage and accommodate domestic sociability.

"We consider each of these rooms a composition," Sanderson explains, clearly referring to most if not all of the rooms in the house. Nothing escapes their attention. The placement of every object in every room is carefully considered, akin to the individual elements or components in a painting or symphony.

A broad hallway that was original to the building (and undoubtedly once lined with students' lockers) connects the renovated classrooms, which have been transformed into a large kitchen and dining area, studios, bedrooms, bathrooms, an office, a library, and a small, uncharacteristically crowded room lined with floor-to-ceiling shelves, each filled with traditional Peruvian figurative pottery intermingled with other exotic objects. Although all the other spaces are not nearly so densely crowded, all are furnished and decorated with rare, special, or unusual objects and fixtures.

It's a comfortable home, but it's also a tastefully idiosyncratic, private museum of international art and design through the ages, with its director-curators in long-term residence. Sanderson and Black are approaching ninety, but continue to take care of the entire place on their own, maintaining a daily routine of steady but variable cooperative activity. Waking hours typically find them at one task or another, whether it be working on personal art projects, tending the grounds, keeping the rooms tidy and dust-free, attending to correspondence, or taking care of domestic chores, including the care and feeding of their two dogs, a Rat Terrier named Zephyr and a Jack Russell Terrier named Bunky. It's a regimen they appear to carry out with consistent enthusiasm, and it seems to have served their physical and mental health exceedingly well. They're clearly prepared to pursue it until they run out of steam, whenever that happens. To prepare for that inevitability, they have lately dedicated a share of their time to planning the disposition of their collection and financial assets to benefit various art institutions and related organizations, including substantial contributions to NC State's Gregg Museum of Art & Design.

A handful of North Carolina's veteran cultural insiders have long been aware of Ormond Sanderson and Robert Black and their contributions to contemporary art and design in the region, but their efforts and extraordinary achievements deserve to be far more widely known and celebrated while they're still around to join in. The present exhibition and this publication are a long-overdue and much deserved step toward honoring and recognizing them for their rare creative legacy.

Notes

EPIGRAPH, PAGE V

Gunnar Ekelöf, *Selected Poems*, W.H. Auden and Leif Sjöberg translators, Penguin Books, London (1971): 14. Originally published as "Jag hörde i drömmen . . ." in *Diwan över fursten av Emgión*, 1965.

ROGER MANLEY ESSAY

1   Lao Tzu, *Tao Te Ching*. D.C. Lau translation, Penguin Books, London (1963): 52.
2   "Die Kunst des Lebens zu meistern ist die Voraussetzung für alle weiteren Formen des Ausdrucks, ob es sich um Gemälde, Skulpturen, Tragödien oder musikalischen Kompositionen," http://www.paul-klee.org/de/zitate/
3   "Zeichnen ist die Kunst, Striche spazieren zu führen," *Bildnerische Gestaltungslehre*, 1921-31, Centrum Paul Klee, Bern, unpaginated facsimile.
4   In paintings where the overall pattern seems determined by a strict grid, the crisscrossing lines are even more subtle, created when blocks of repeated colors draw attention to each other. As the eye finds all the yellows or blues of a particular hue and shade, imaginary intersecting webs of lines form between them.
5   An earthen berm hidden in the densely wooded landscaping around the property completes the effect by deflecting all sound from the nearby roads as well.
6   Diana Lobel, *The Quest for God and the Good: World Philosophy as a Living Experience*, Columbia University Press (2011): 62.

TOM PATTERSON ESSAY

1   Biographical information in this essay, including any otherwise unattributed quotations or paraphrasing, is from interviews with Black and Sanderson during the summer and fall of 2017 and/or printed material they provided the author.
2   In 1990, the name was changed to Barton College to honor Barton Warren Stone, a founder of the Christian Church, also known as Disciples of Christ.

3   The college was relocated to Winston-Salem, NC, in 1956, and restructured as Wake Forest University.

4   Renamed the School of Design in 1948 and College of Design in 2000, the original faculty included a lineup of exceptionally gifted architects hired by dean Henry Kamphoefner, including Eduardo Catalano, James Fitzgibbons, George Matsumoto, Matthew Nowicki, and Edward Waugh. International luminaries such as Buckminster Fuller, Ludwig Mies van der Rohe, Lewis Mumford, and Frank Lloyd Wright participated as visiting professors. This pool of architectural talent eventually led to the Triangle Area having the nation's third largest concentration of modernist houses, after only Los Angeles and Chicago.

5   By now, more than two hundred companies, organizations, laboratories, studios and educational institutions are located in RTP.

6   Designed by Edward Durell Stone and opened in 1963, the NC Legislative Building's strikingly exotic modernist style—shared with the US embassy in New Delhi, India, and the Pakistan Institute of Nuclear Science & Technology in Islamabad (both also by Stone)—remains controversial.

7   From a Cogswell/Hausler-produced flyer advertising available rentals at Strawvalley and promoting it as an alternative to inconvenient, generic shopping mall environments.

8   A triple-net lease specifies tenant responsibility for building insurance, real-estate taxes, and maintenance on a property as well as rent, utilities, and other tenant fees.

Plates

All photographs are by John Mark Hall unless otherwise credited.

Ormond Sanderson's 1972 stoneware and pewter sculpture, *Hodie Christus Natus Est*, stands at the end of the courtyard arcade. Antique English chimney toppers of saltglazed stoneware serve as planters.

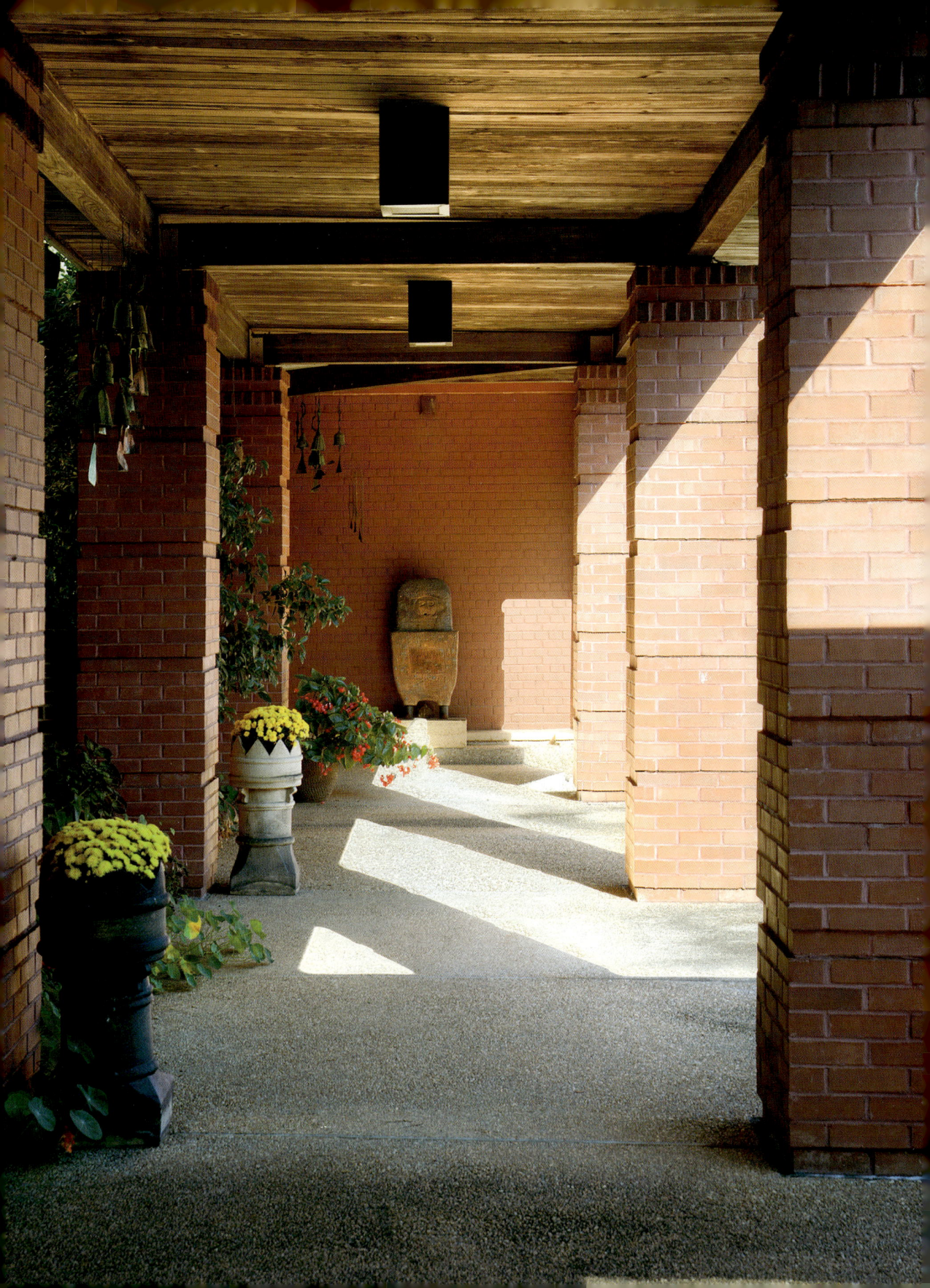

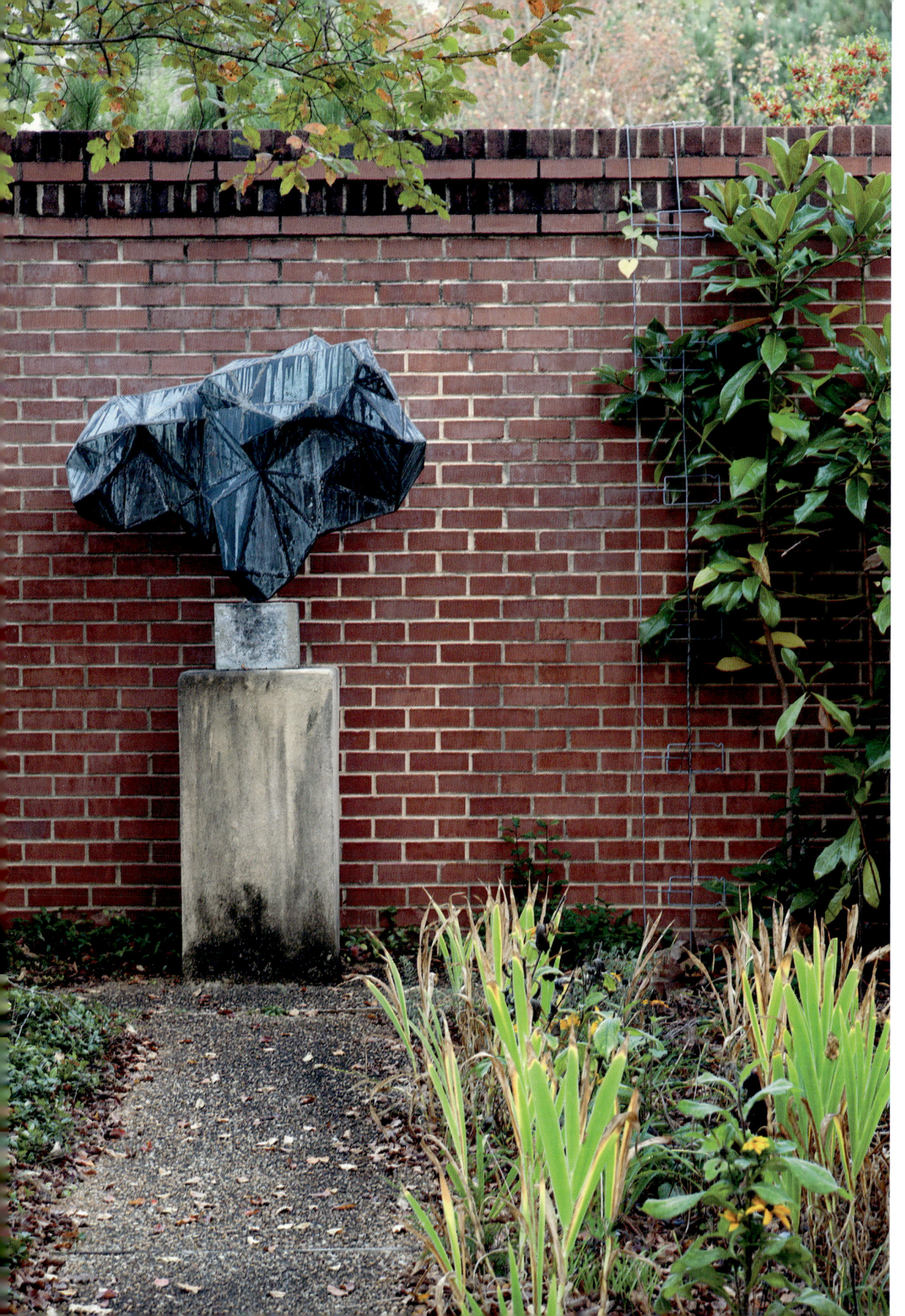

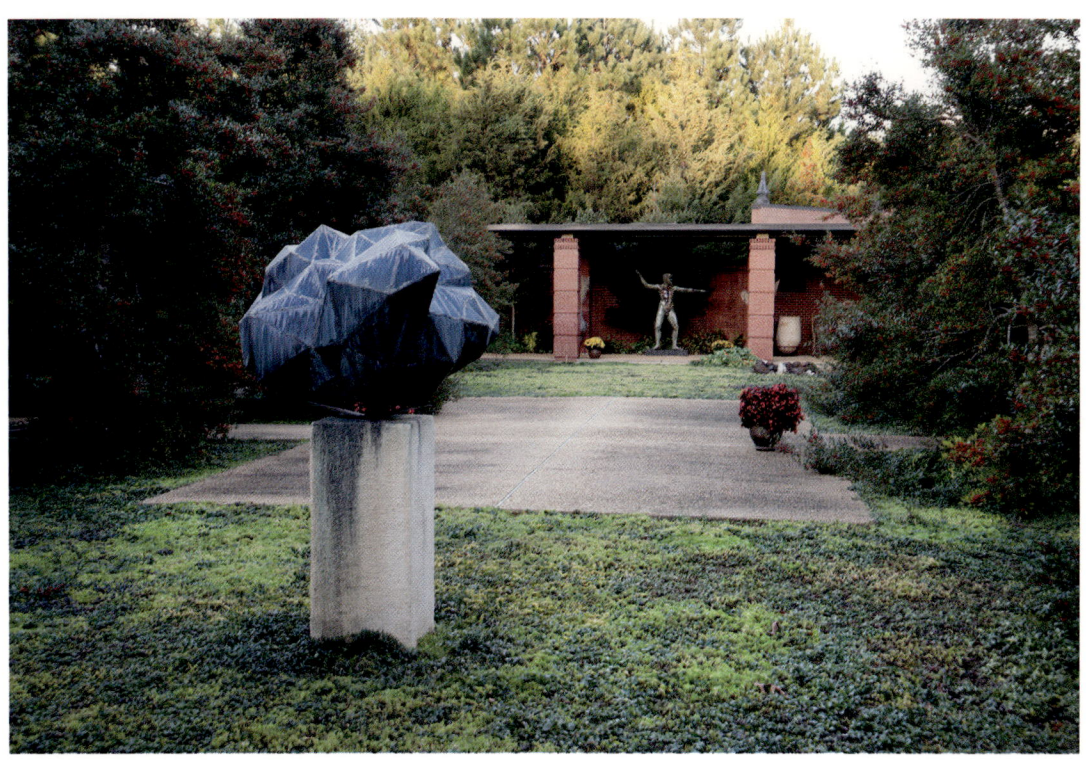

Black's large copper *Premonition* (1983) provides a major focal point in the large courtyard. A larger than life-sized statue of Zeus or Poseidon stands poised under the arcade at the far end.

———

(*opposite*) In the upper courtyard is Robert Black's 1983 brazed and patinated copper sculpture, *Flight*.

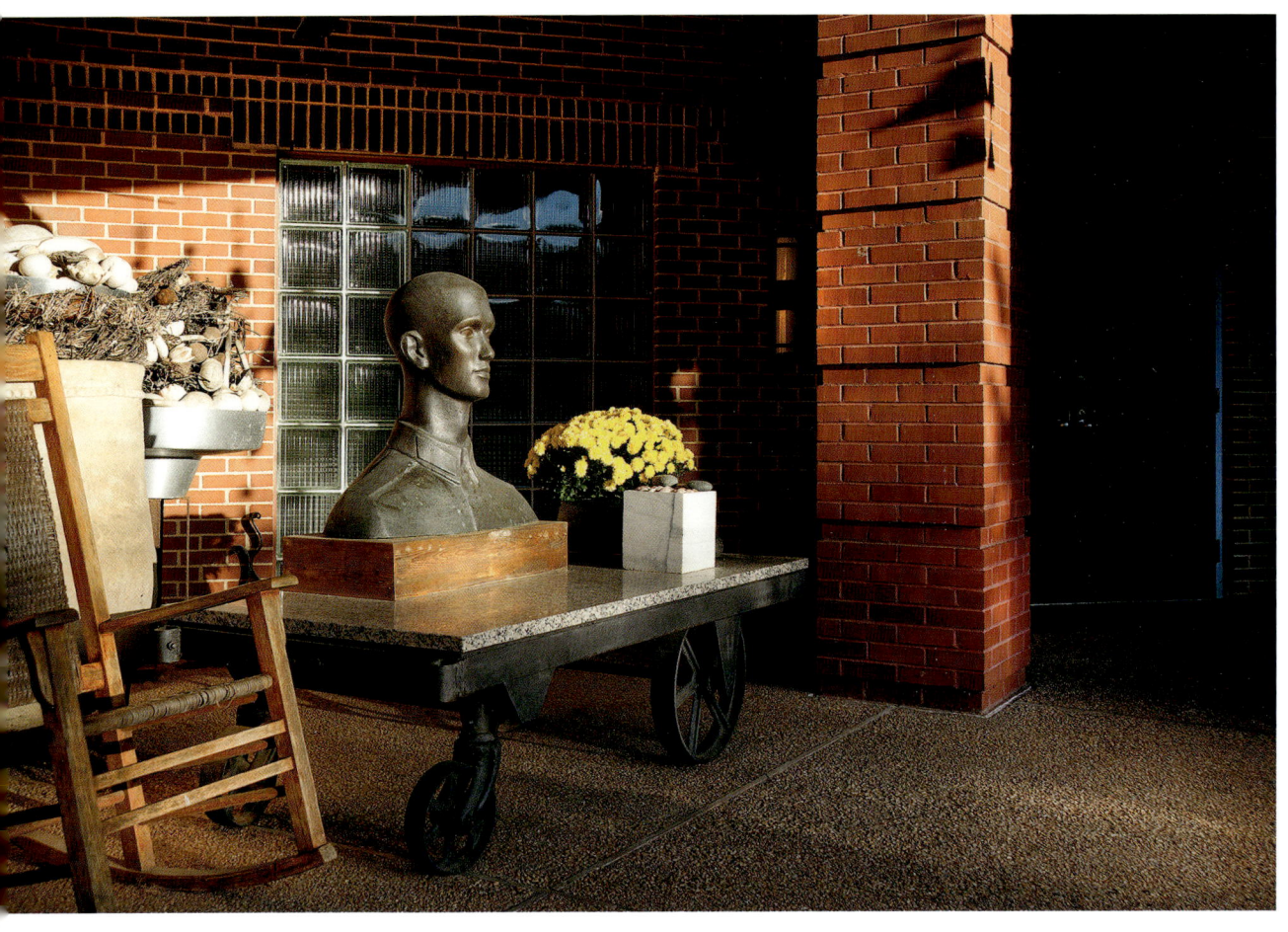

Bust of a Russian soldier purchased from a museum in Estonia, which deaccessioned it following the dissolution of the USSR in 1989. It now rests atop a coal cart that once serviced the heating furnace at the Anderson School, which Black and Sanderson transformed into their home.

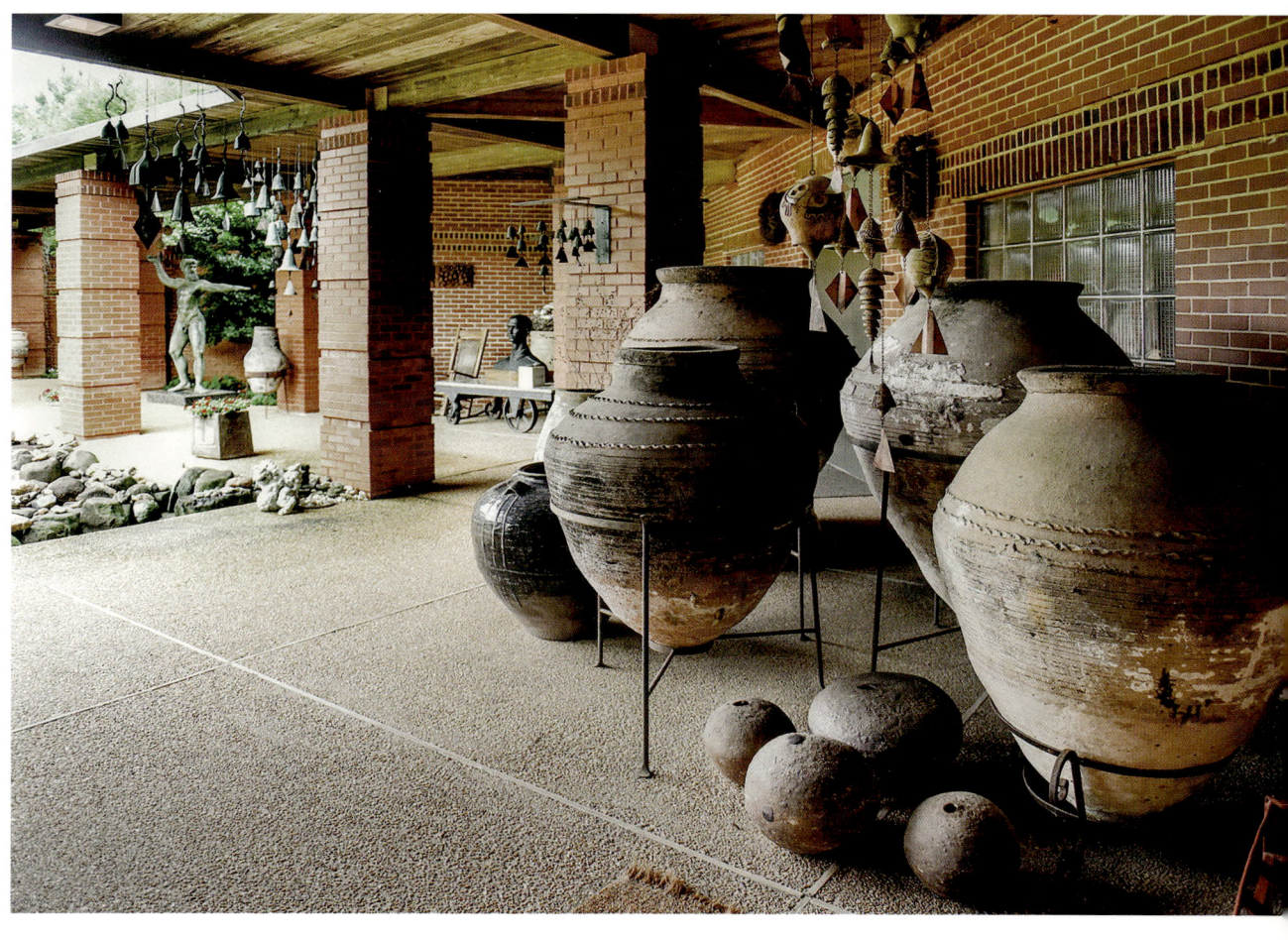

Just inside the main entrance, huge antique Mediterranean olive oil jars in metal stands crowd a dark-glazed Ming Dynasty storage jar on the pavement just beyond. In the foreground are smaller bulbous pots by Ormond Sanderson. Paolo Soleri's Arcosanti bells dangle above.

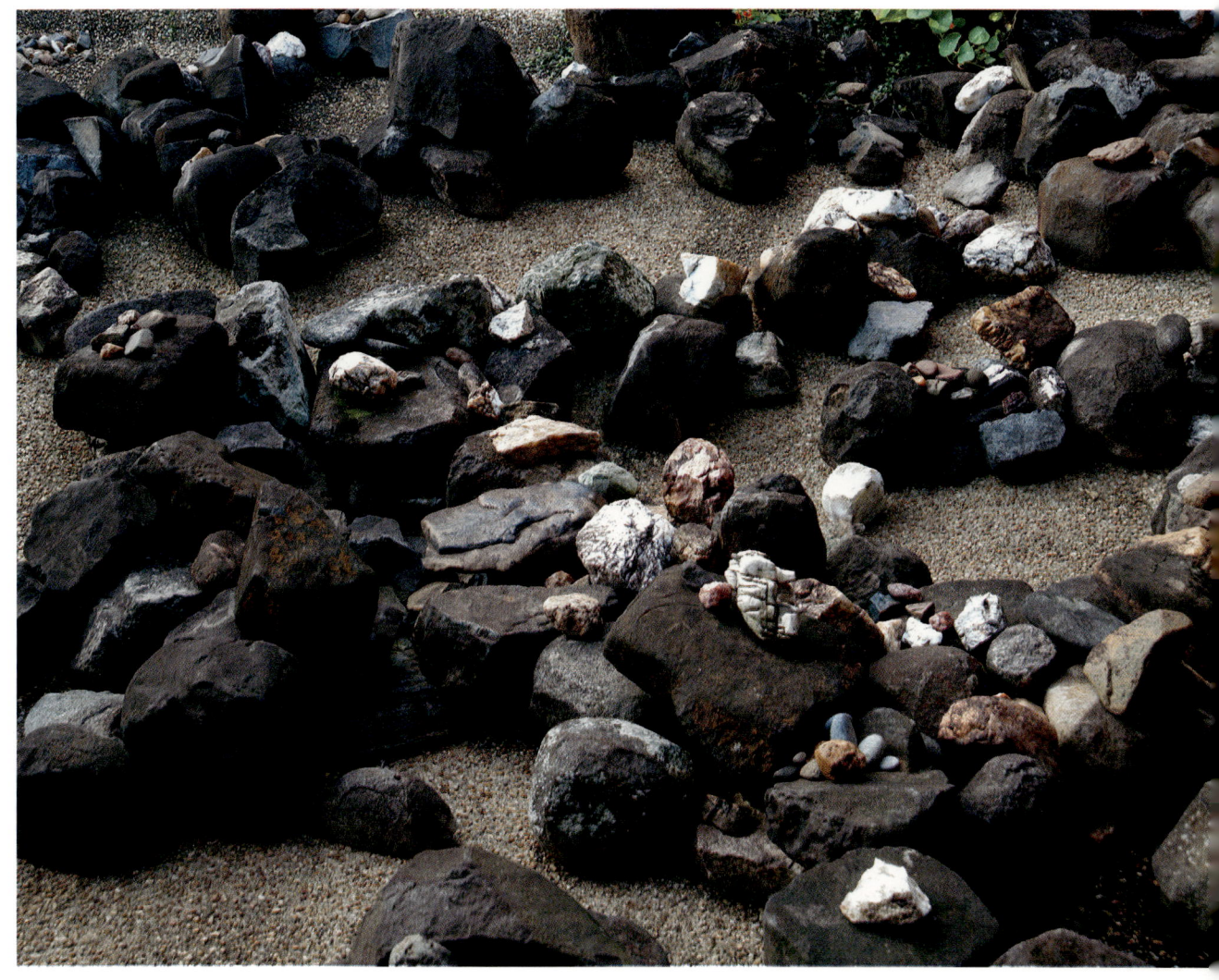

Along with all the art, decorative objects, and designer furniture that Black and Sanderson moved to their new home north of Burlington, they brought the stones that had once formed the foundation of their cabin and farmhouse at Strawvalley, three or four at a time in the trunk of their car.

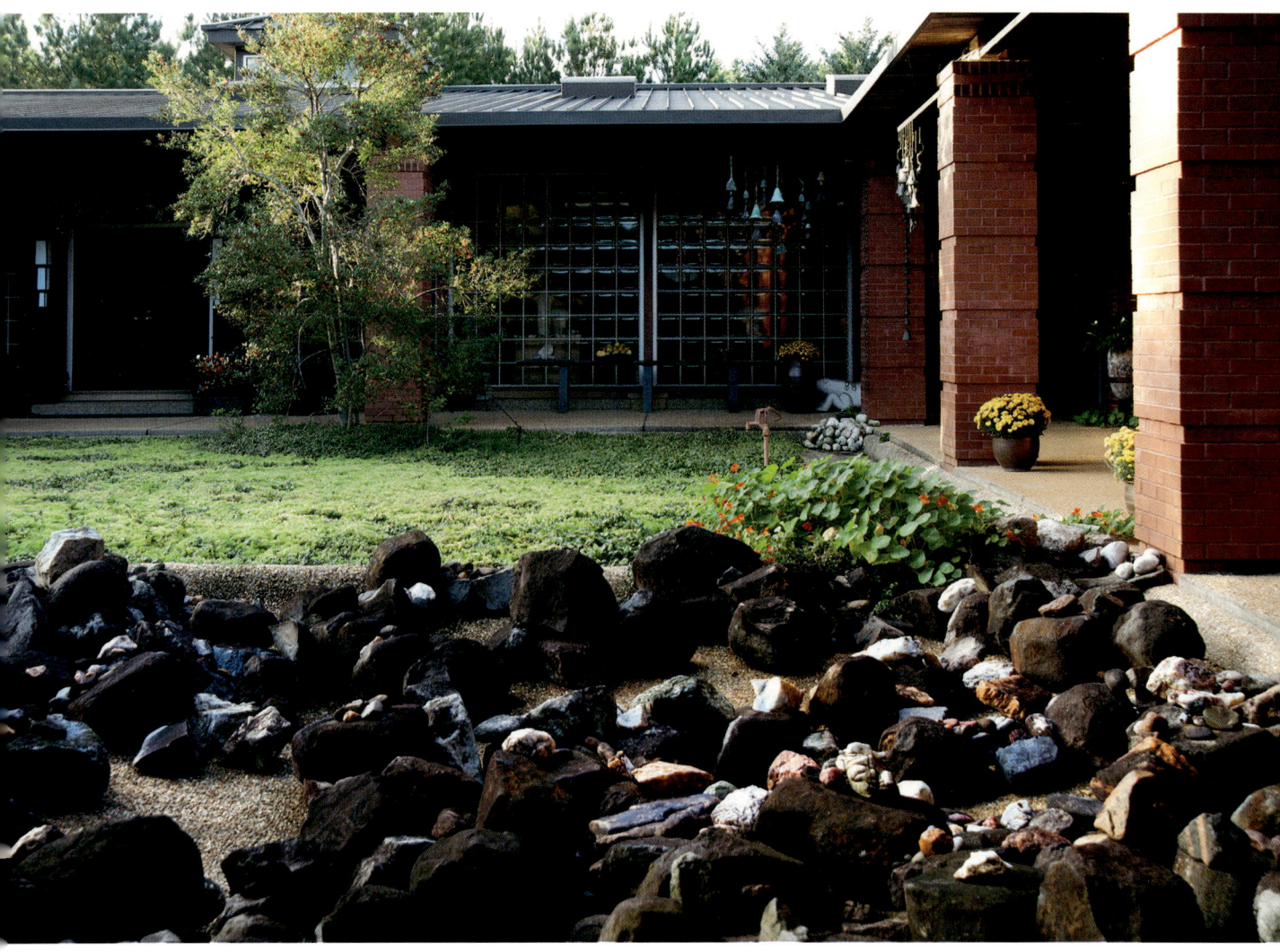

The stones are now a rock garden in one corner of the large courtyard, where rainwater collects after each storm.

(*opposite*) A statue of Zeus or Poseidon ready to hurl a thunderbolt or trident is a replica of the ca. 460 BCE "Artemision Bronze" preserved in the National Archaeological Museum of Athens. Bronze bells by Paolo Soleri chime in the breeze.

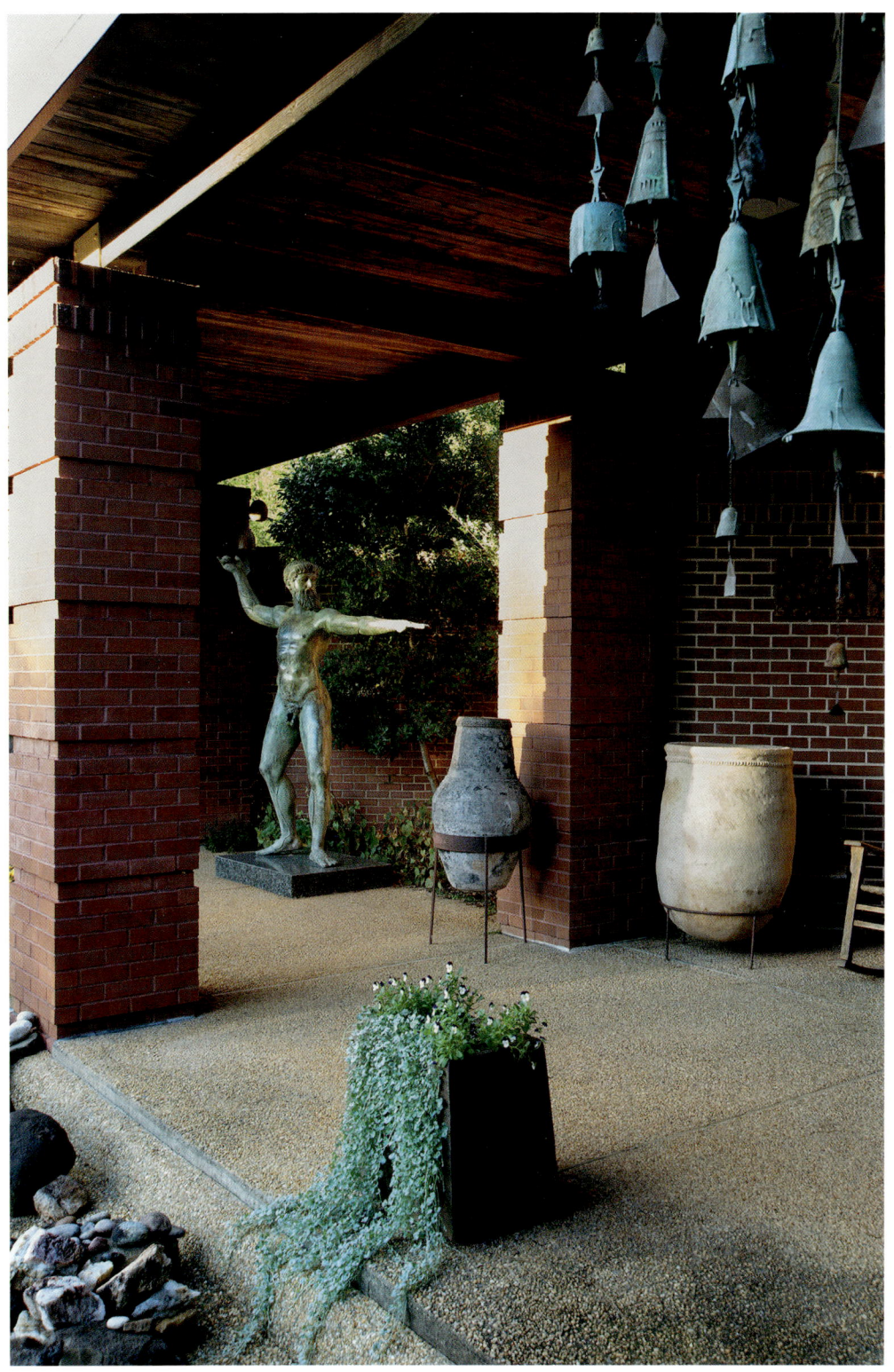

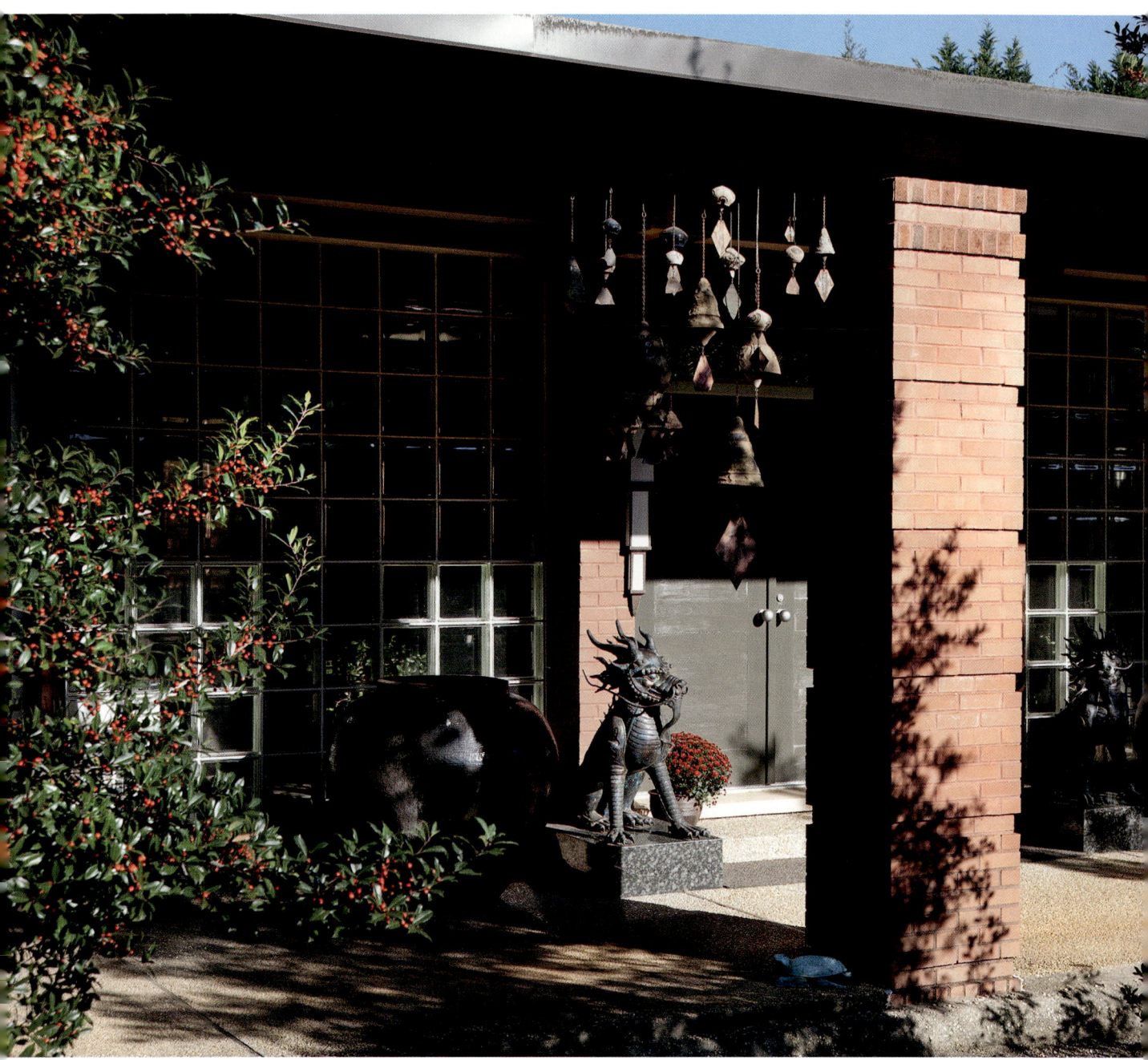

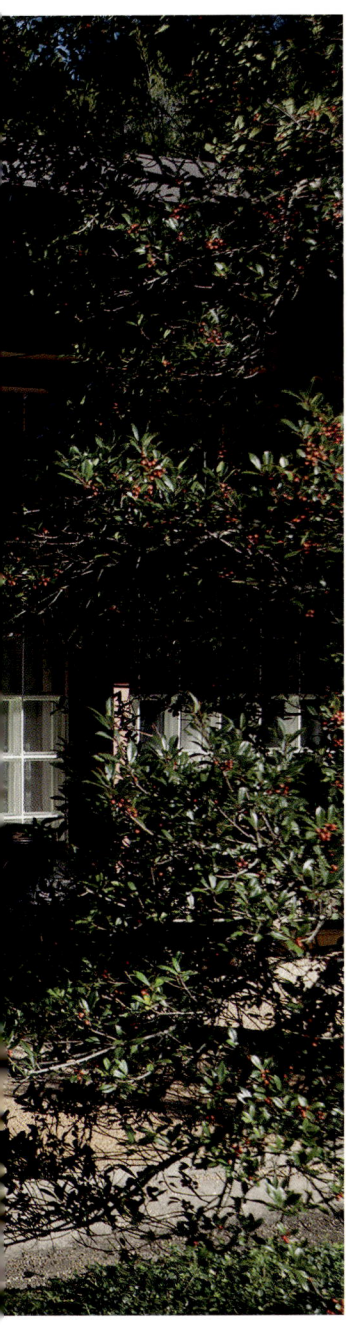

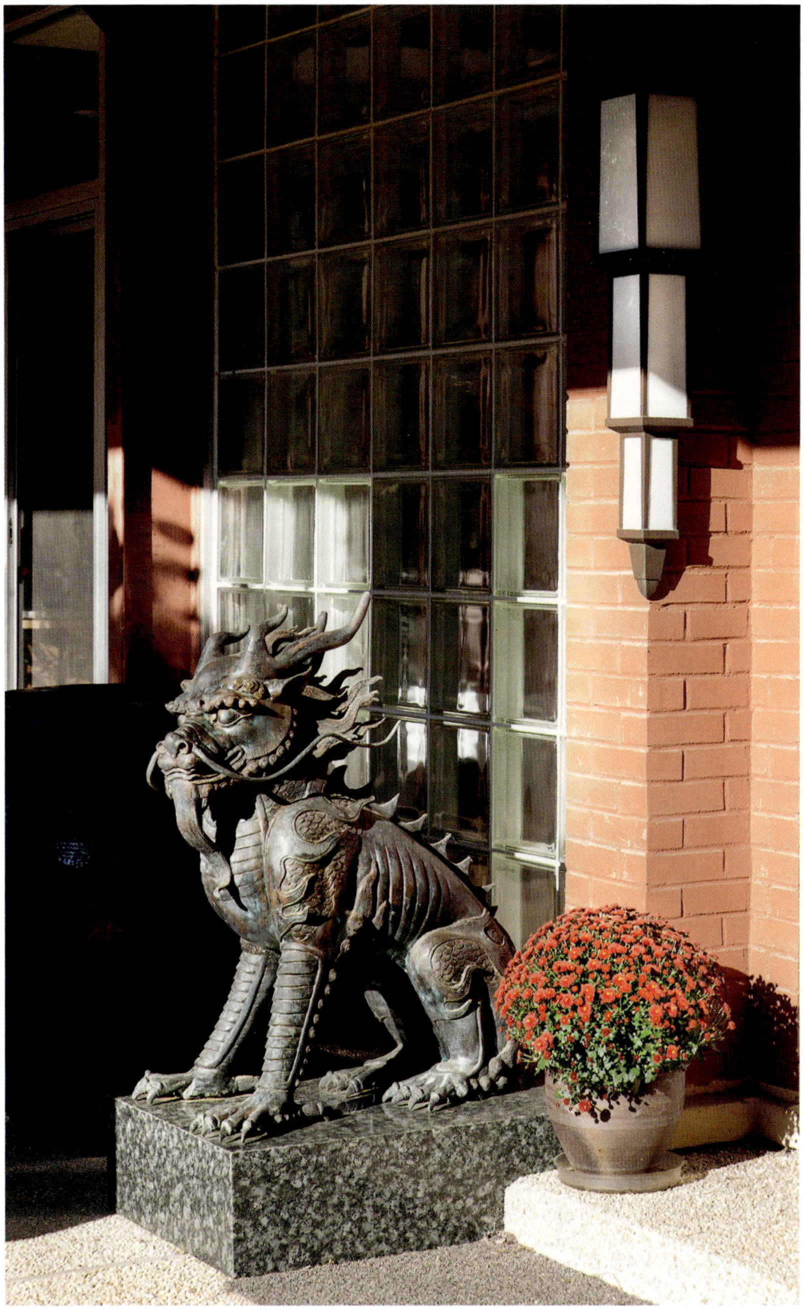

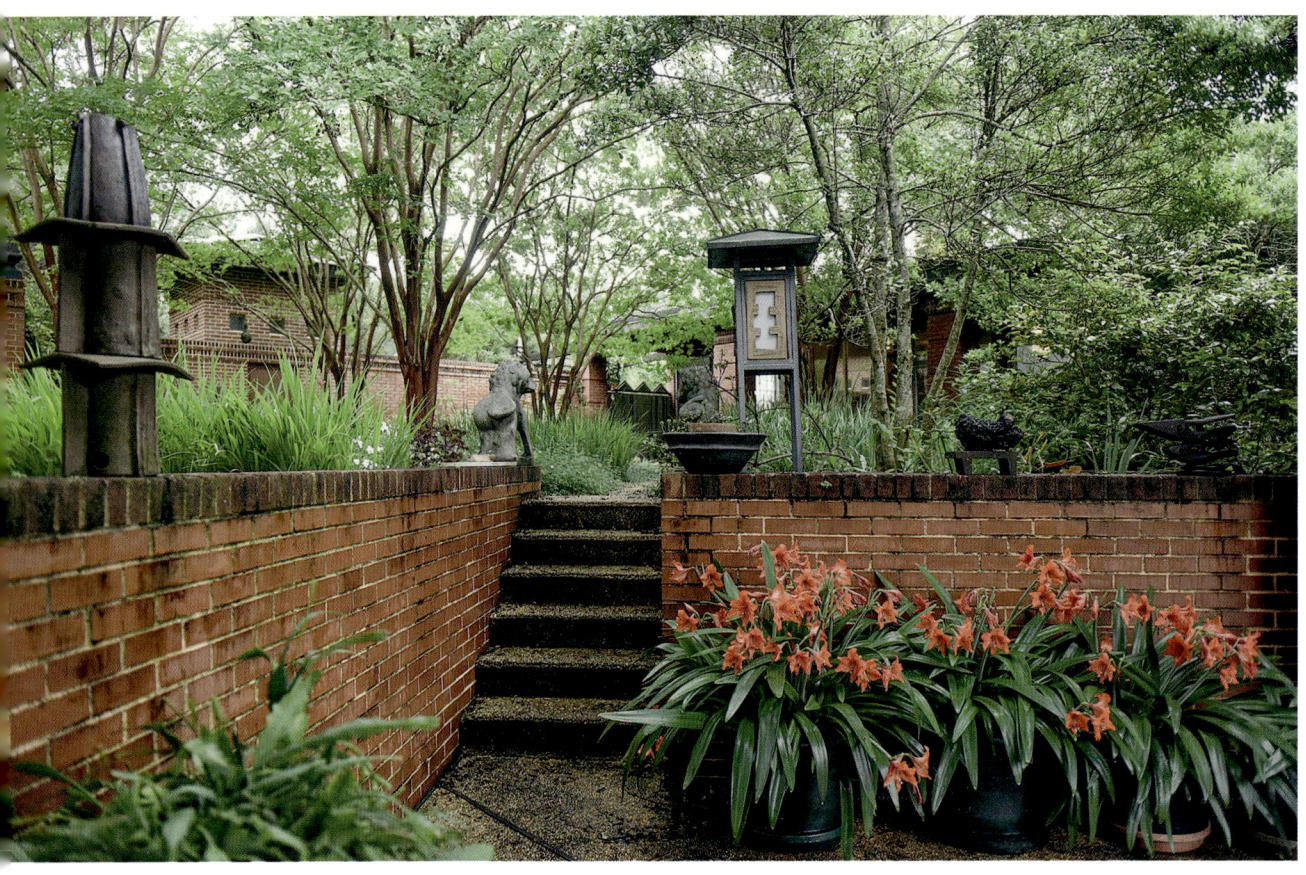

The upper courtyard provides dappled shade for perennials. A lantern that Robert Black originally made on commission for the balcony of a suite at the Watergate Hotel overlooks a sweep of what Sanderson calls "Yarborough lilies."

———

(*overleaf*) Bronze Chinese dragons guard the doors to the house proper. Ming storage jars and Art Deco lamps that once graced the Carolina Theater in Durham, North Carolina, also flank the entrance.

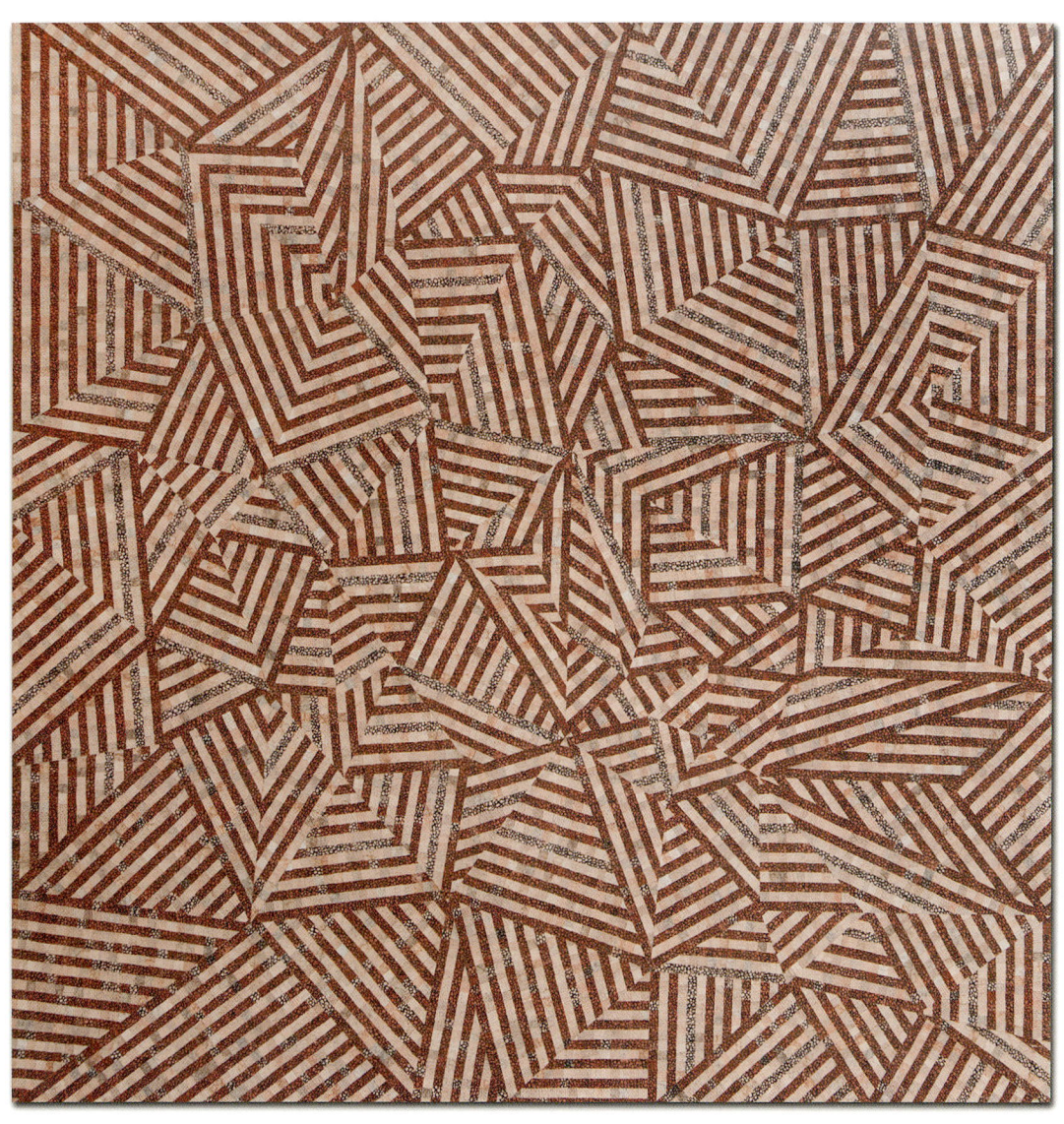

Robert Black, *Cataclysm*, 1993, acrylic over paper on canvas, 56½" x 56½".

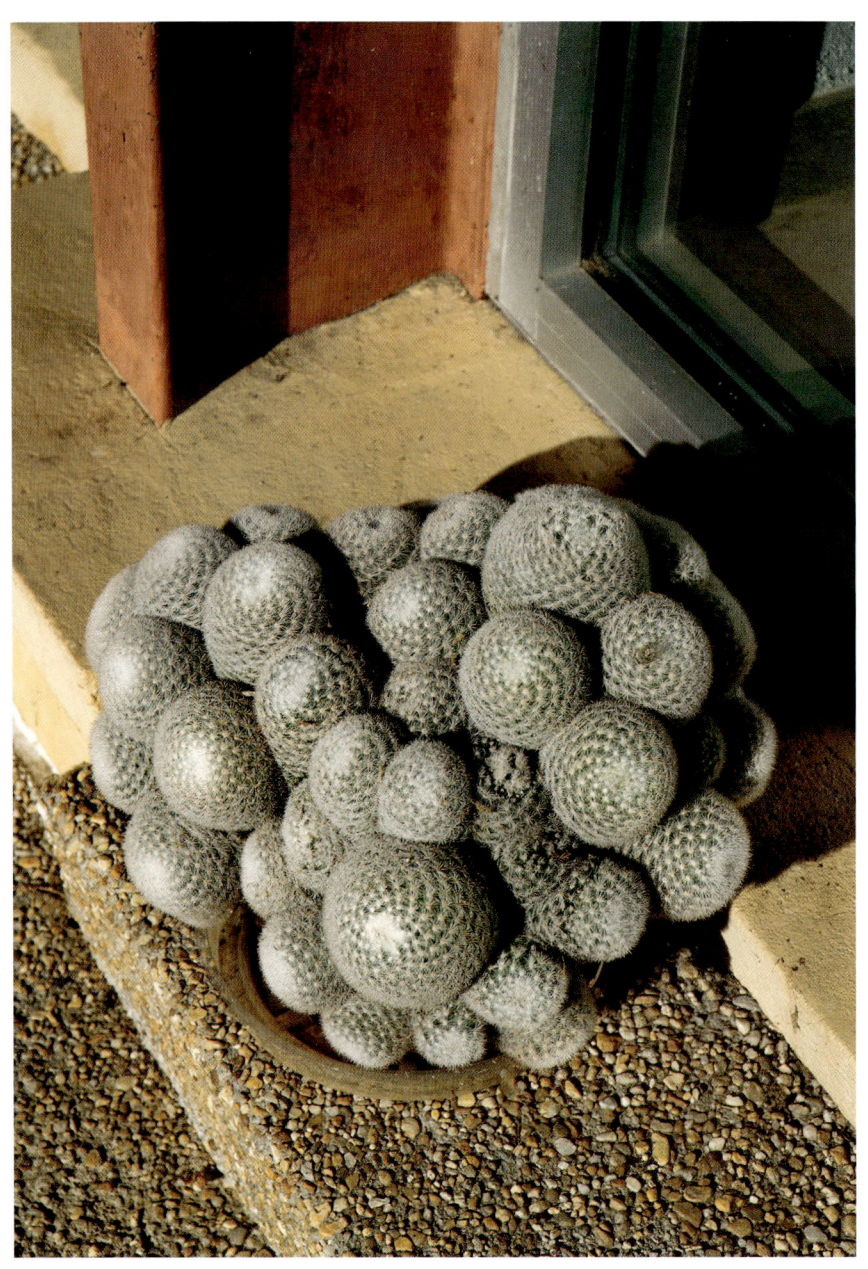

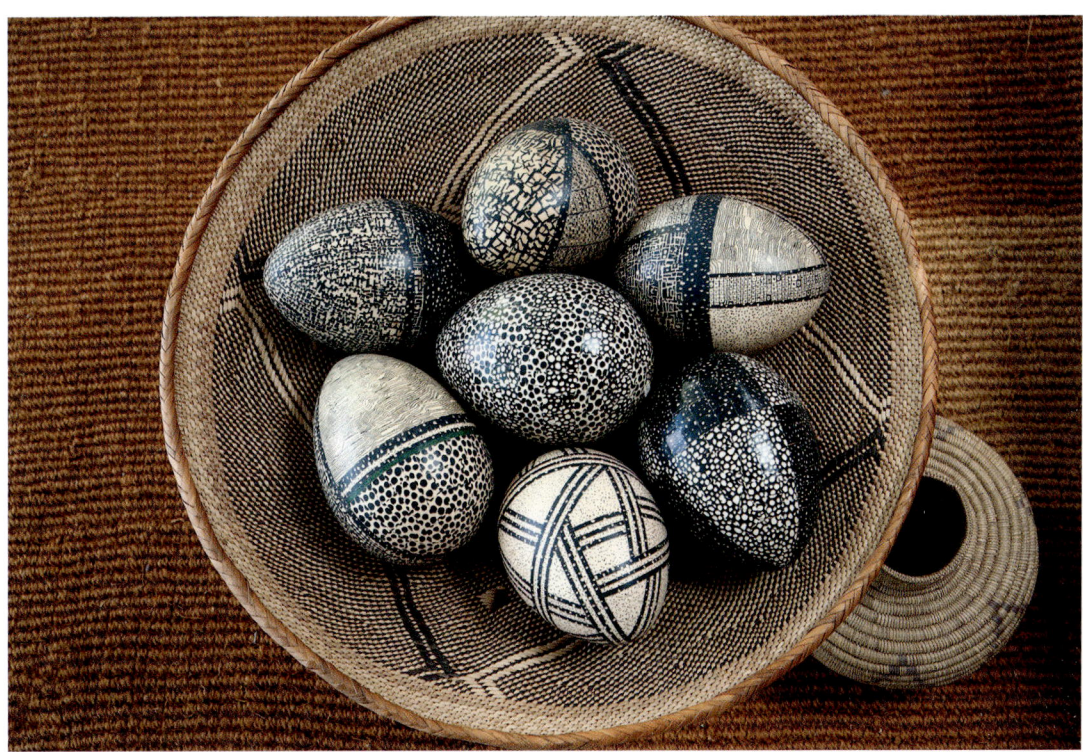

A clutch of wood and papier-mâché eggs covered with dot-patterned paper by Ormond Sanderson fills an African basket. See examples of similar dot patterns at the front and back of this publication.

––––––

(*opposite*) A cactus from Sanderson's collection of succulents.

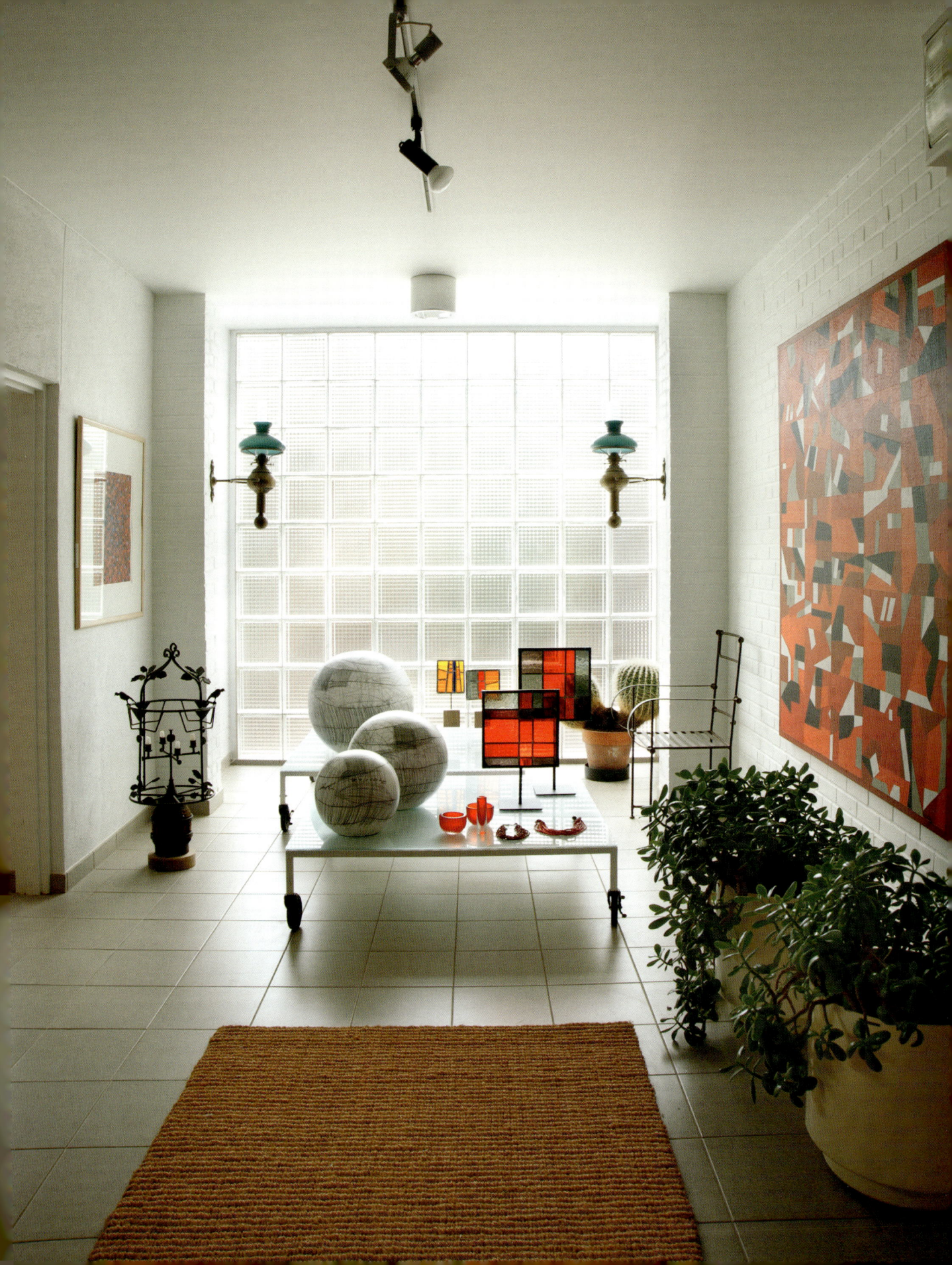

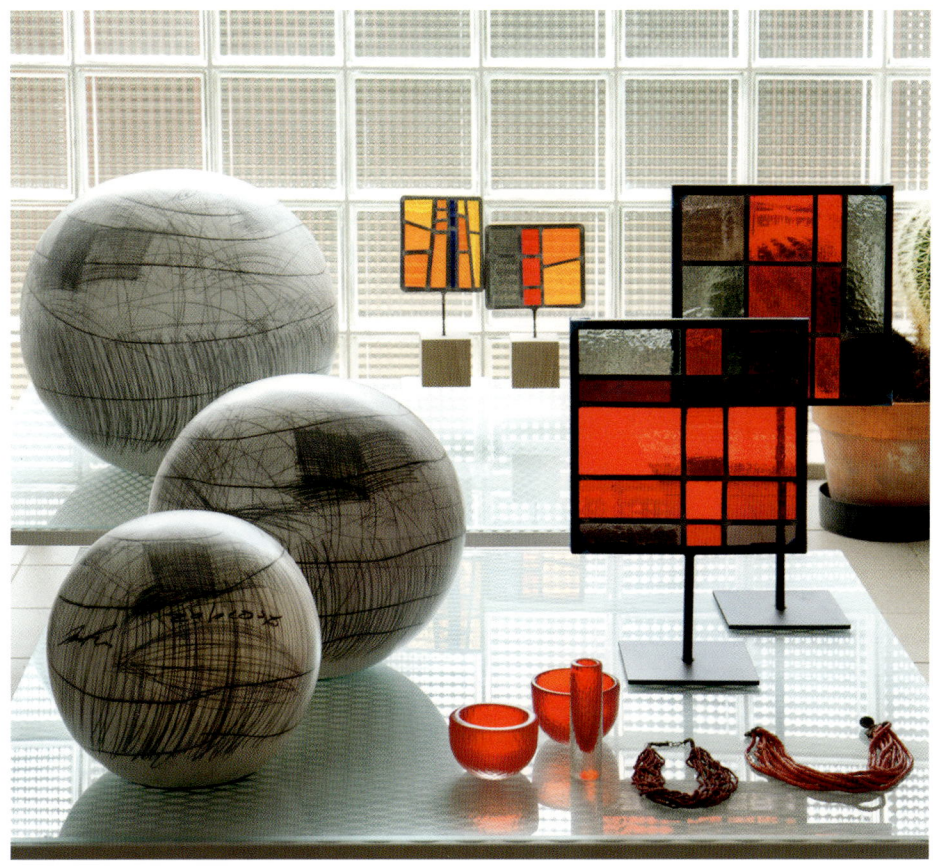

Glass-topped rolling tables designed and built by Black and Sanderson for their Strawvalley showrooms now support examples of Black's stained glass. An iron chair and candelabra in the style of Diego Giacometti and Black's *Scarlet Dawn* painting complete the scene.

In one of the largest rooms in the house, an Arco floor lamp by Pier Giacomo and Achille Castiglioni (1962) leaps over furniture by Poul Kjaerholm and Tobia Scarpa, accompanied by slender white Eero Saarinen end tables. Glass by Venini and Carlo Moretti and a platter by Shoji Hamada grace the décor. Beyond the central cluster are gatherings of Black's sculptures and collage paintings from his *Exuberance* series (the largest seen here is 64" x 64").

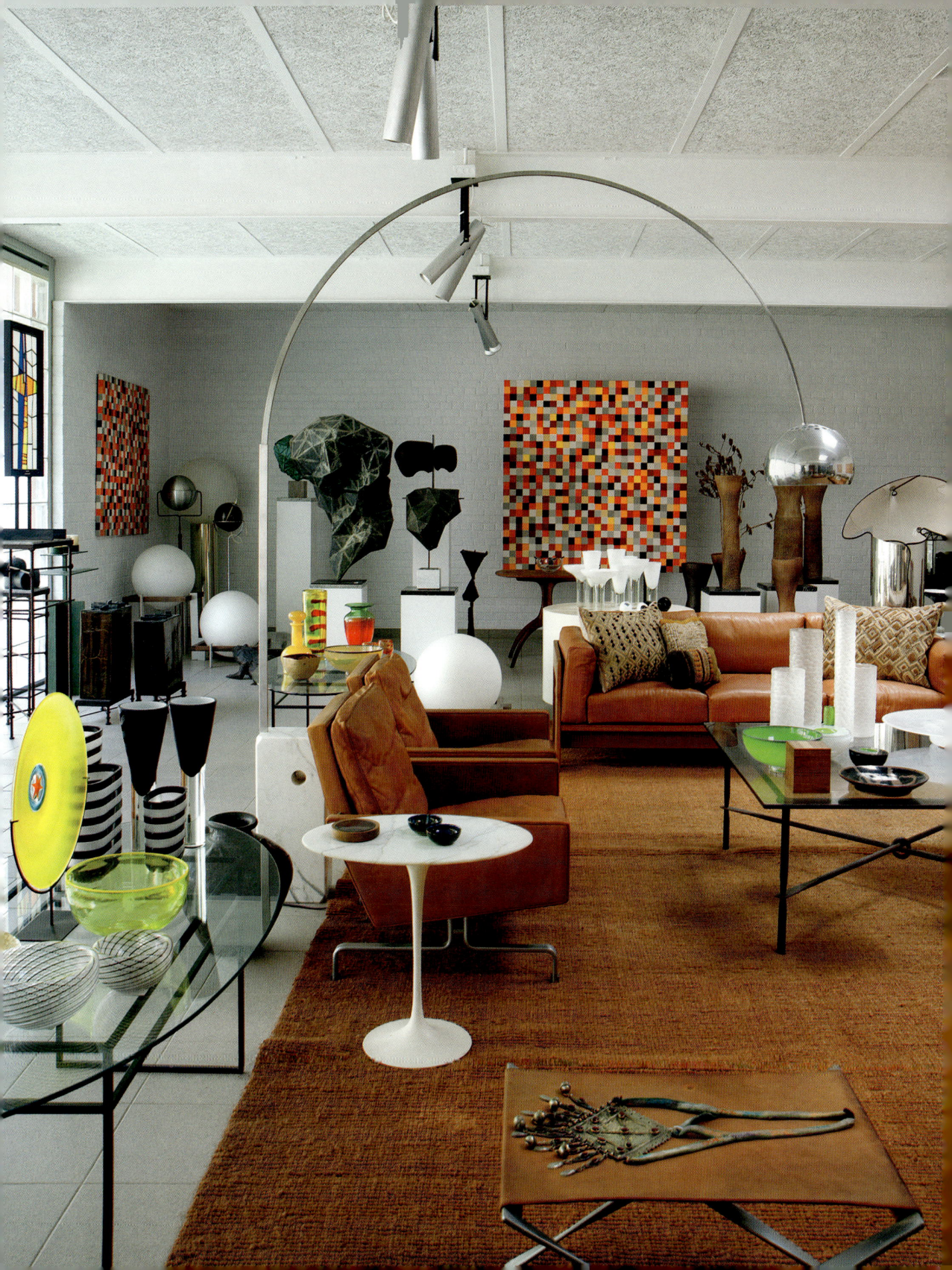

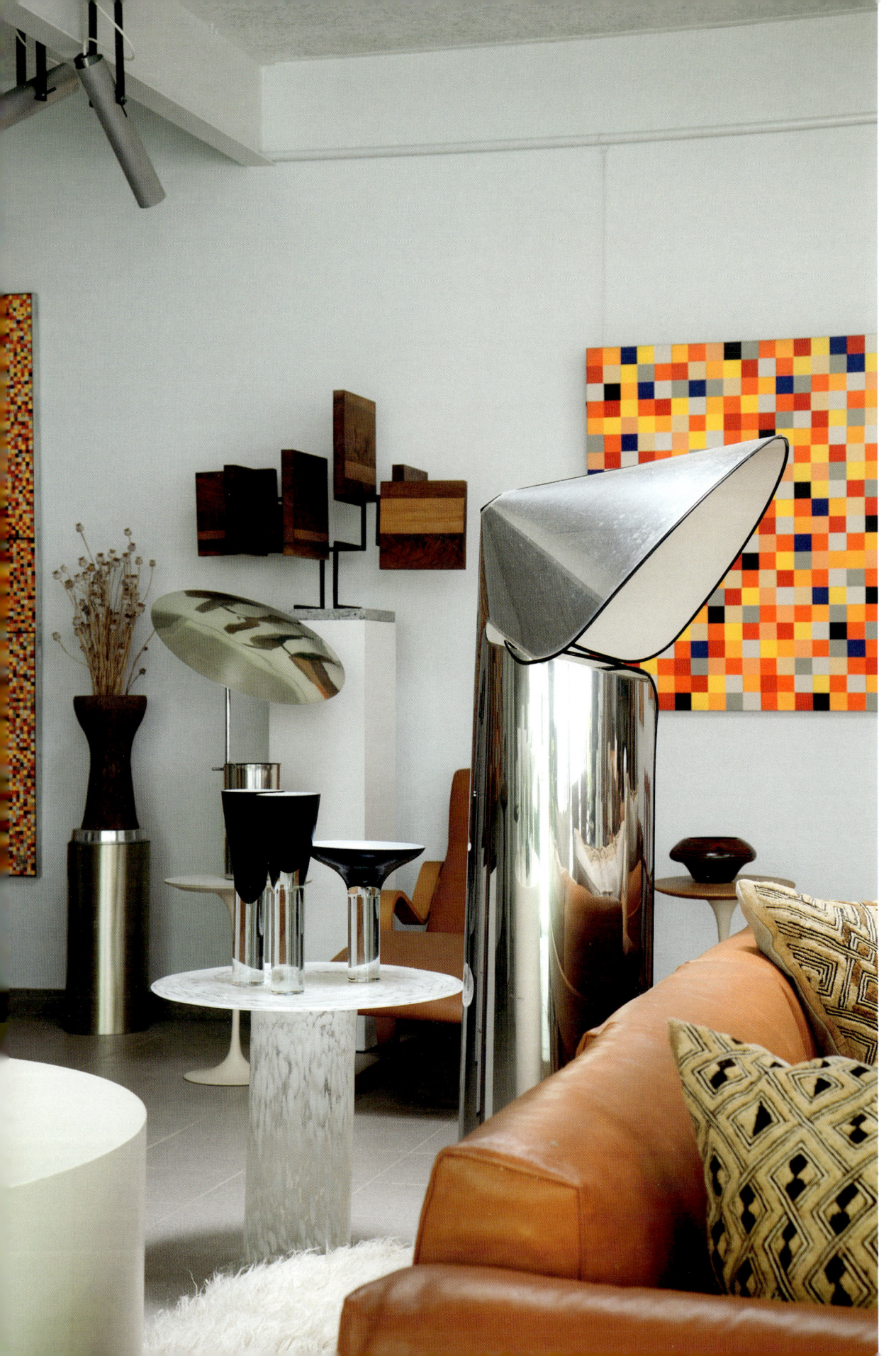

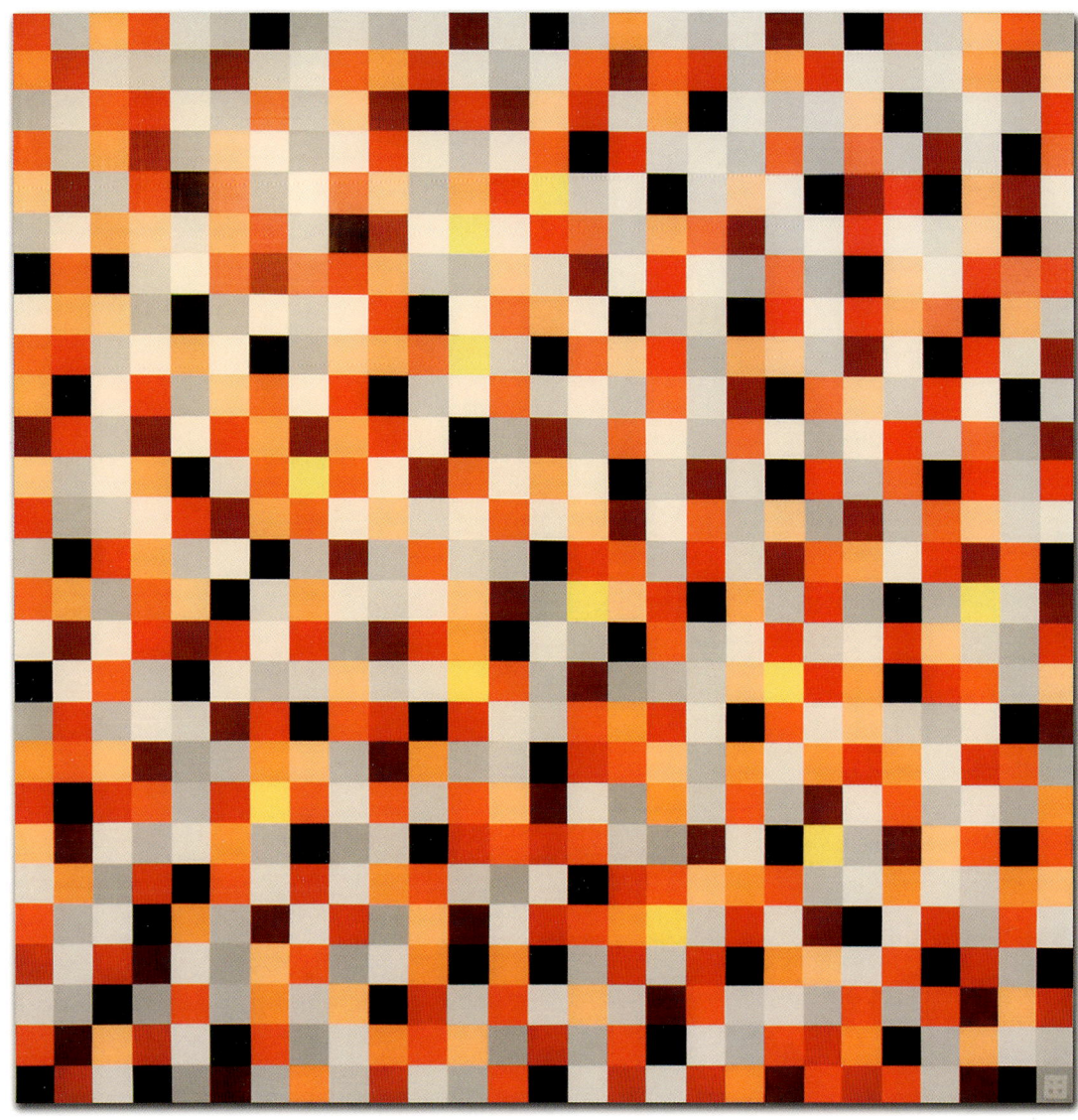

Robert Black, *Exuberance #5*, 1997, acrylic over paper on canvas, 64" x 64".

———

(*opposite*) Looming behind a Tobia Scarpa leather sofa with Kuba cloth pillows, the stainless steel Chiara floor lamp by Mario Bellini (1964) became known as the "nun" lamp for its resemblance to the habits worn by the Sisters of Charity. Ormond Sanderson's wood and steel sculpture, *Divergence* (1982), tops a pedestal next to Robert Black's collage painting, *Exuberance #4* (1997, 32" x 32").

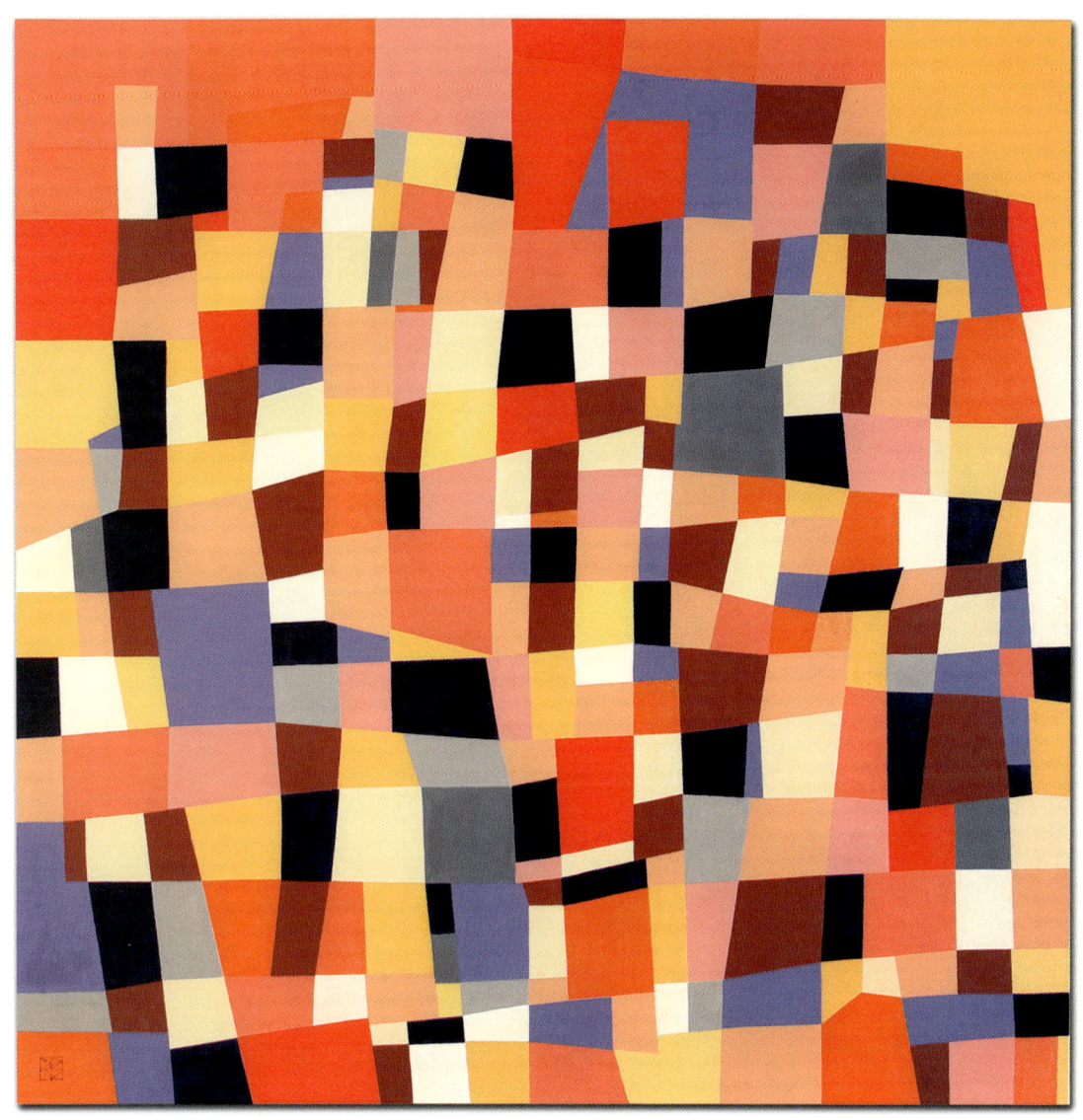

Robert Black, *Mystique #2*, 2010, acrylic on canvas, 60" x 60".

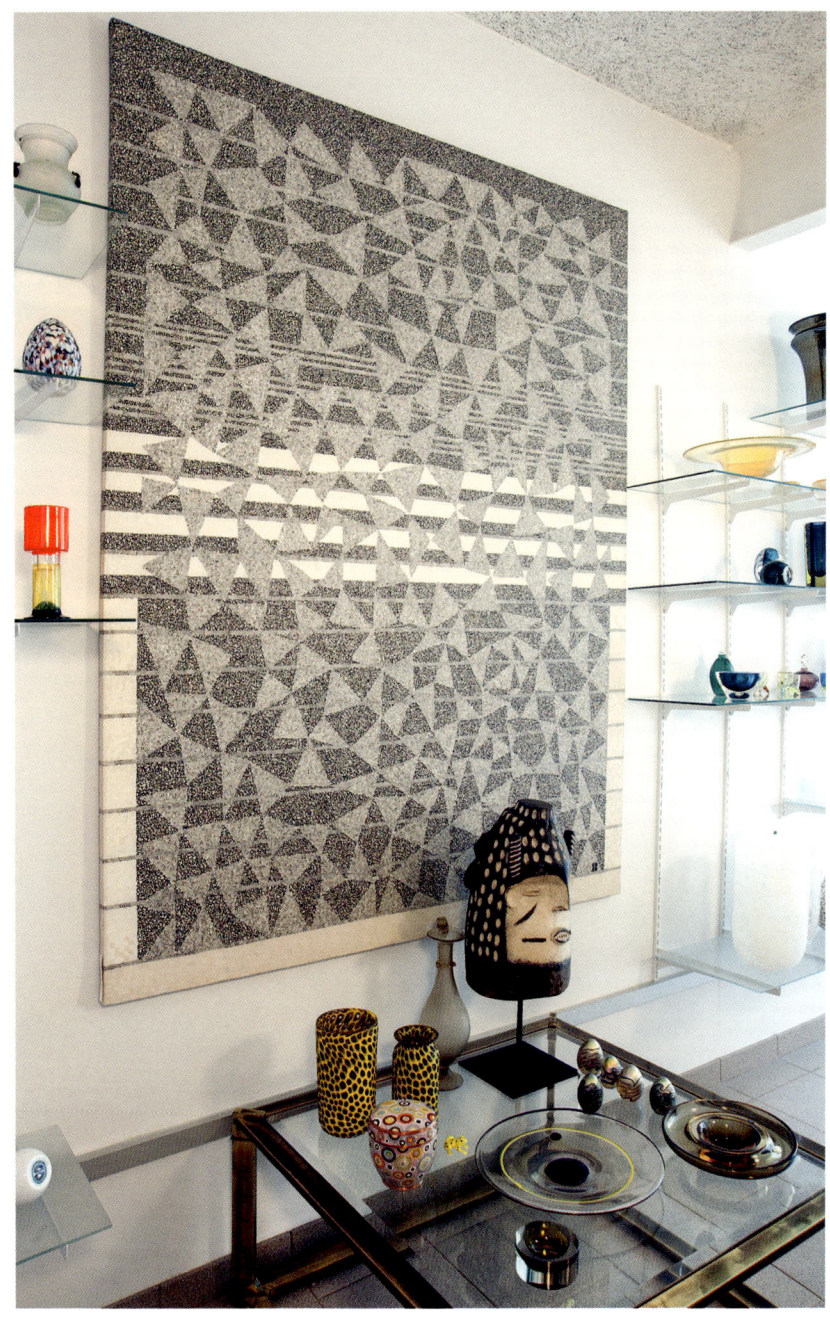

The myriad tiny dots that form the pulsating pattern of Black's collage painting, *Awakening* (1986, 74" x 56½"), are echoed in the dots that appear on an African mask, a lidded cloisonné "Rondo" jar by Fabienne Jouvin, and glassware by Venini, Kosta Boda, and Orient and Flume.

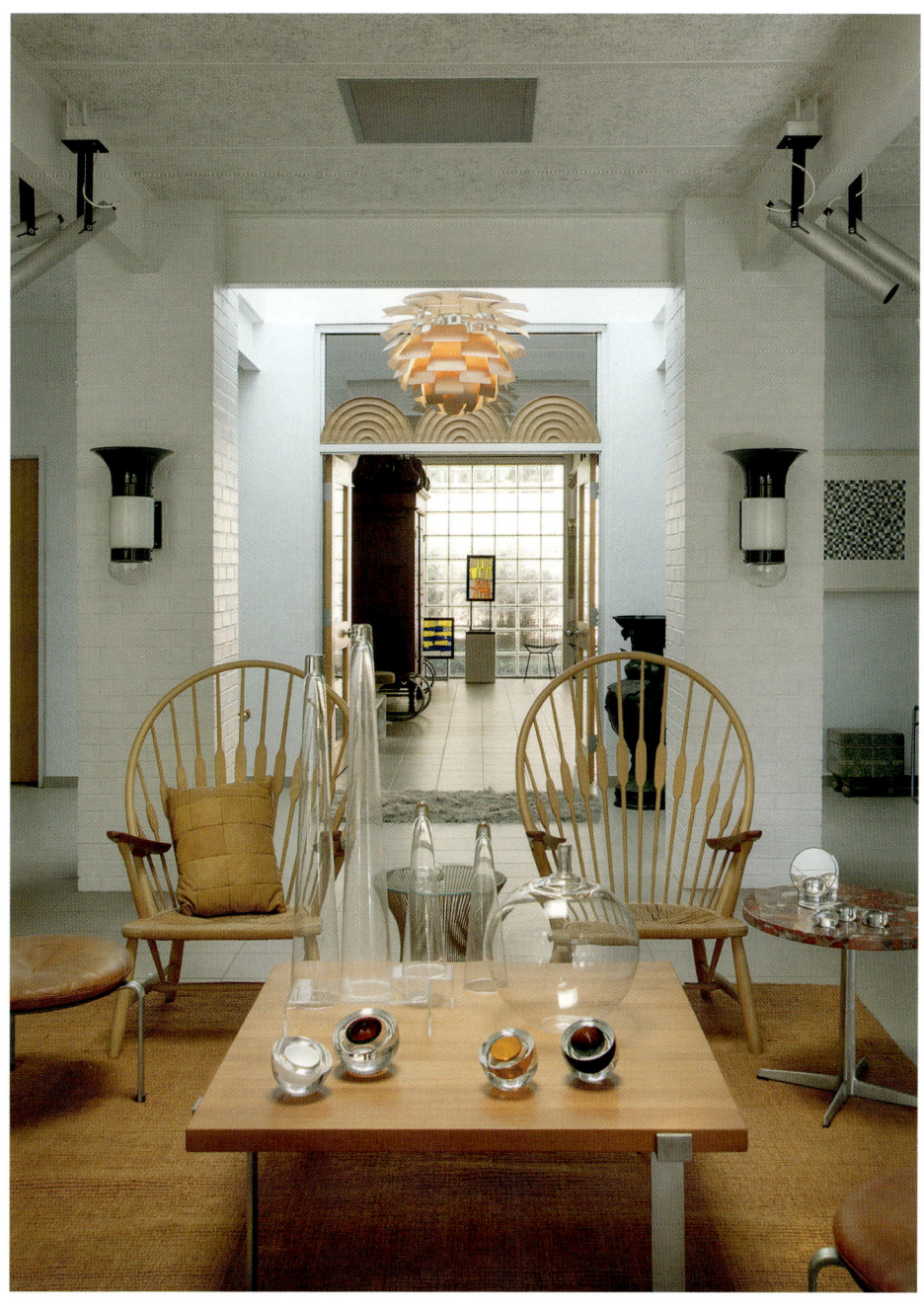

Two "Peacock" chairs by Hans Wegner (1947) face a table flanked by Poul Kjaerholm stools. A Warren Platner wire and glass side table (1962) stands between the chairs, while a Poul Henningsen "Artichoke" lamp (1958) hangs beneath one of two belvederes that allow natural light into the central hallway. Robert Black designed the spotlights attached to the ceiling, using tubes rescued from old soft drink vending machines.

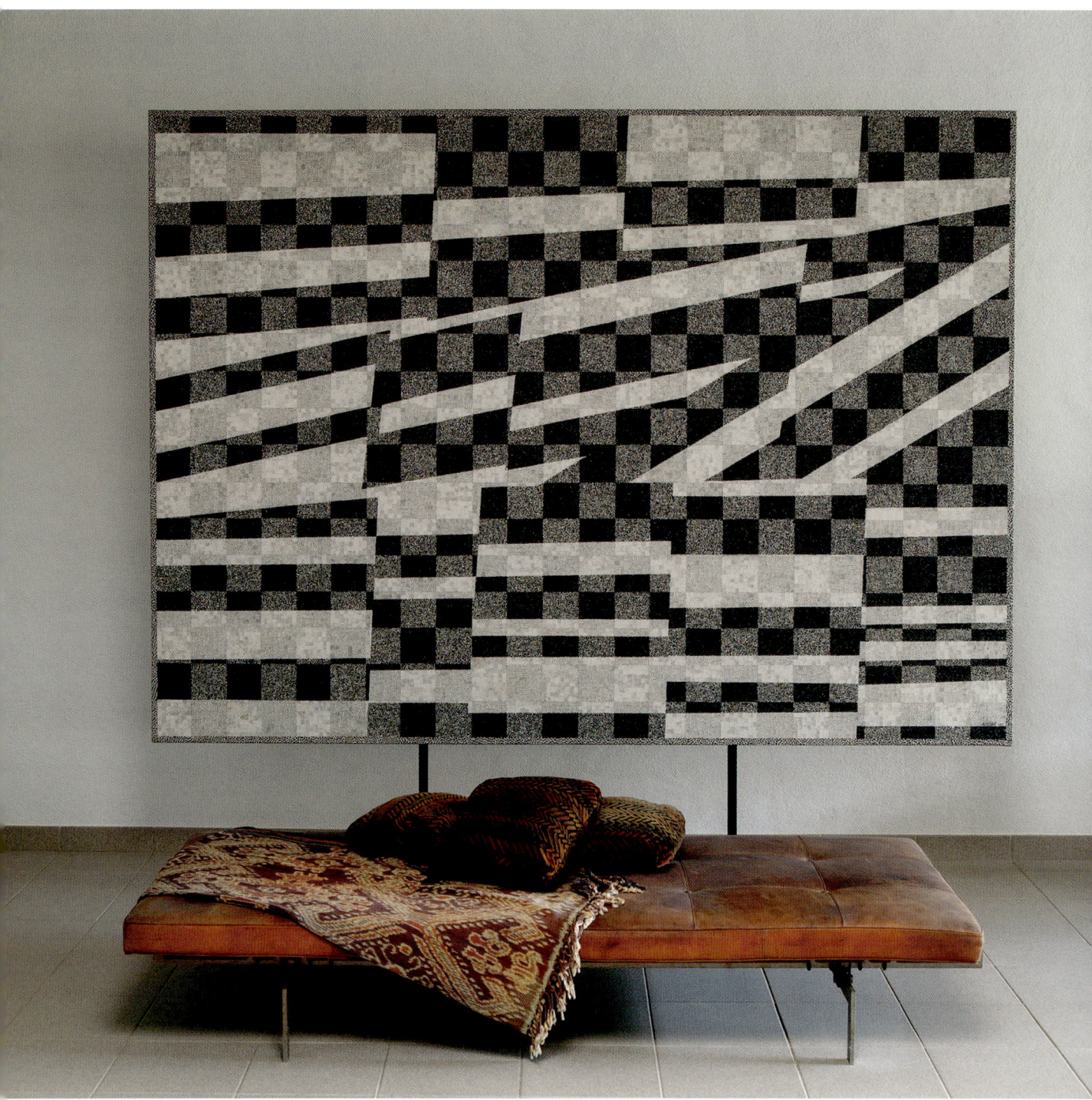

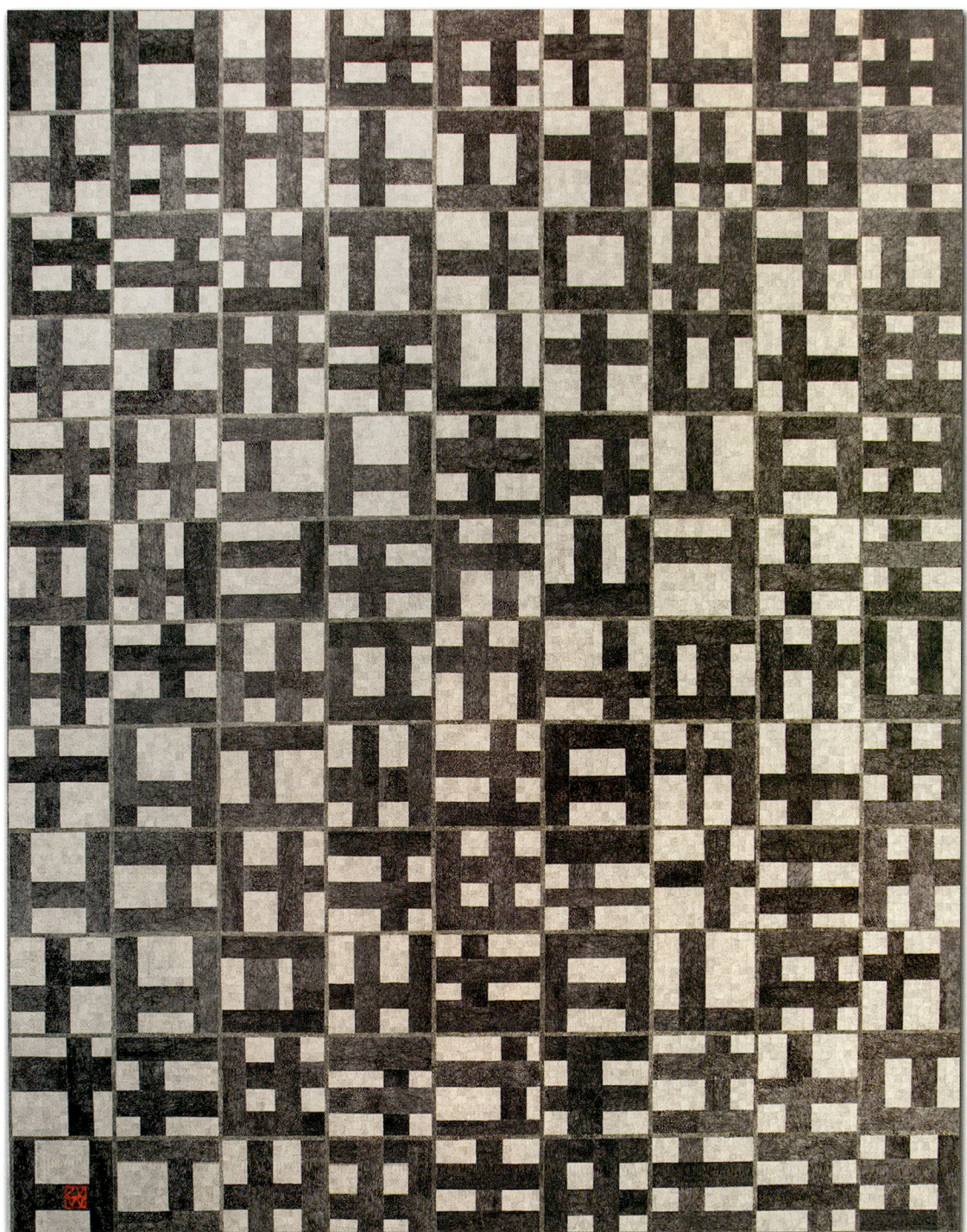

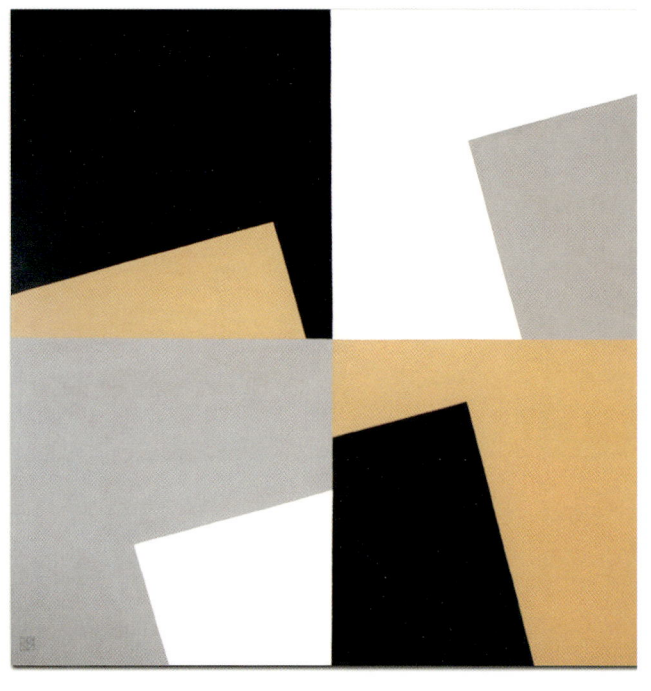

(*overleaf, left*) An Indonesian ikat drapes over a leather upholstered PK80 daybed designed by Poul Kjaerholm (1957). Floating off the wall behind it, on a stand designed by Robert Black, is Black's *Shadowcast* (1985, acrylic over paper on canvas, 69¼" x 97¼").

(*overleaf, right*) Robert Black, *Hieroglyph*, 1997, acrylic over paper on canvas, 72" x 56¾".

 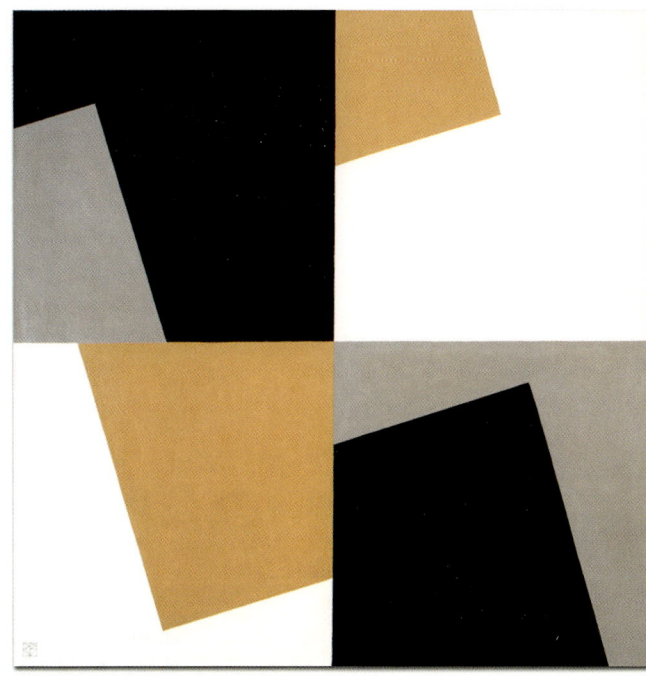

Robert Black, *Contemplation* series, 2012, acrylic on canvas, each 60" x 60".

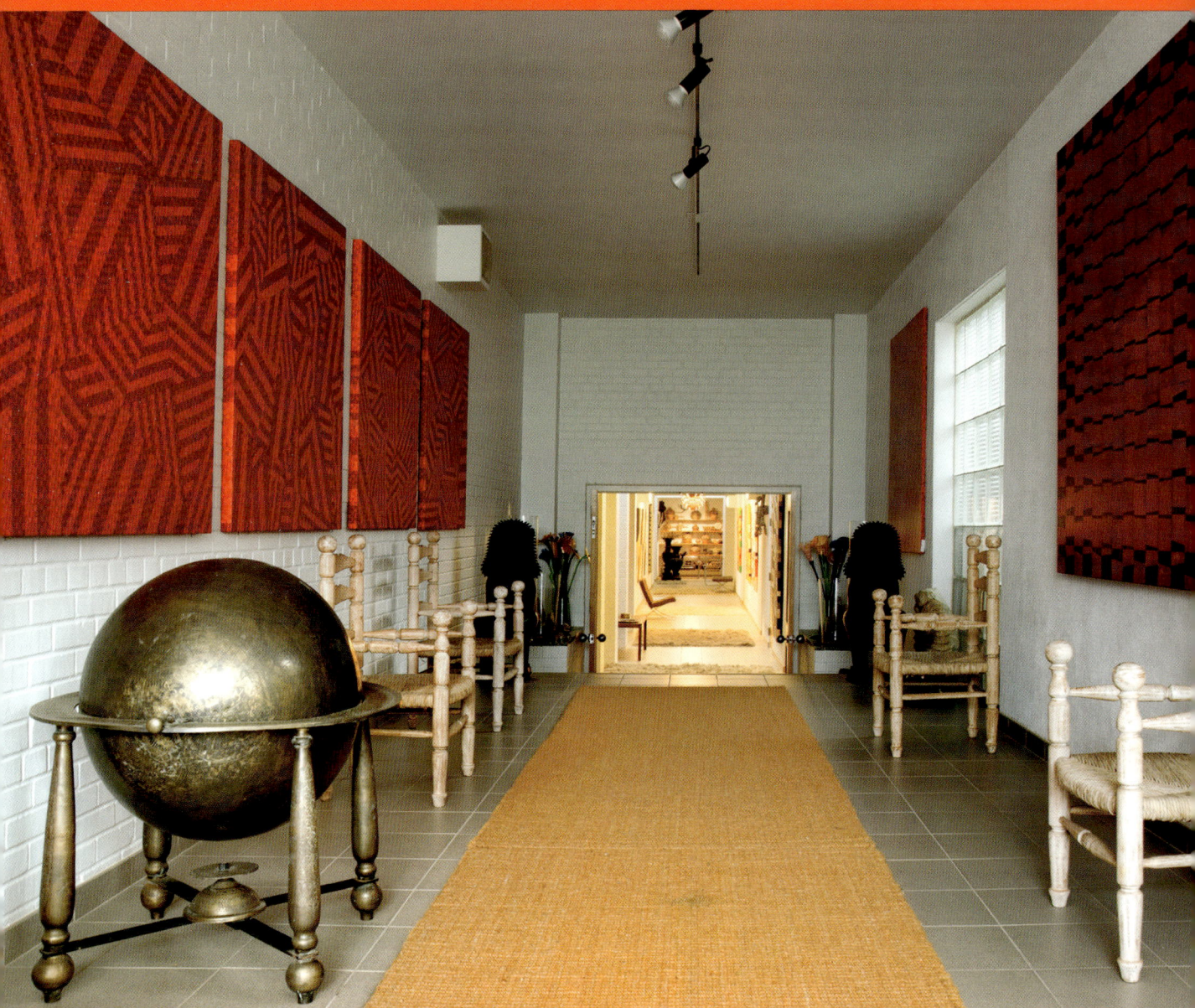

The long central hallway, once lined with students' lockers when the building was still the Anderson School, now serves as a private display gallery. On the left are four collage paintings from Black's 1999 *Fire Drake* series (each 48" x 48"), while on the right are *Logarithm* and beyond it, *Cosmic Fire #2*. Colonial chairs and a brass celestial globe from India feature legs terminating in round knobs.

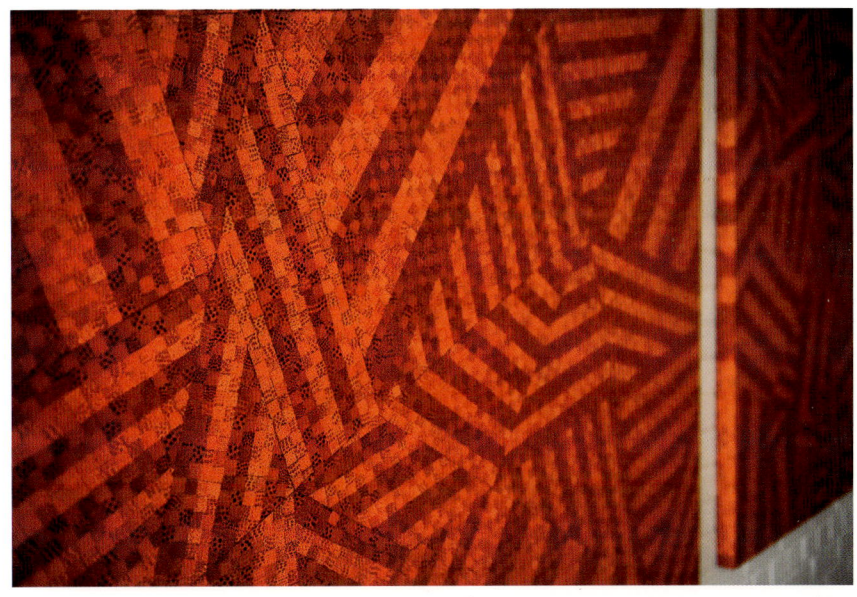

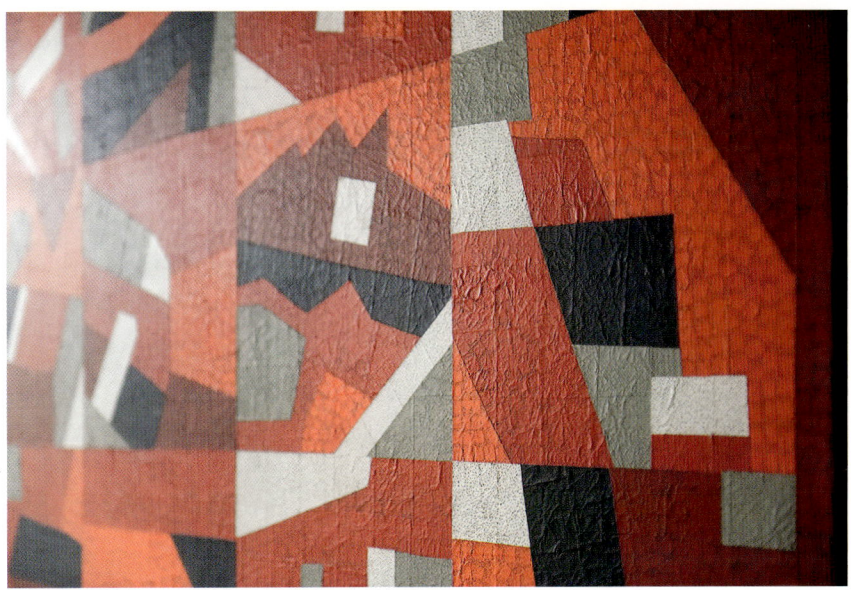

Close-ups of Black's *Fire Drake* and *Scarlet Dawn* collage paintings reveal his exacting technique. Tiny squares of dot-patterned paper are applied like mosaics and then painted over with transparent color washes to create vivid, pulsating surfaces that become even more intricate and lively upon close inspection.

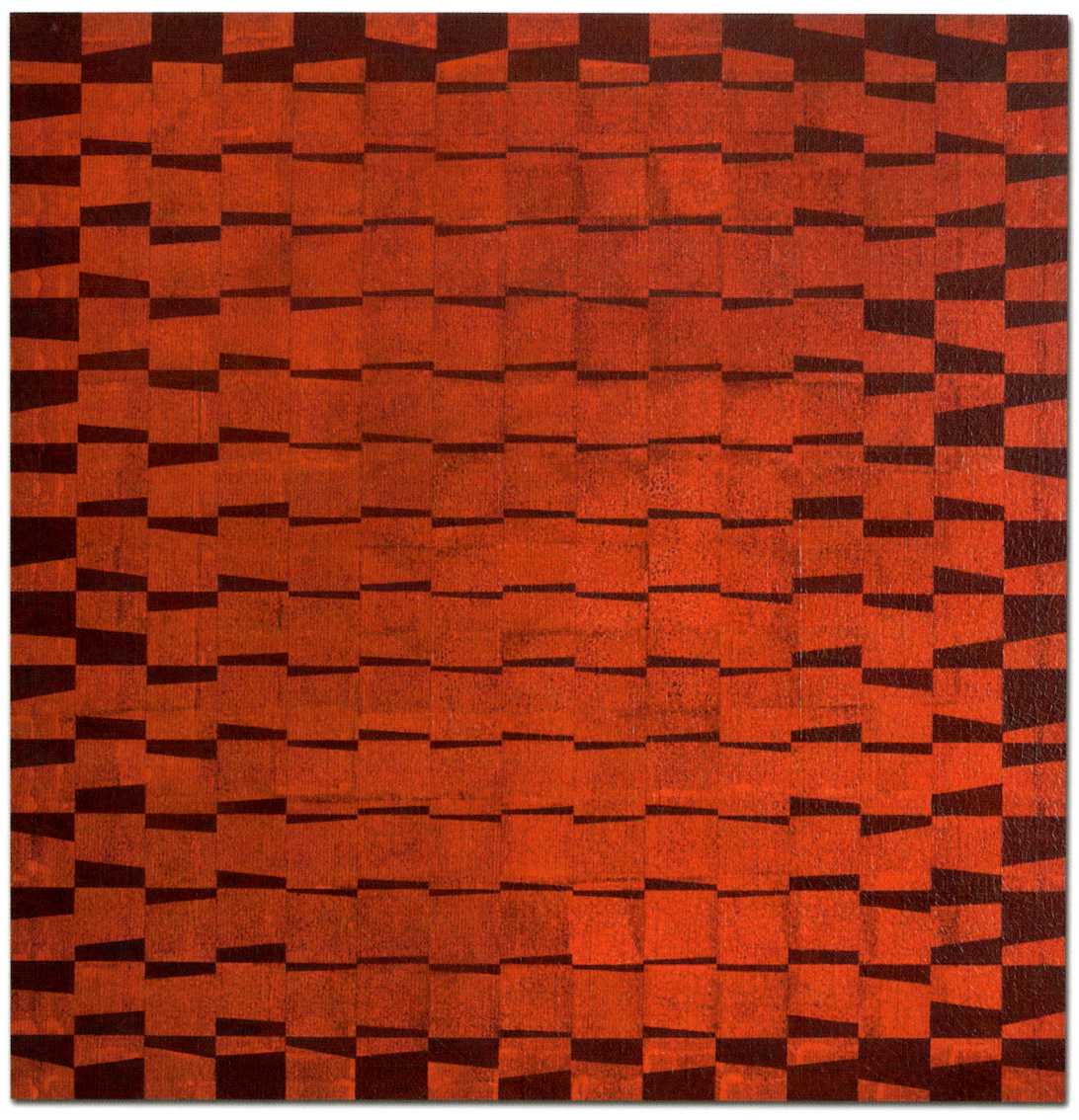

Robert Black, *Logarithm*, 1996, acrylic over paper on canvas, 64" x 64".

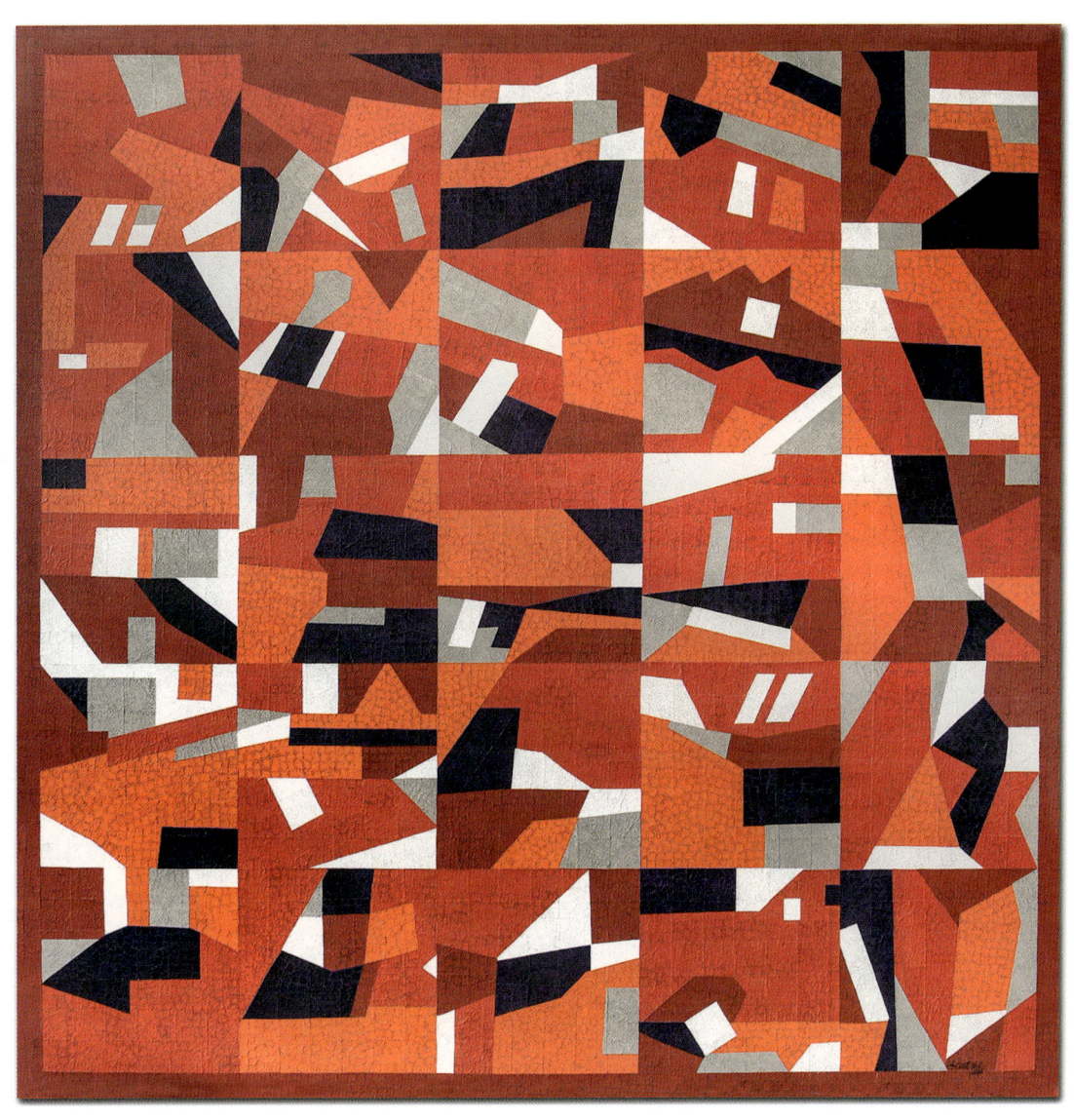

Robert Black, *Scarlet Dawn*, 1990, acrylic over paper on canvas, 64" x 64".

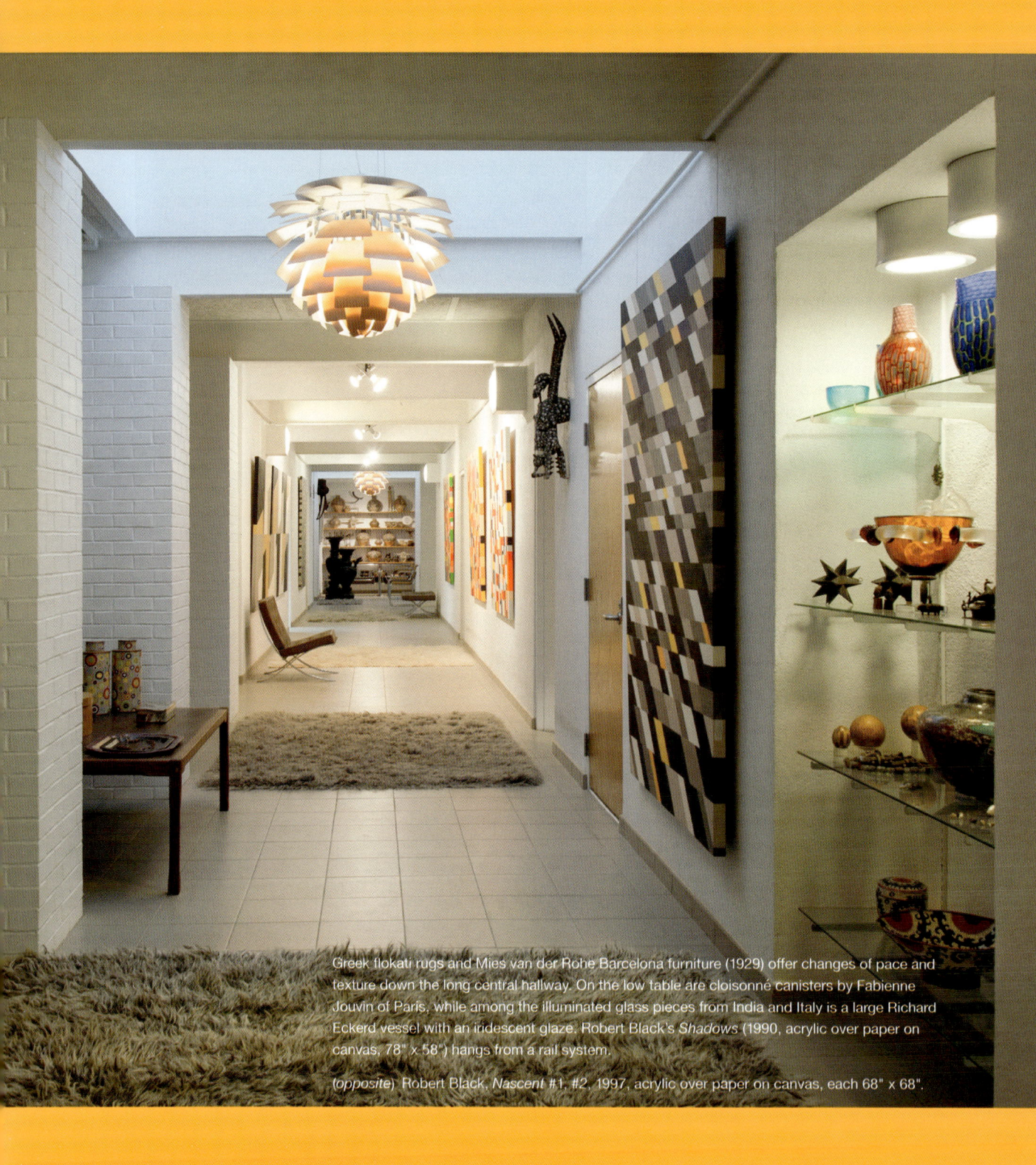

Greek flokati rugs and Mies van der Rohe Barcelona furniture (1929) offer changes of pace and texture down the long central hallway. On the low table are cloisonné canisters by Fabienne Jouvin of Paris, while among the illuminated glass pieces from India and Italy is a large Richard Eckerd vessel with an iridescent glaze. Robert Black's *Shadows* (1990, acrylic over paper on canvas, 78" x 58") hangs from a rail system.

(*opposite*) Robert Black, *Nascent #1, #2*, 1997, acrylic over paper on canvas, each 68" x 68".

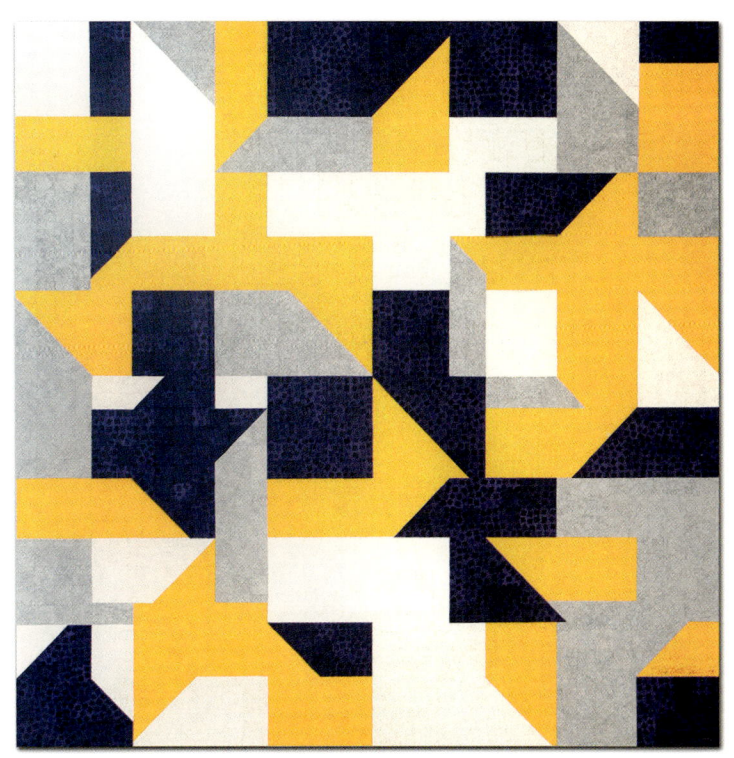

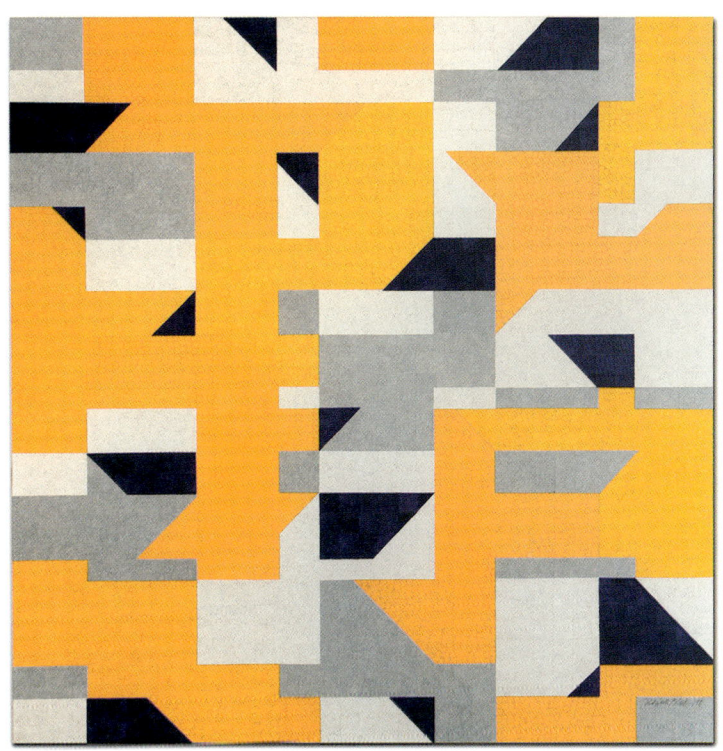

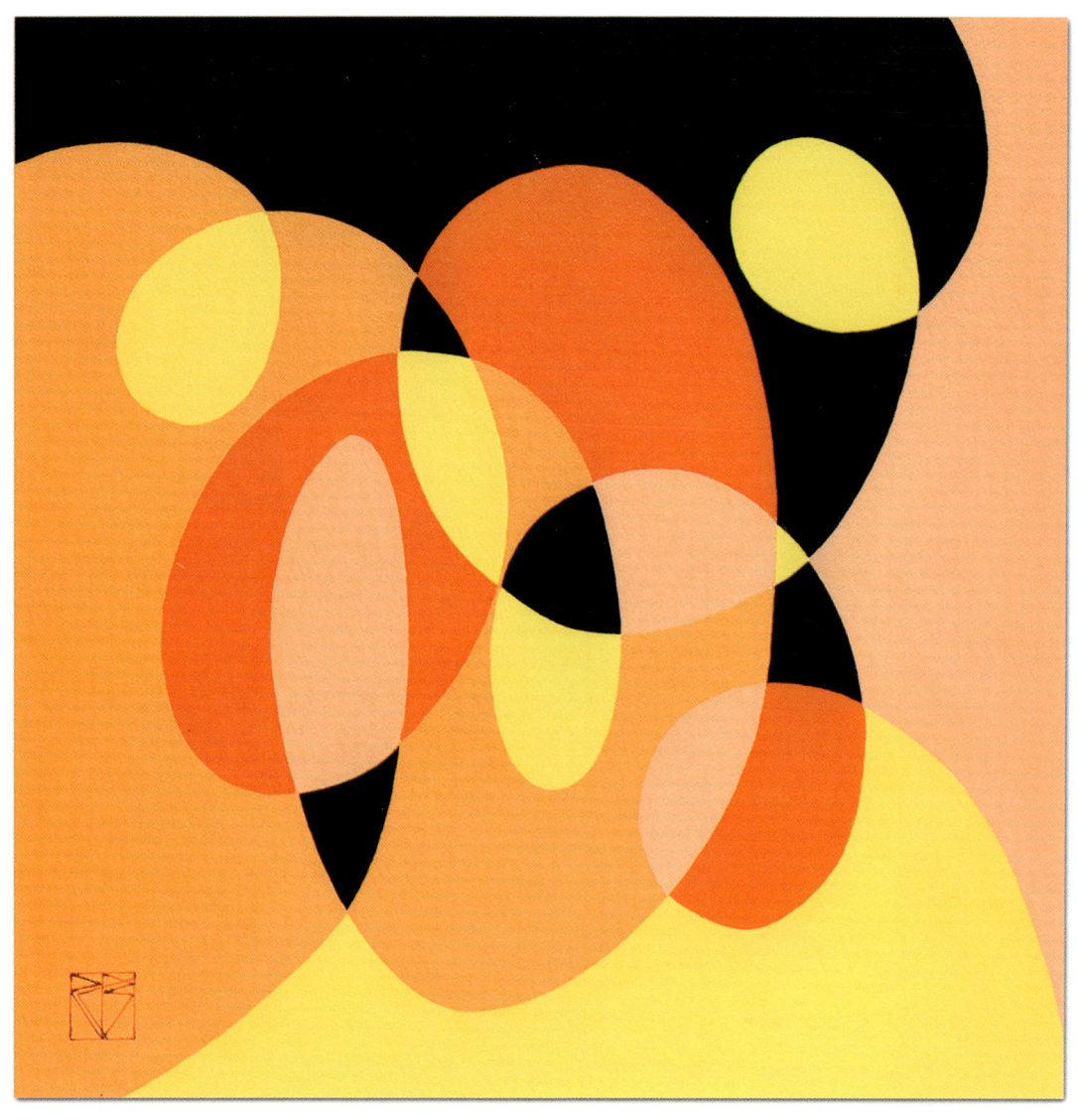

Robert Black, *Vortex #1* (opposite, *Vortex #2*) both 2010, acrylic over paper, 19" x 19".

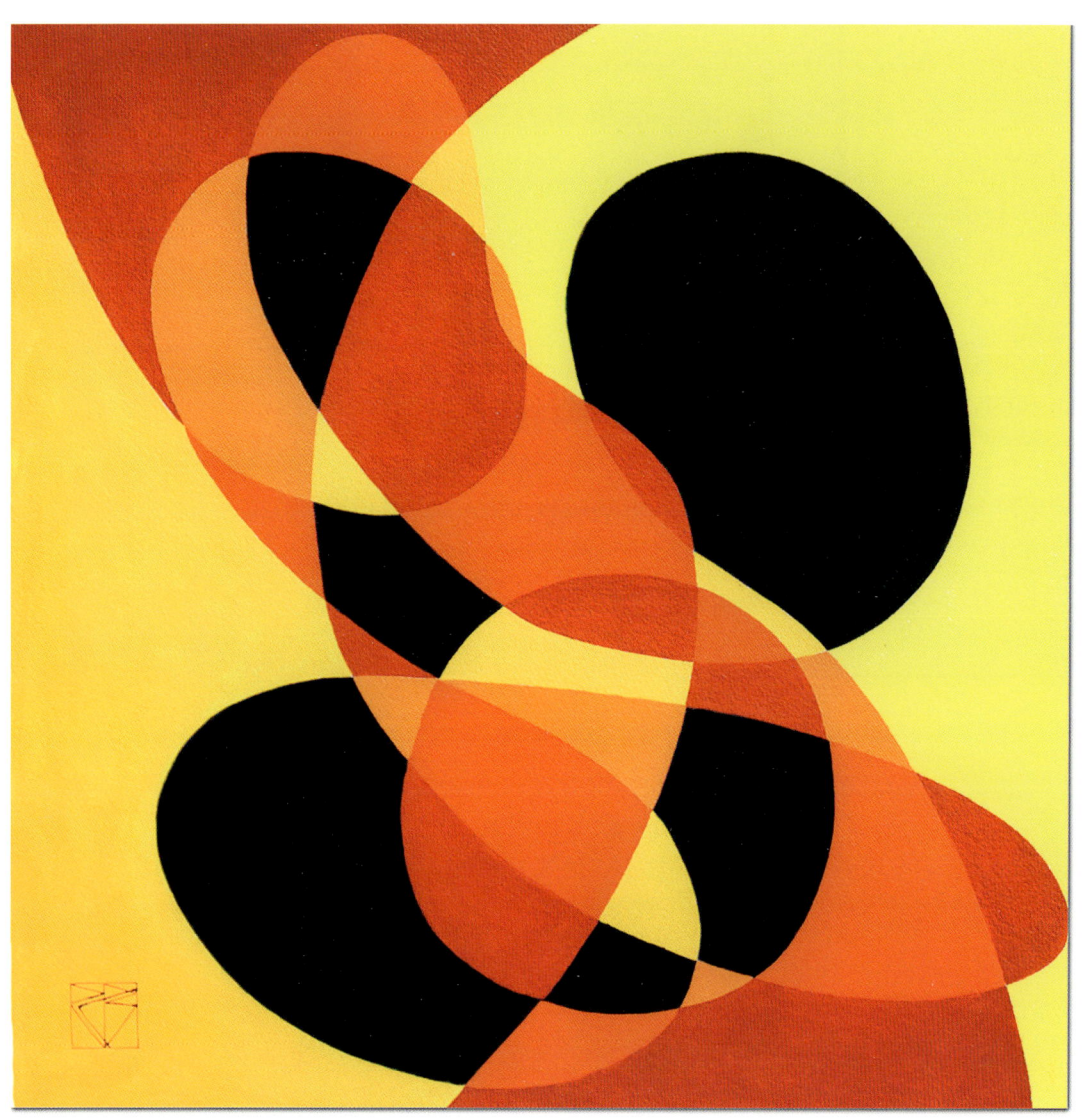

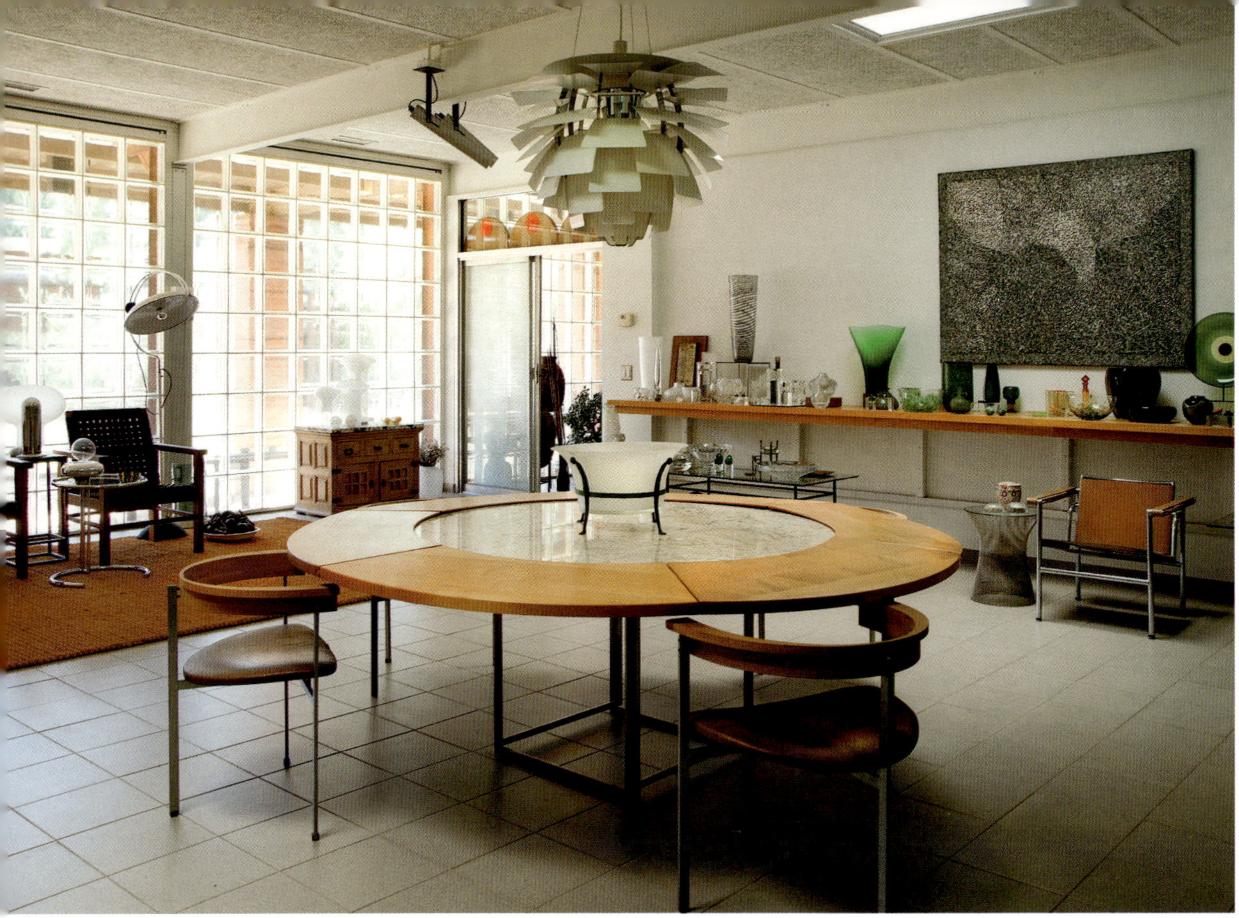

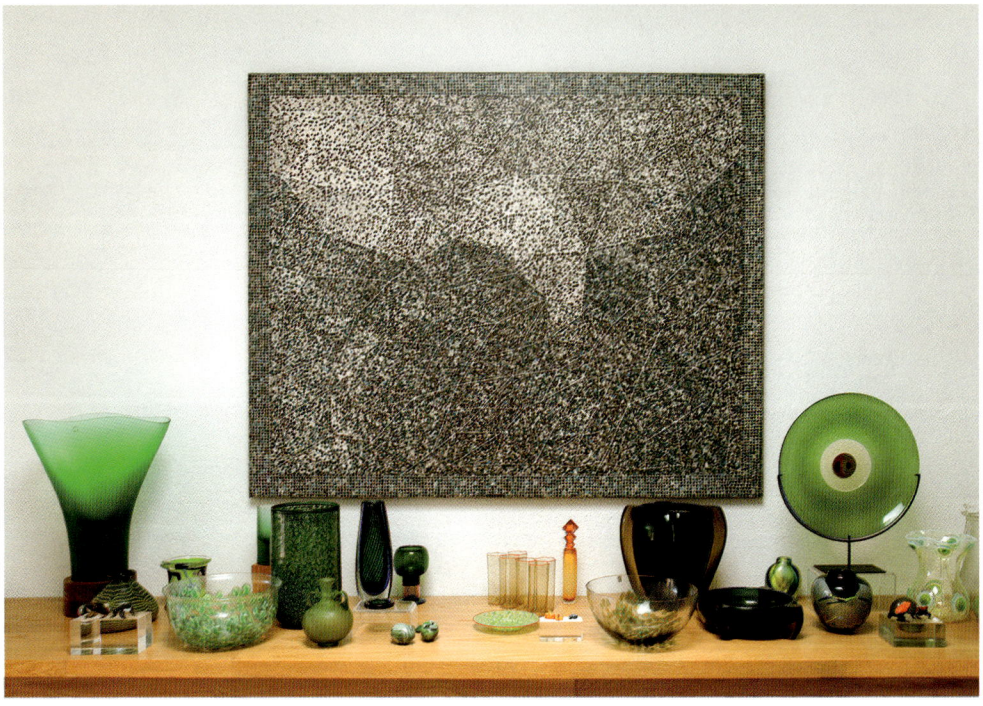

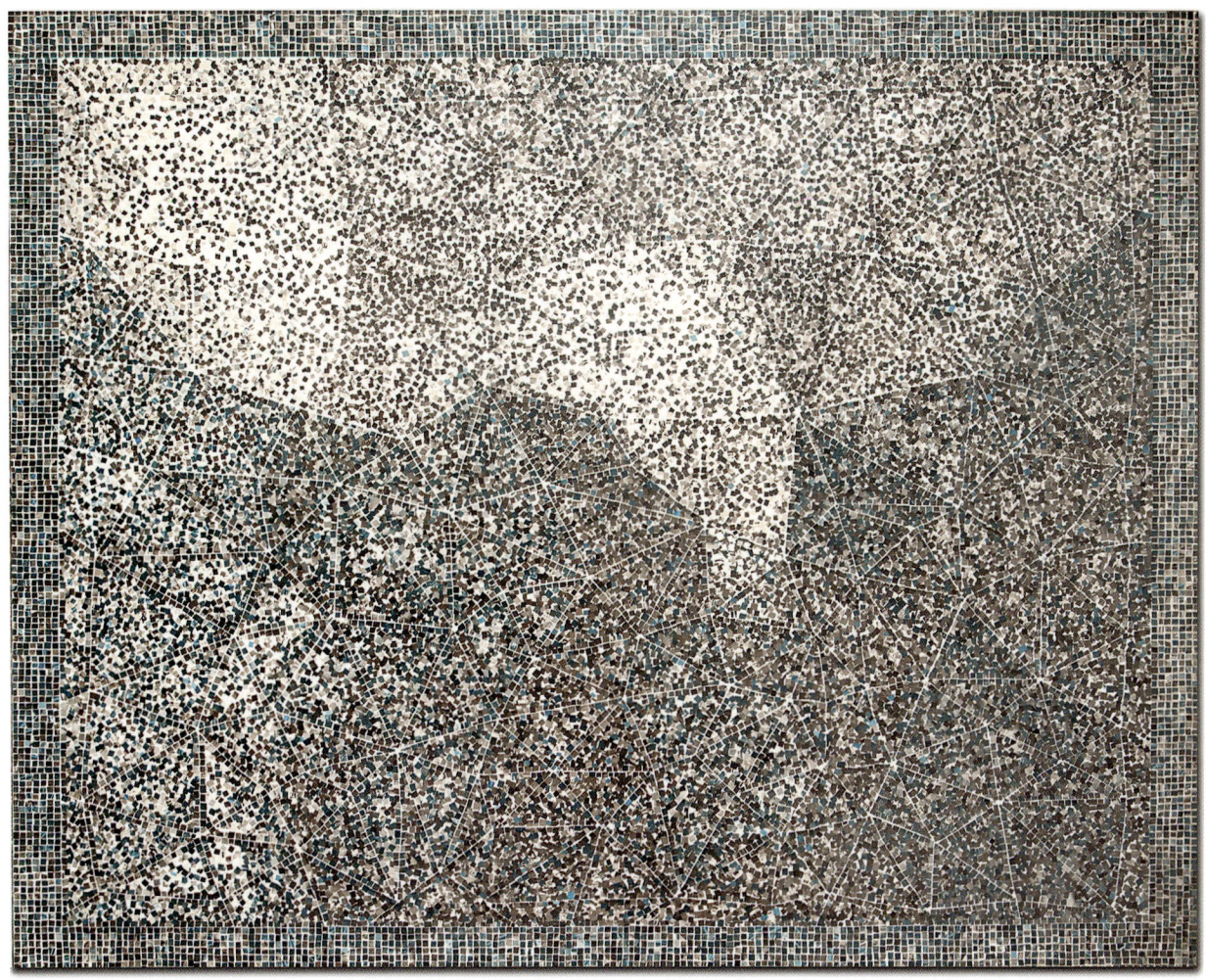

Robert Black, *Starry Night*, 1985, colored papers on gessoed canvas, 46" x 58".

———

(*opposite, above*) A Poul Kjaerholm PK54 Cipollino marble table with removable wooden exten-
sion leaves (1963) and PK11 tripod chairs (1957) take pride of place in the dining room. At left, an
Eileen Gray adjustable side table (1927) stands between wood and leather chairs designed by
Robert Black. At right, a chrome Basculant LC1 sling chair by Le Corbusier (1928) and a Warren
Platner side table (1962) sit beneath Black's *Starry Night* painting.

(*opposite, below*) Greenish glasswares by Venini and Leerdam resonate with some of the painting's subtle hues.

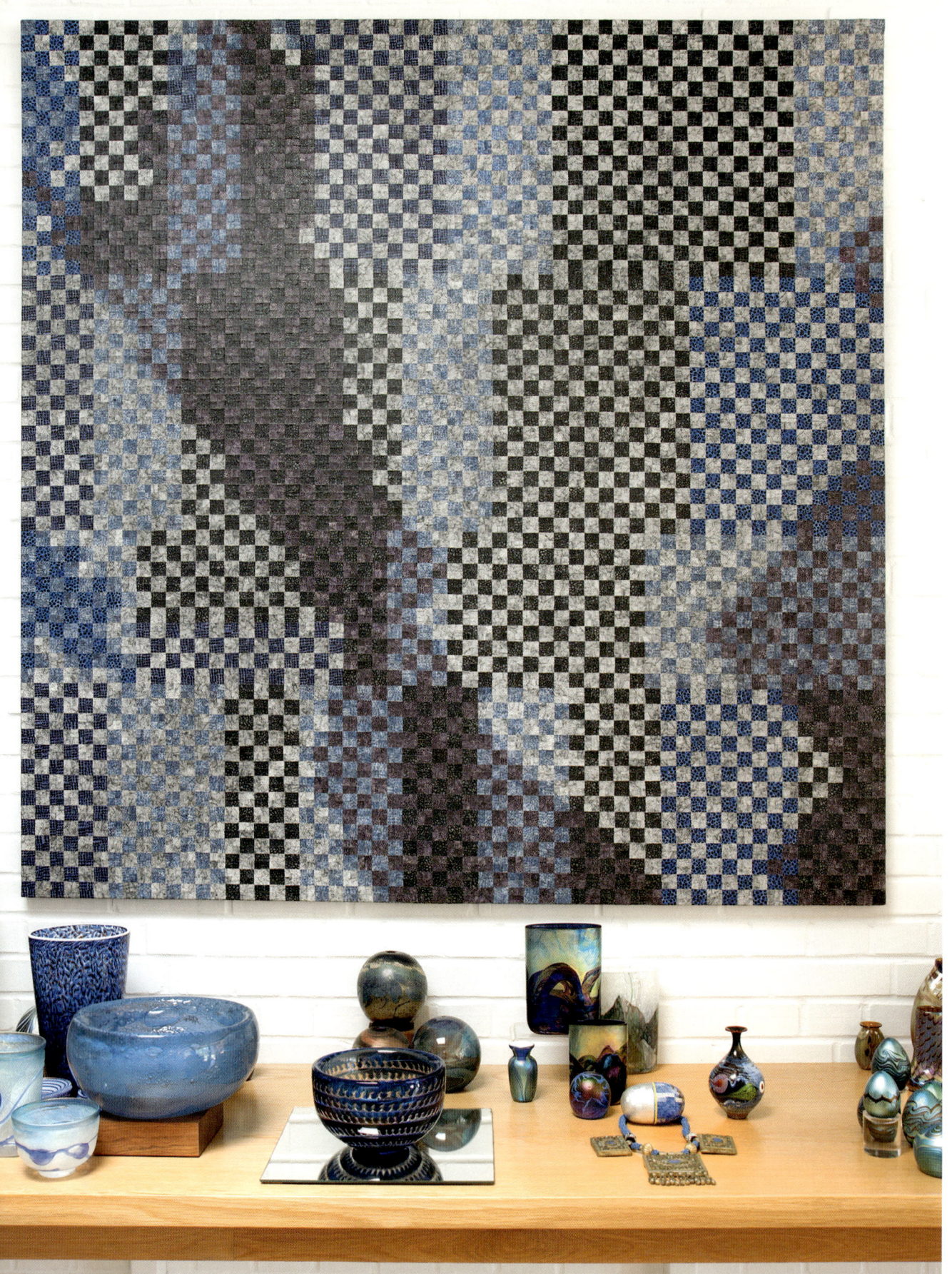

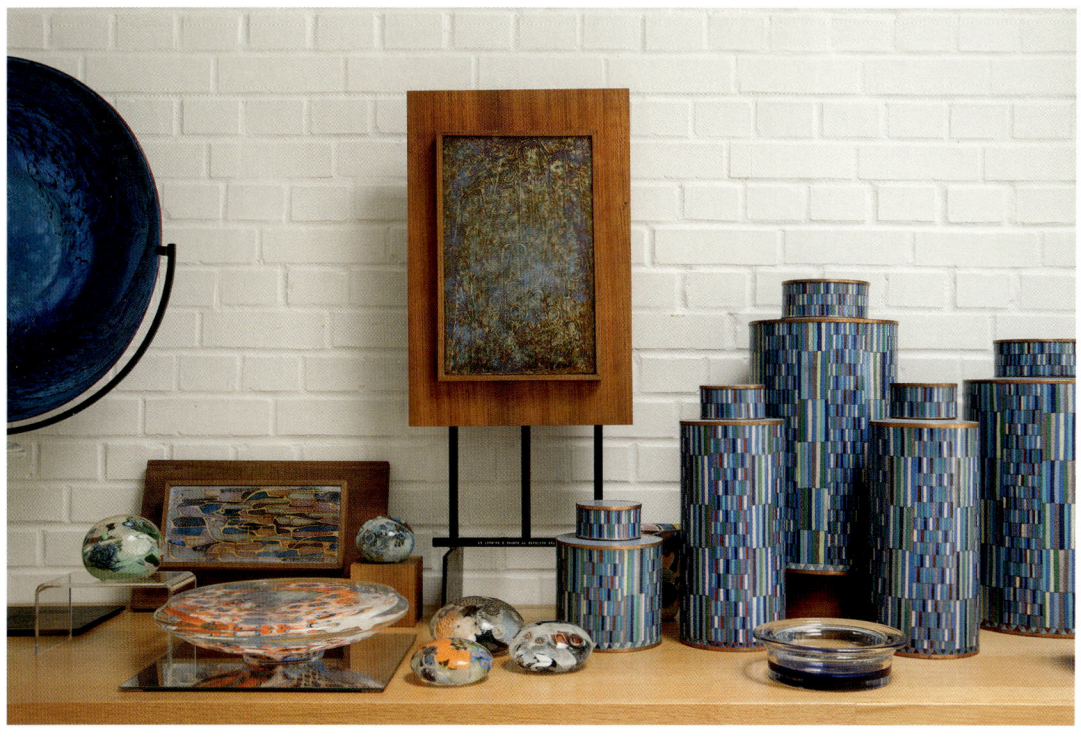

Ormond Sanderson's enamel panels harmonize with late 1970s glass *murrini, millefiori,* and electroformed works by Richard Ritter, translucent disks by Venini and "Sticks"-patterned metal cloisonné tea jars by Fabienne Jouvin (1996).

─────────

(*opposite*) Robert Black's acrylic over paper on canvas painting, *Blue Ridge* (1988, 58" x 58"), hangs above blue-toned glass objects by Kosta Boda, Orrefors, and Orient and Flume.

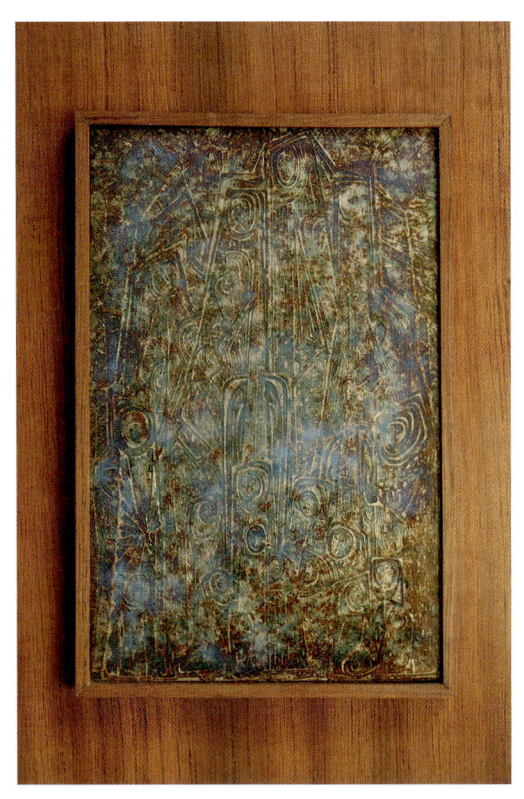

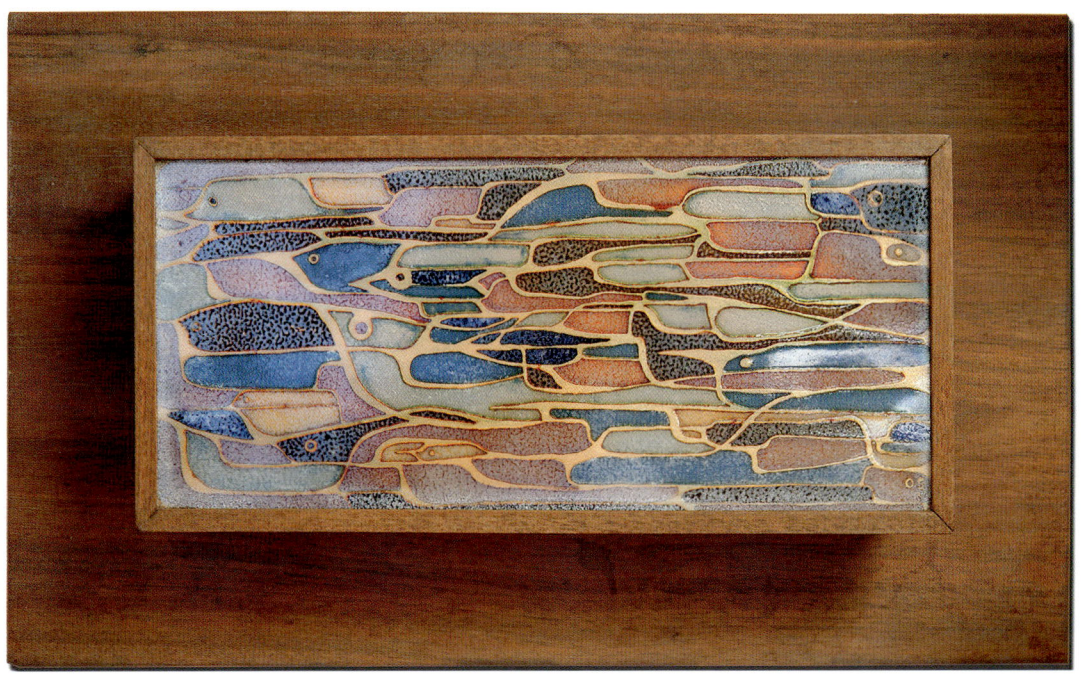

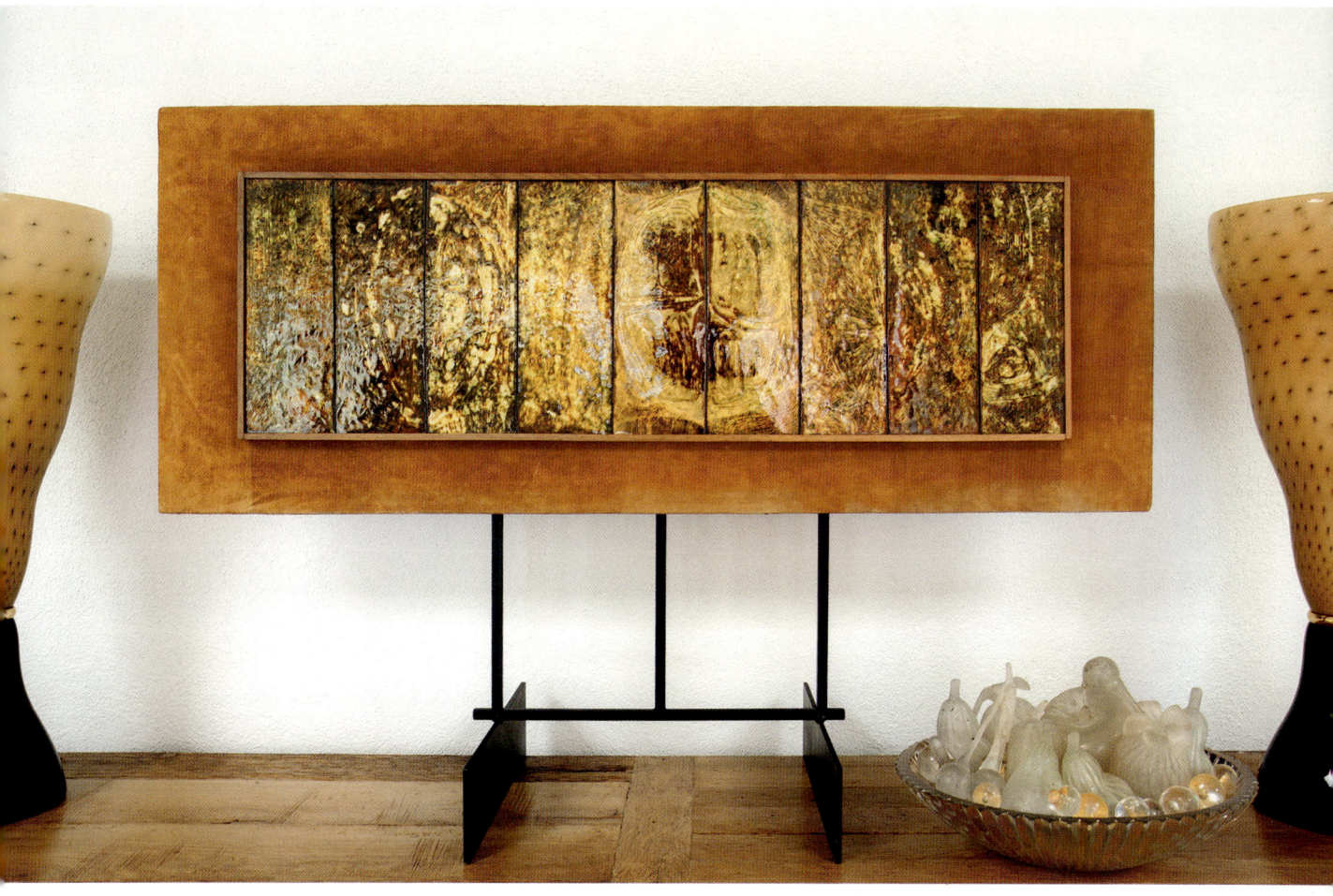

Ormond Sanderson, *Germination*, ca. 1963, enamel panels on suede-covered mount, 19" x 48", on welded steel stand designed by Sanderson and Black. Flanked by Vivia T lamps by Renato Toso for Leucos.

———

(*opposite, above*) Ormond Sanderson, *Le Lagrime d'Amante al sepolcro d'Amata*, enamel on etched copper, 19" x 13".

(*opposite, below*) Sanderson, *Migration*, cloisonné enamel on copper, 9" x 15". Both are from the early 1960s.

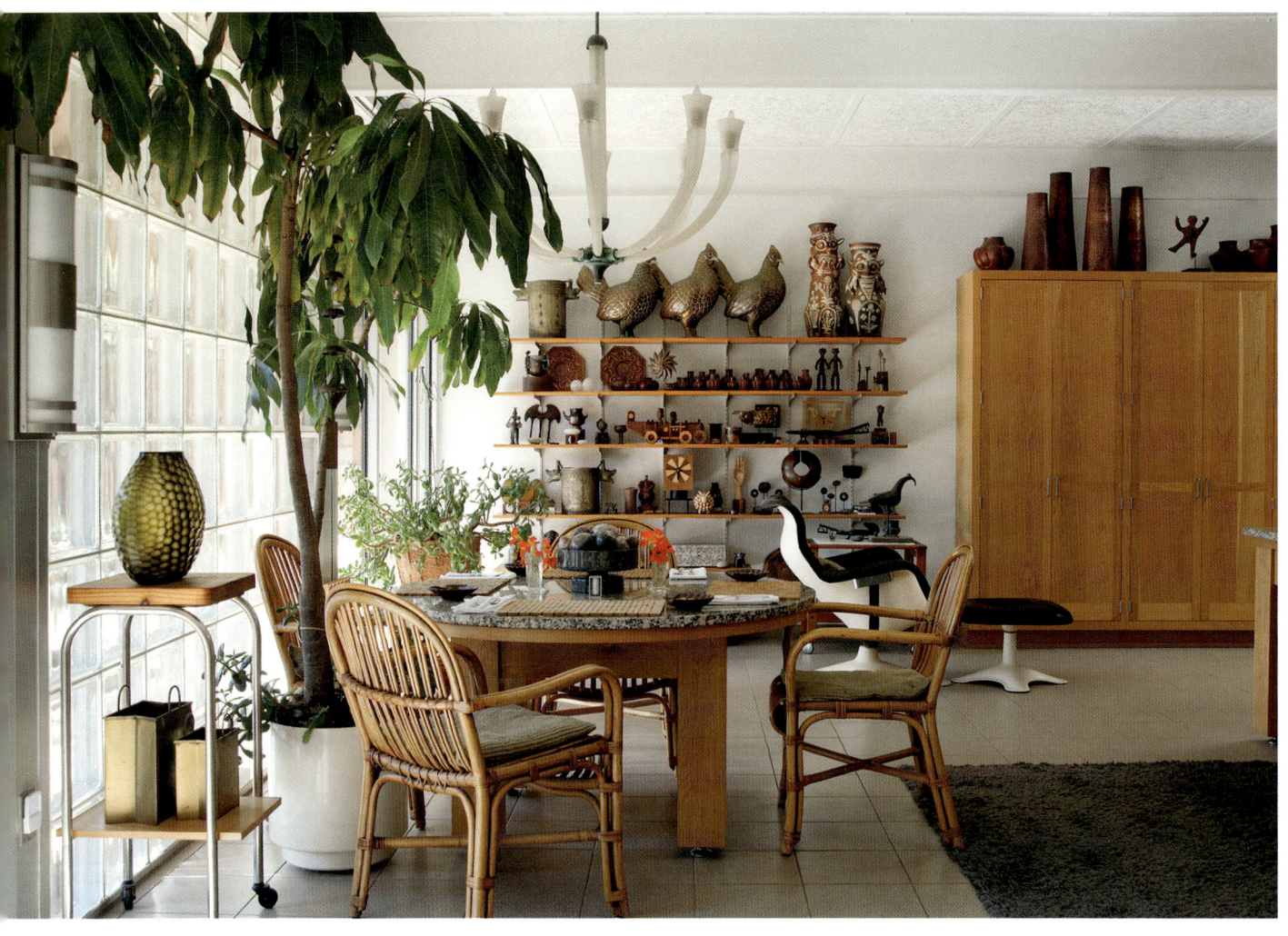

In the kitchen, above a table that Robert Black made, is a Seguso chandelier in frosted glass. A white fiberglass and leather Karuselli lounge chair and ottoman by Finnish designer Yrjö Kukkapuro (1964) is beyond it, in front of shelves filled with Mexican copper pieces. On the left is a faceted glass vase from India and at the upper right is one of Black's ceramic *Acrobat* figures.

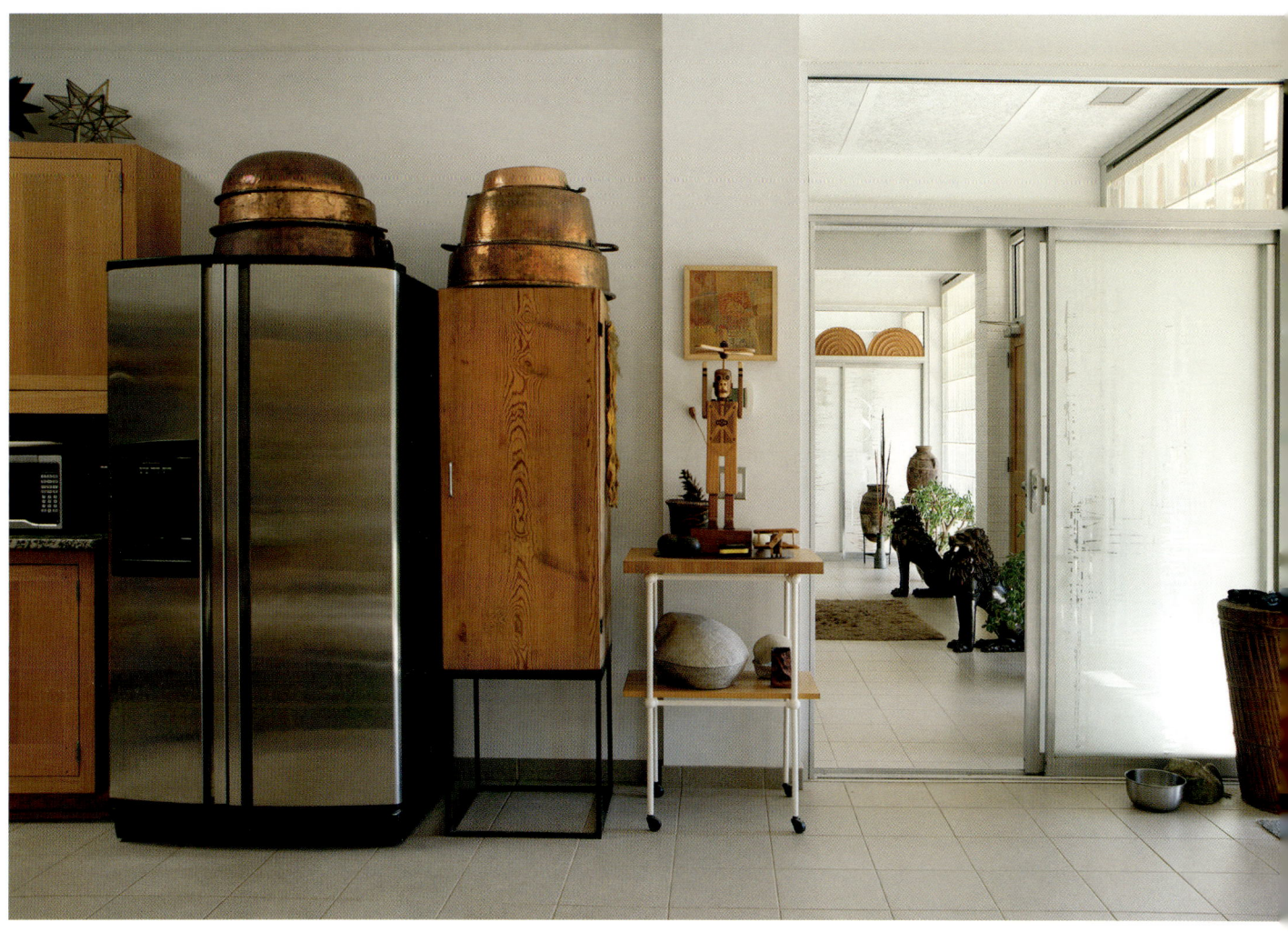

Turned on end, an antique blanket chest with a single heart pine board for a lid serves as a cupboard in the kitchen. Turkish copper vessels top it and the fridge. Frosted patterns created by Sanderson were sandblasted into the sliding glass doors.

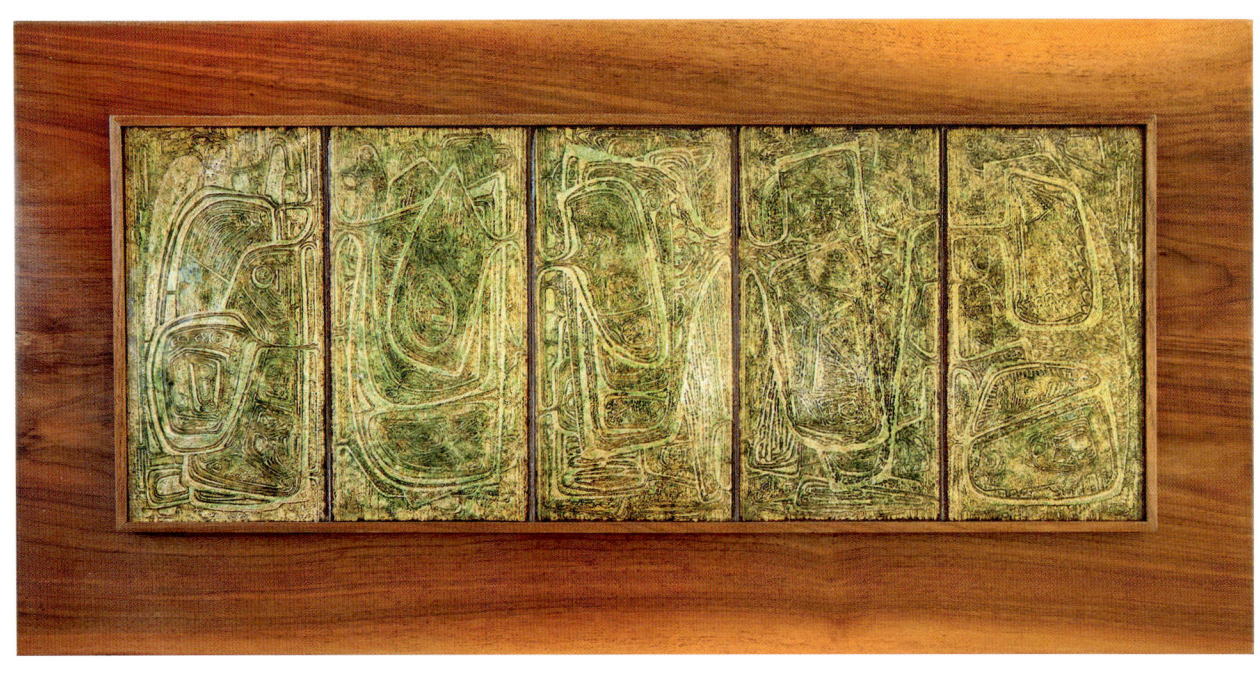

Ormond Sanderson's taille basse enamel, *Metamorphosis* (1963, 19" x 38"), was among the pieces selected for exhibition in the American Pavilion at the 1964 World's Fair in New York City.

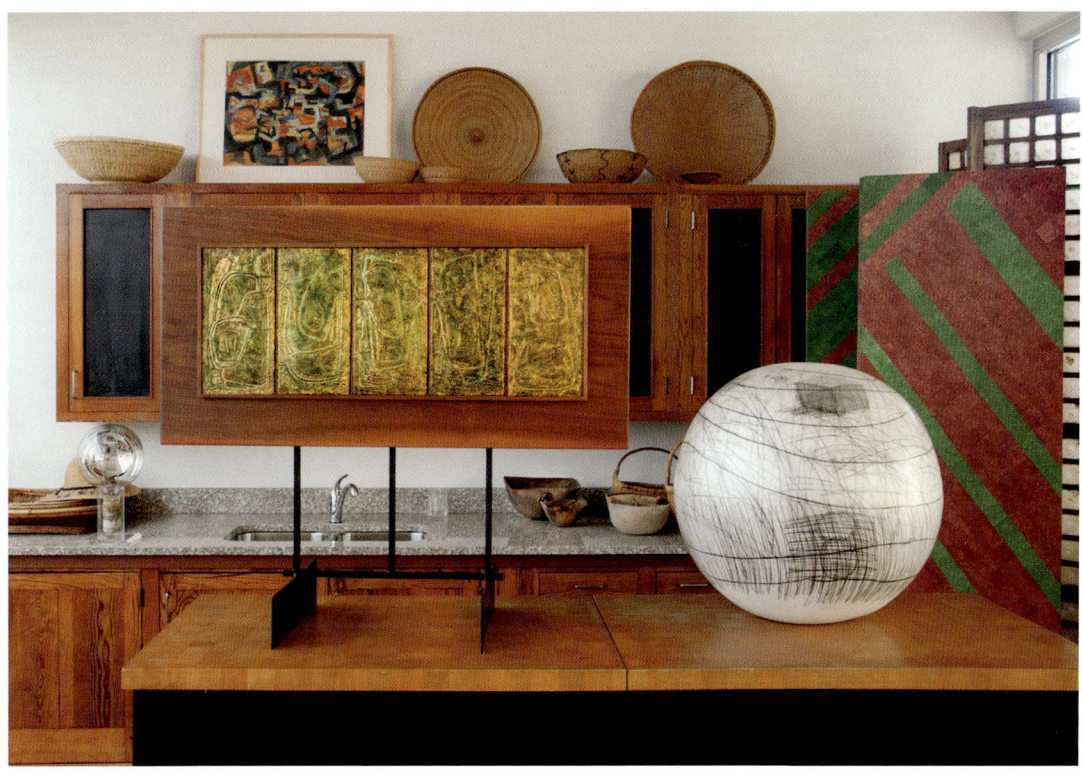

Metamorphosis is now displayed atop a counter in the room that once served as the Anderson School's science lab. On the right is a folding screen by Robert Black.

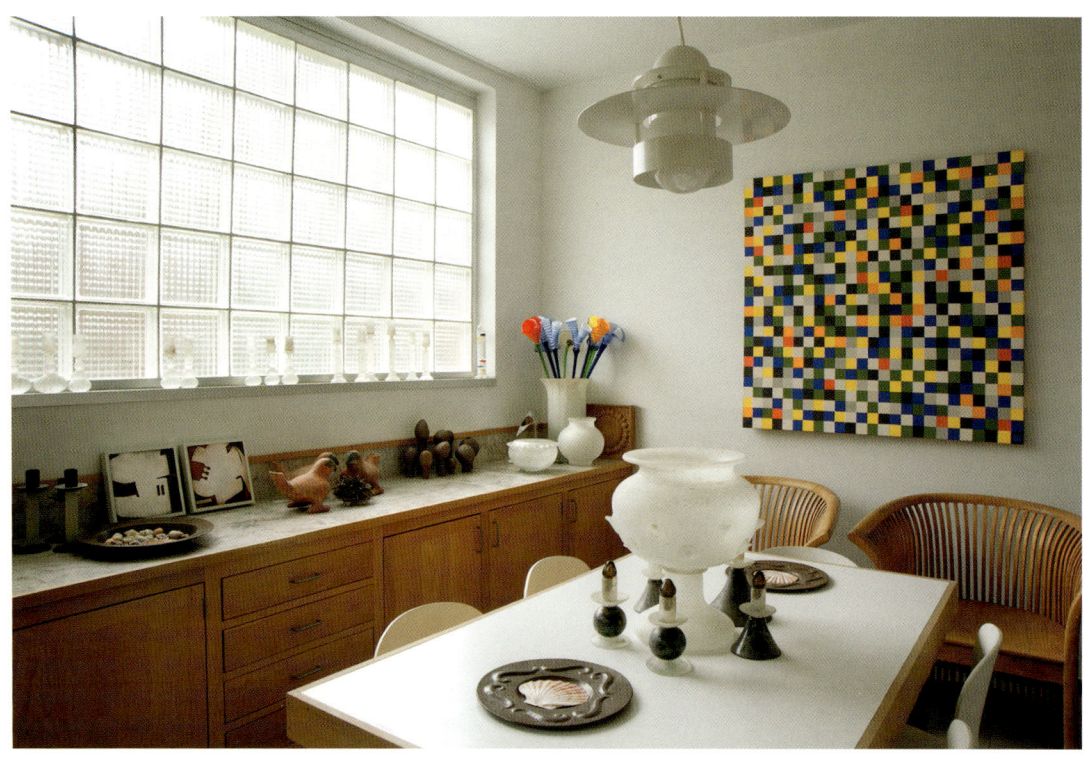

In Sanderson's office, a rare variant of Poul Henningsen's PH5 lamp (1958) hangs above a frosted glass urn by Seguso. The table is surrounded by "Ant" chairs that Arne Jacobsen first created for Novo Nordisk (1952). Behind it is Black's *Reticulation #1*, (1996, acrylic over paper on canvas, 50" x 50").

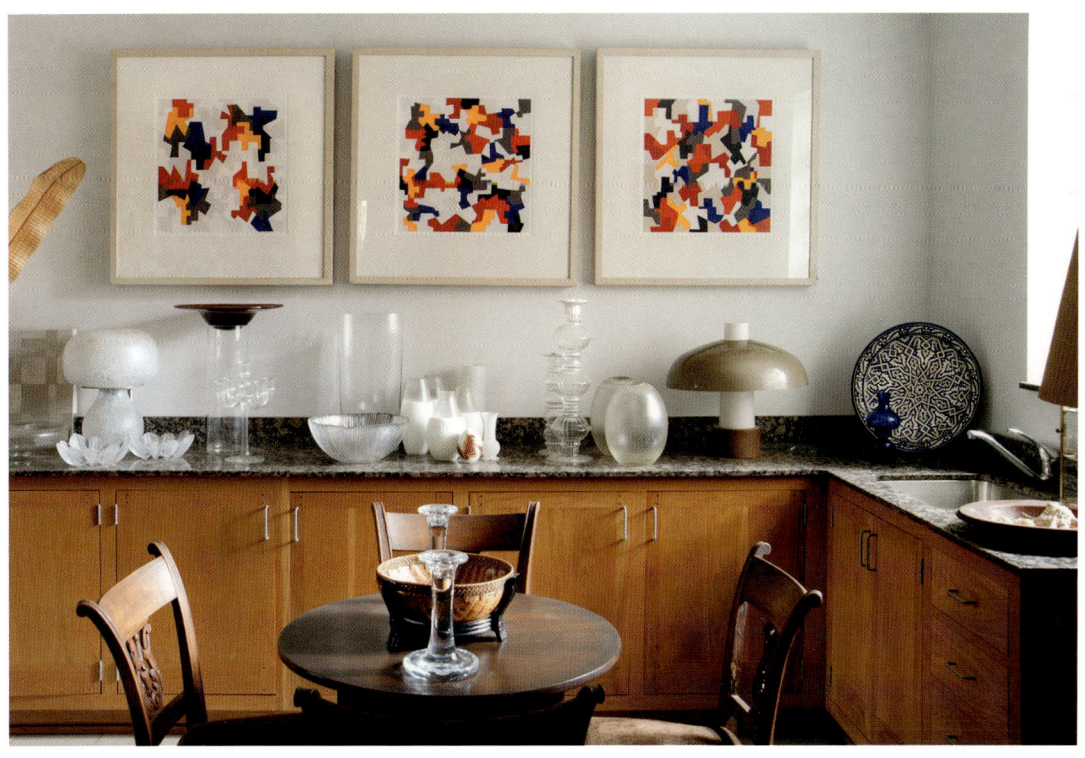

A table from Robert Black's family home is surrounded by chairs that once belonged to Ormond Sanderson's mother in a small guest apartment at one end of the house. On the counter, a glass-shaded Vistosi lamp rests below three acrylic on paper paintings from Black's 1996 *Kaleidoscope* series (each 19½" x 19½").

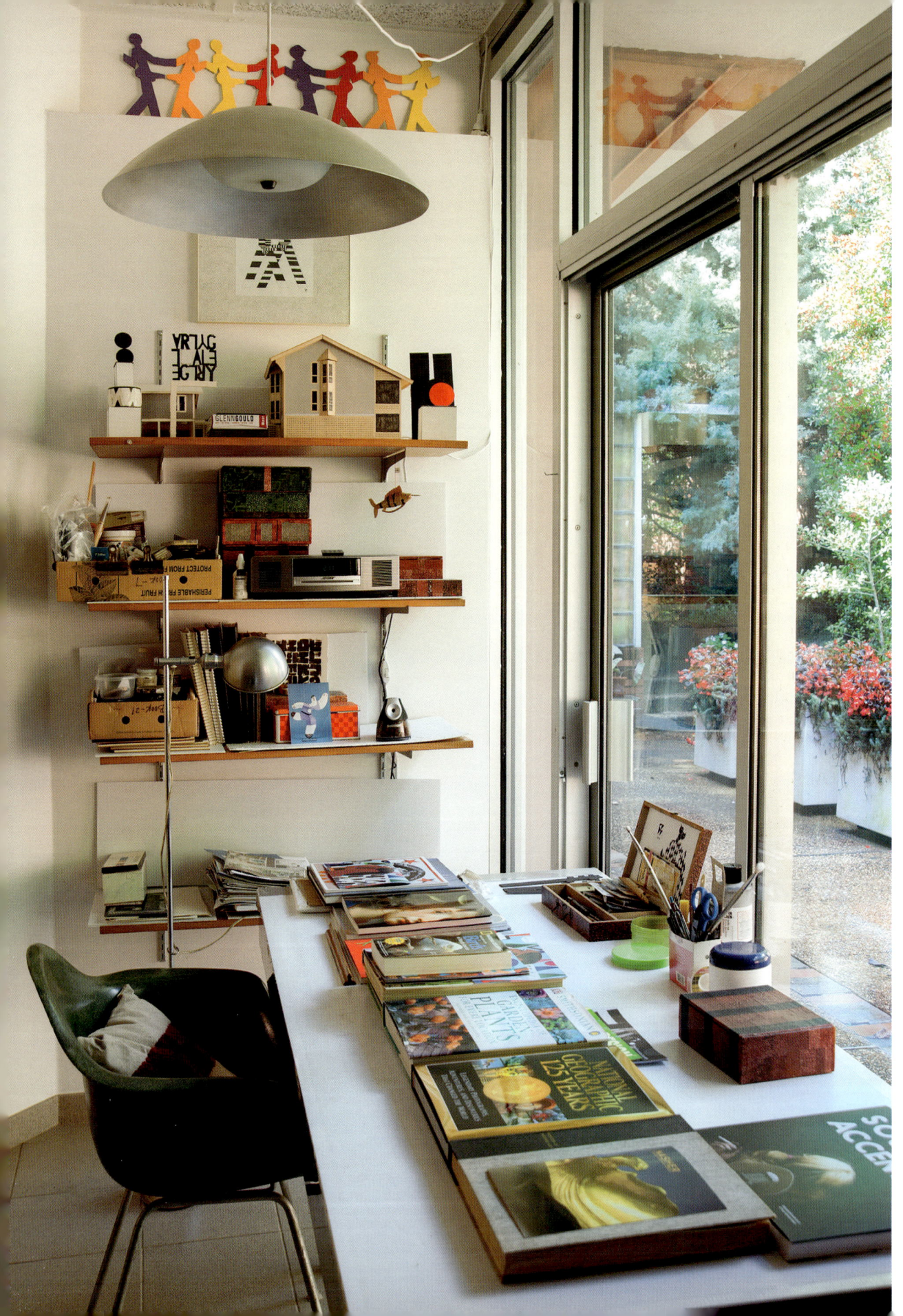

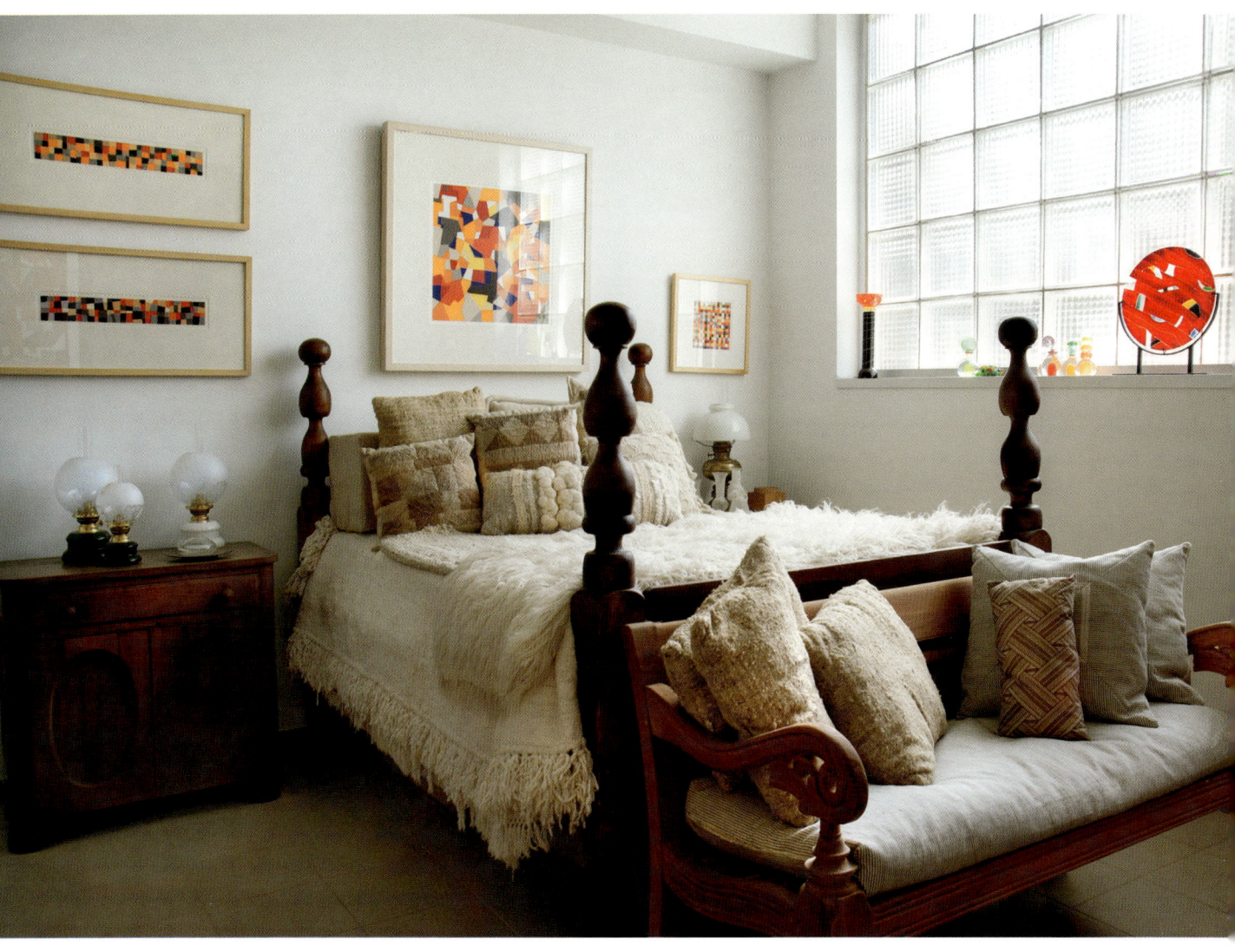

Pillows by Chapel Hill, North Carolina, textile artist Sandy Milroy cluster at the head of a guest bed covered with a Greek flokati spread. Black's 1957 panoramic paintings, *Caravan* and *Procession* (tempera on paper, each 3" x 19¼"), and *Kaleidoscope #4* (1996, acrylic over paper, 19½" x 19½") hang on the wall. Colorful Italian glass catches the sunlight shining through glass bricks.

———

(*opposite*) The study at the back of the house faces out onto the narrow third courtyard filled with Sanderson's flowers. A molded fiberglass armchair by Charles and Ray Eames (designed 1948, in production in 1951) offers a comfortable place to read or paint.

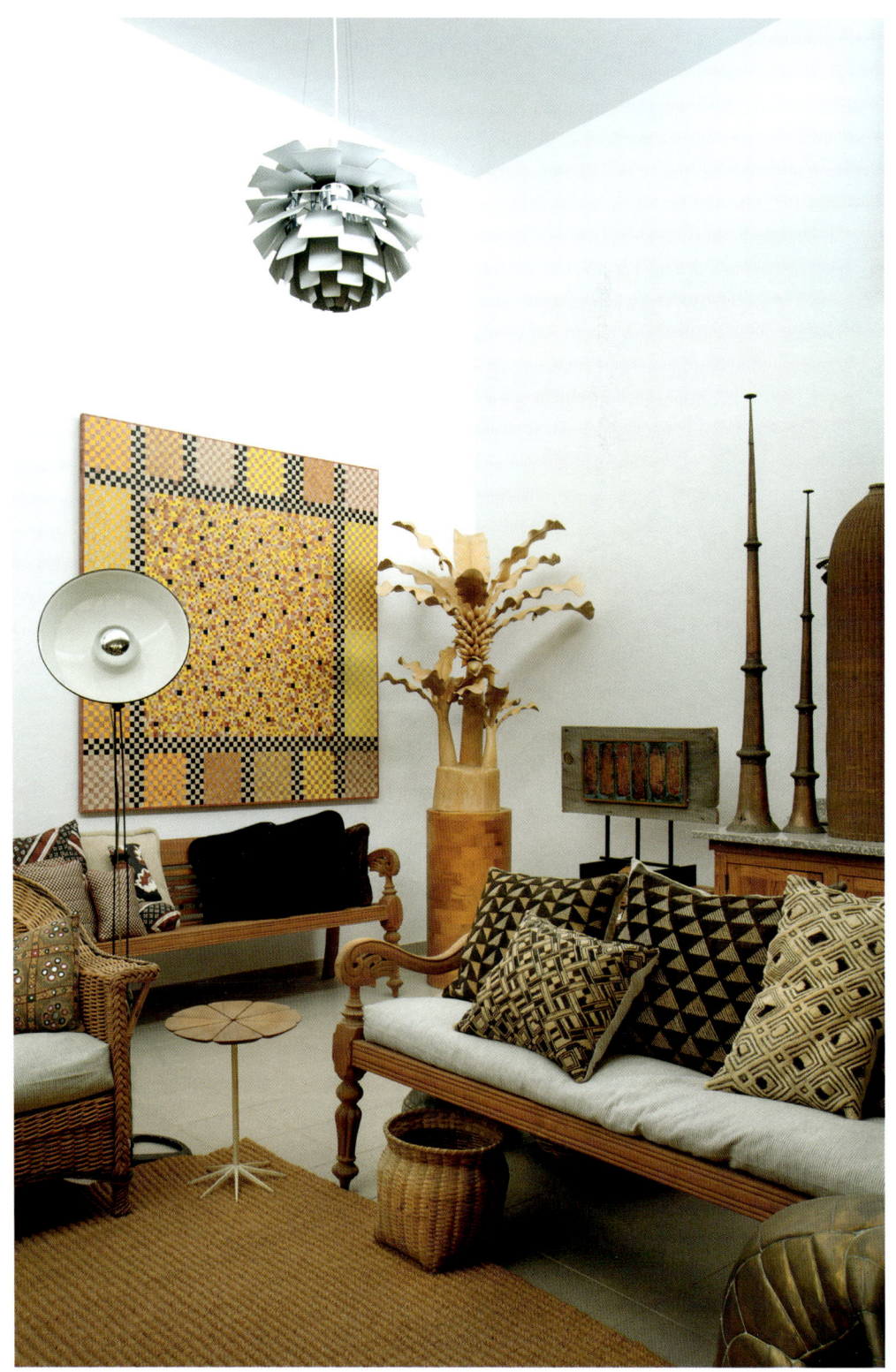

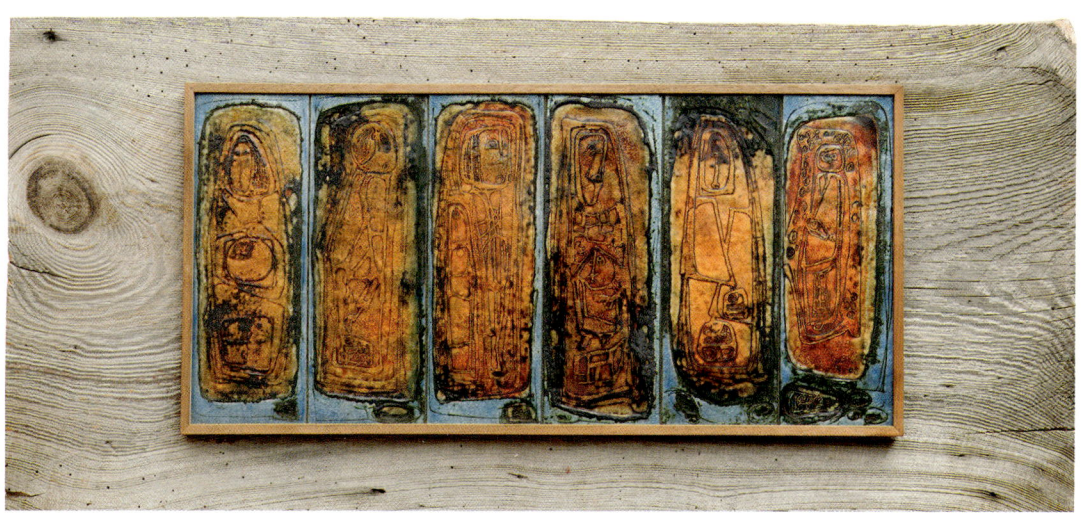

Ormond Sanderson, *The Cloister*, ca. 1960, vitreous enamels on etched copper, 17" x 37½".

———

(*opposite*) A vintage Italian floor lamp stands before Black's S*unlit Parterre* (1988, acrylic over paper on canvas, 69" x 71".) A carved wood banana plant from Indonesia occupies a corner of the former science lab, next to Sanderson's enamel panel, *The Cloister.* Tibetan horns, pillows covered with "Kuba cloth" from Zaire, and a Cherokee basket extend the warm international ambience.

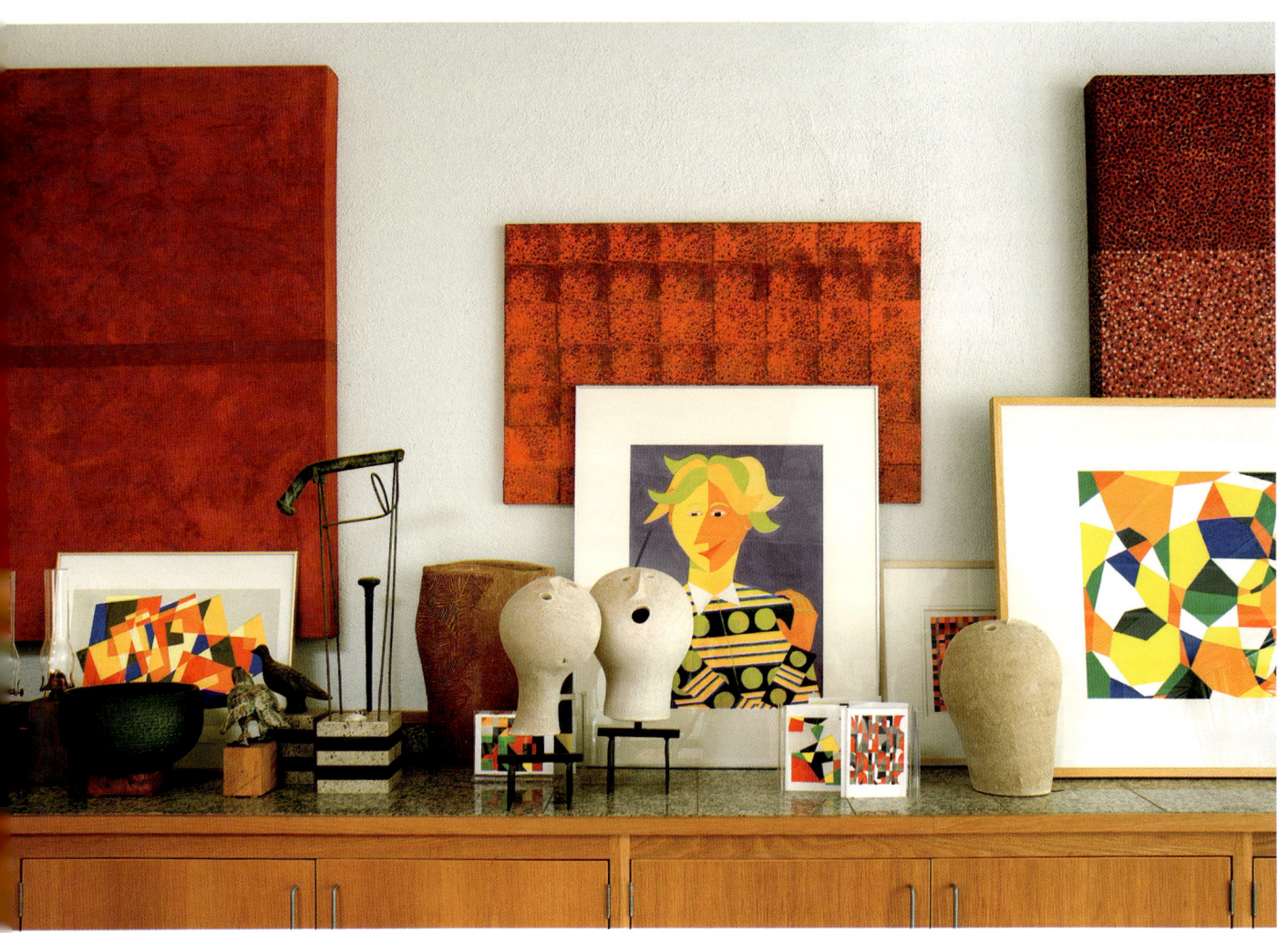

A shelf in the studio includes *Nearsighted Man*, a late-1950s wire and found object sculpture by Roy Gussow, who taught art at NC State's School of Design from 1951 to 1962. Ceramic heads are by Black and Sanderson. White-matted acrylic on paper works by Black are (left to right) *Entrechat*, *Pixie*, and *Fragment #2*. On the wall behind them are *Palimpsest Africana*, *Magma #3*, and *Mutation*, all acrylic over paper on canvas collages.

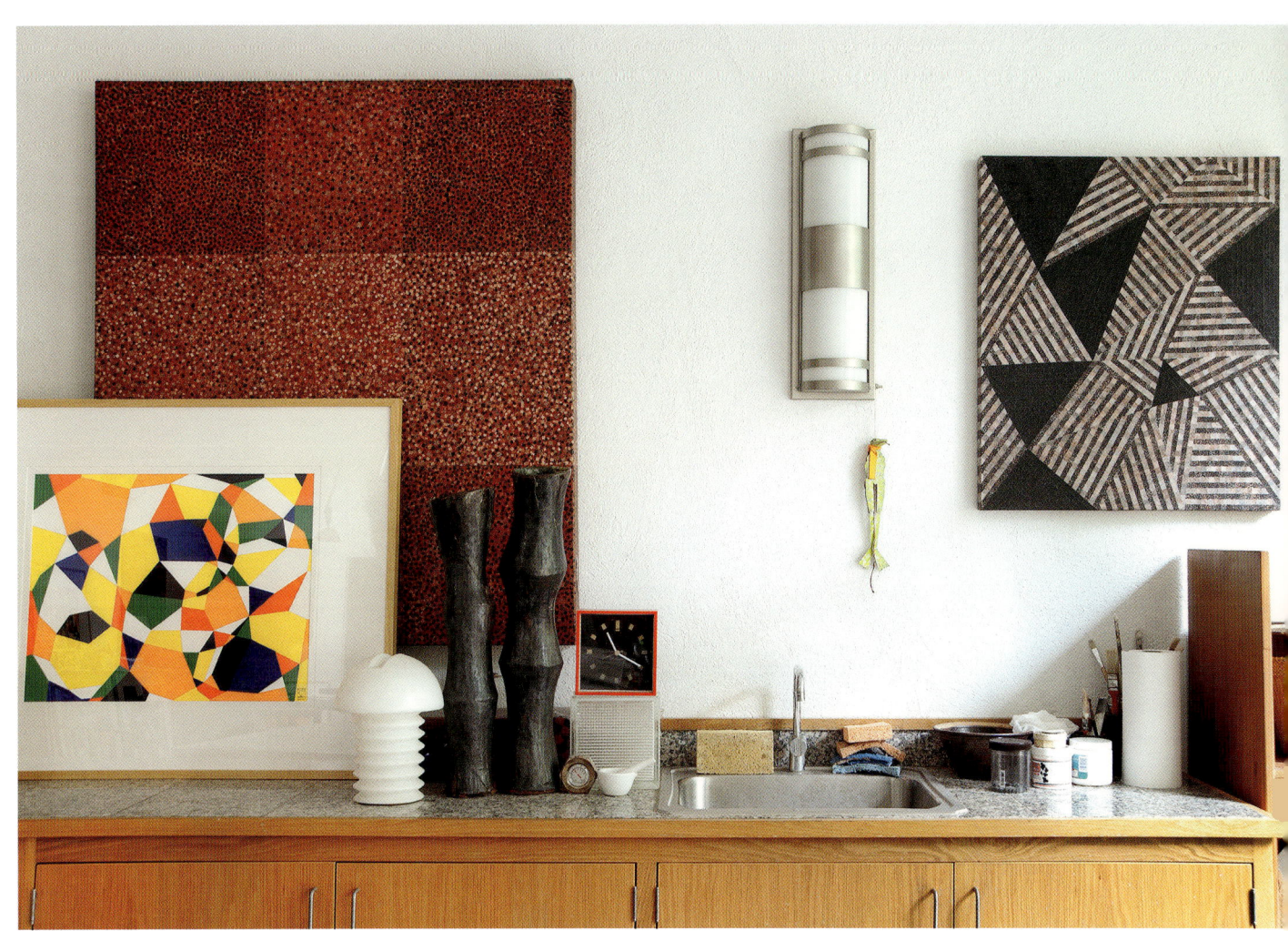

Two undulating vases by Black stand before (left to right) *Fragment #2*, *Mutation*, and *Harlequin #1*.

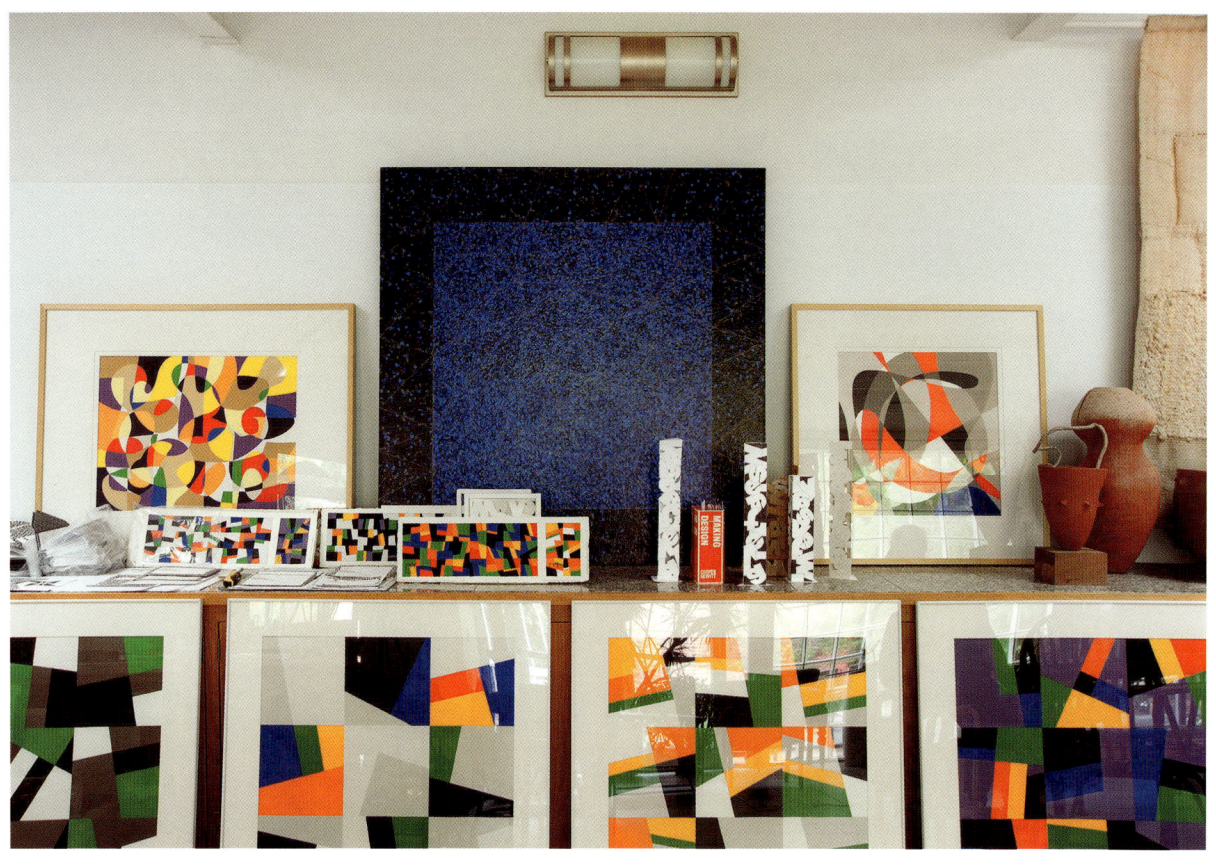

Leaning against another wall of the studio, behind some maquettes for shop signs, are Black's dark blue *Galaxy* (1985, acrylic over paper on canvas collage) flanked by *Serenissima* and *Carnival aux Wien*, both acrylics on paper. Below them are several images from his *Rhythm* series.

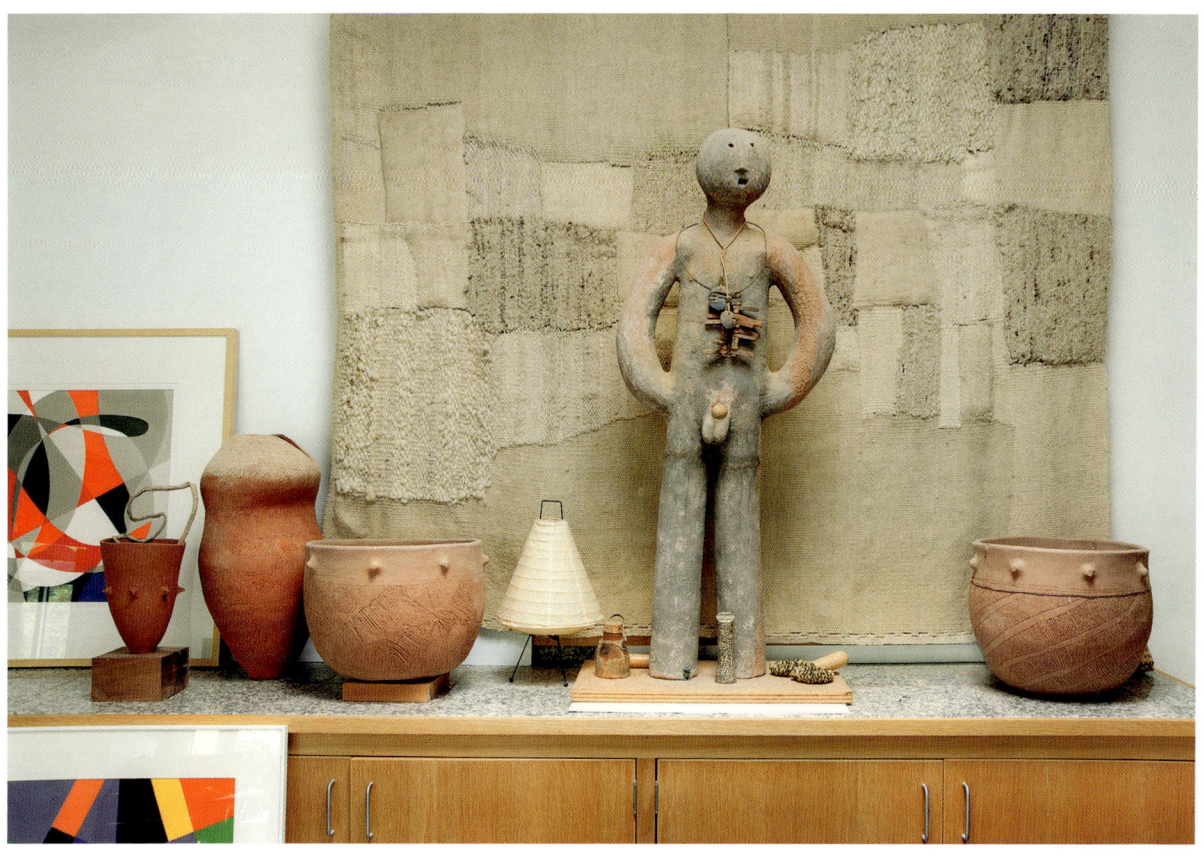

Unfired clay vessels by Black surround his *Primitive Man* sculpture (1981). A subtle tapestry by
Sandy Milroy hangs behind.

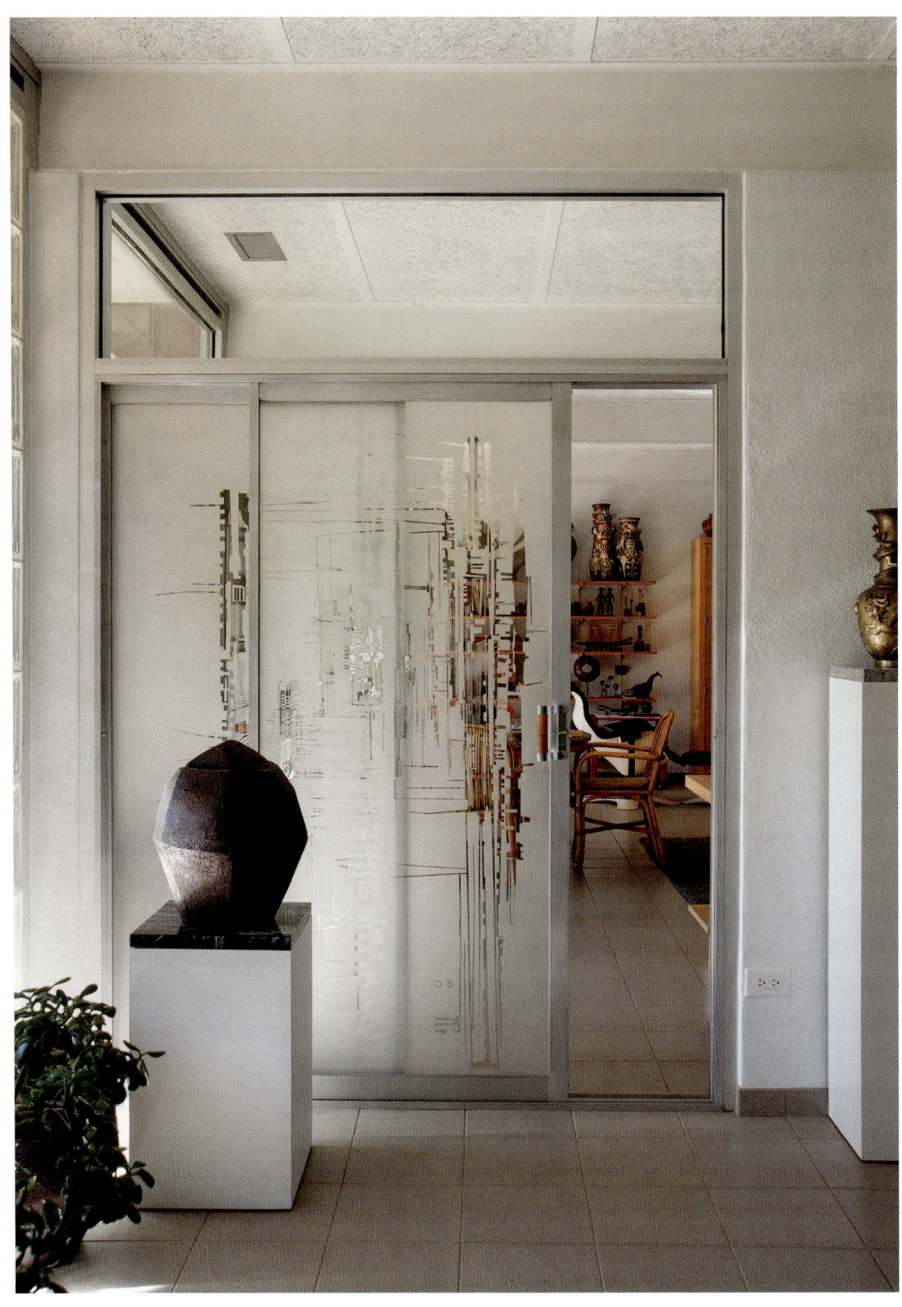

A faceted lidded vessel by Black (1970) is displayed just outside sliding kitchen doors that Sanderson ornamented with a sandblaster, using duct tape as a resist stencil.

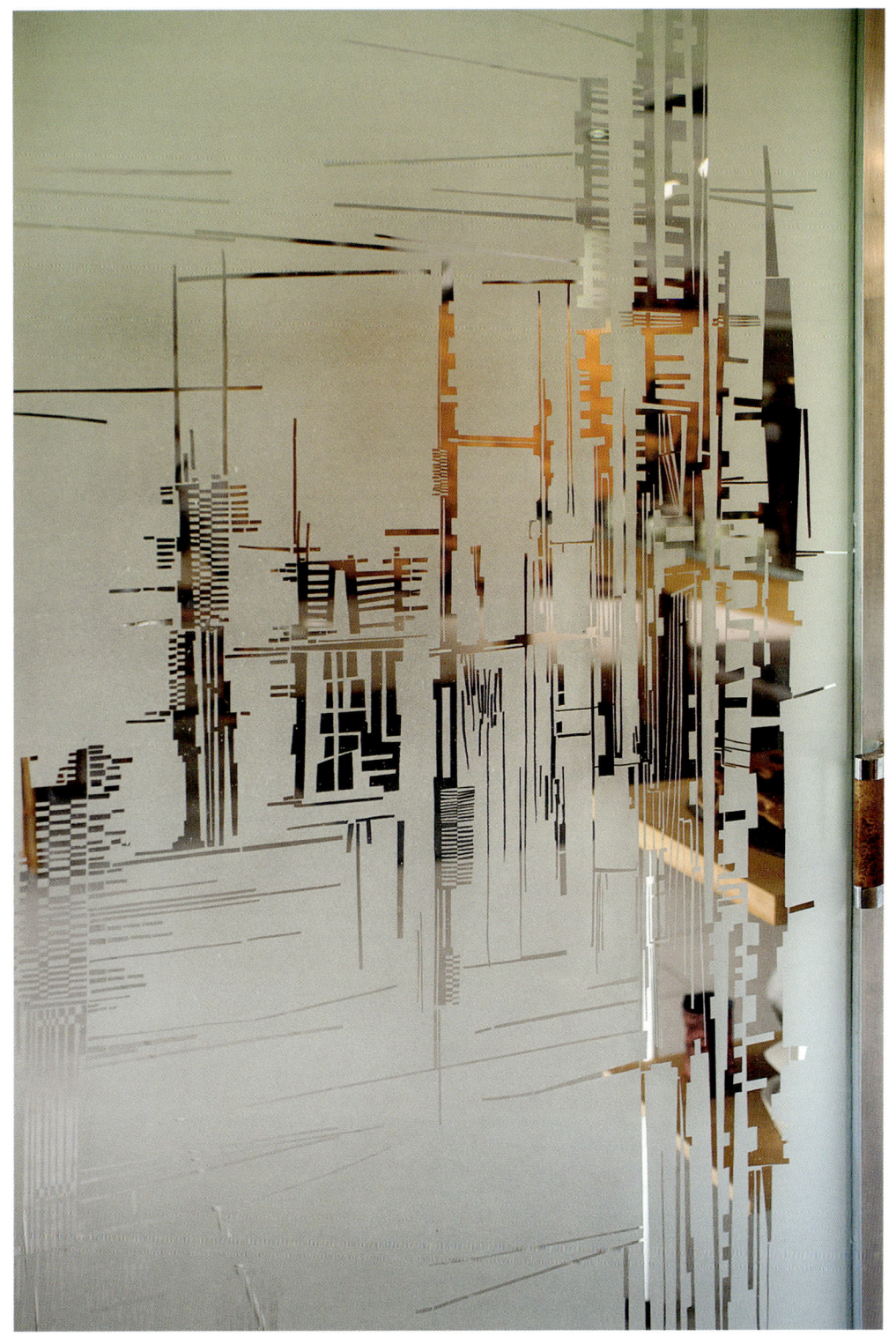

Maquettes for sculptures and signs, miniature pattern tests, and notebooks crowd shelves below a rare realist painting by Black of a house in Athens, Georgia, where he went to graduate school.

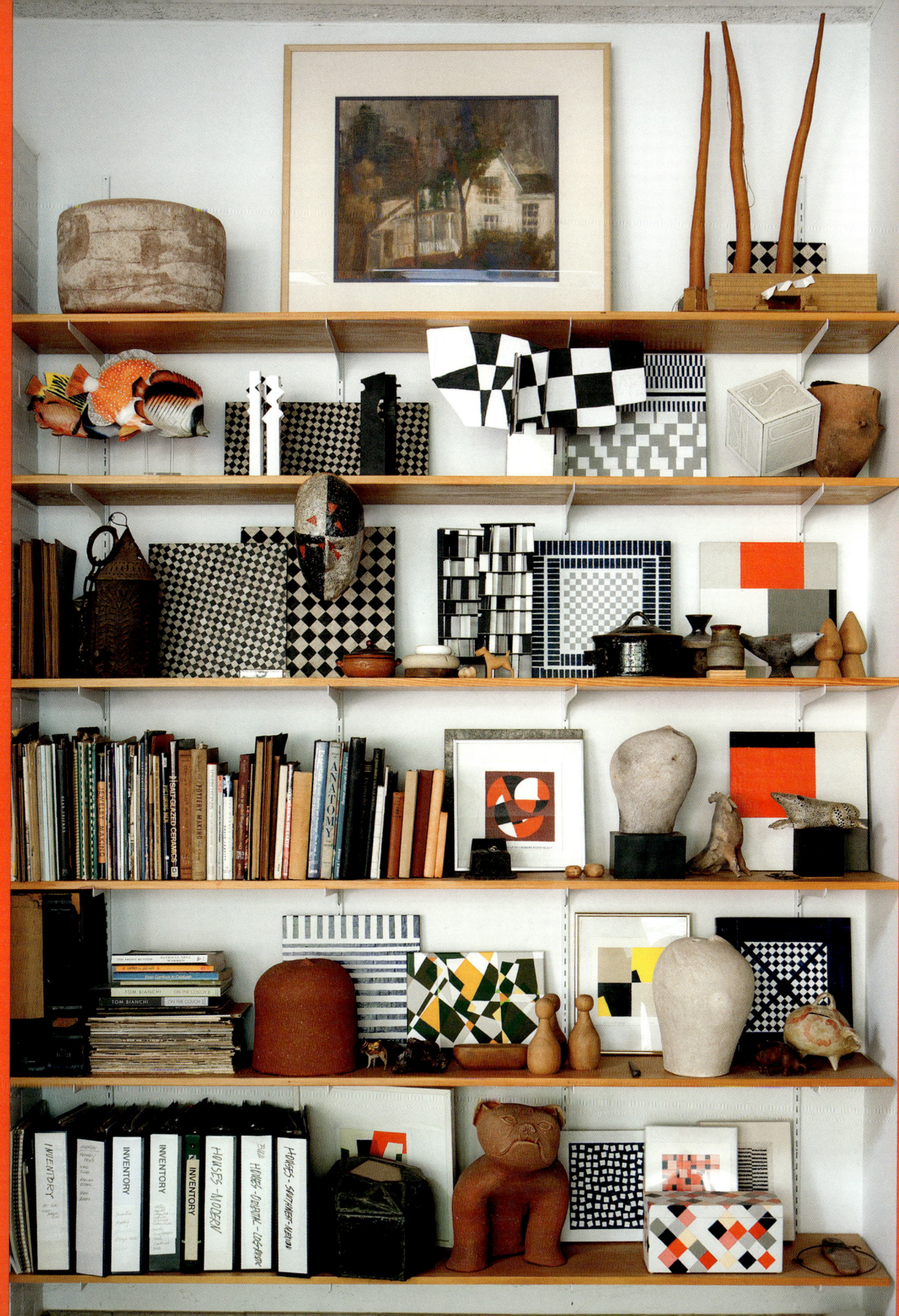

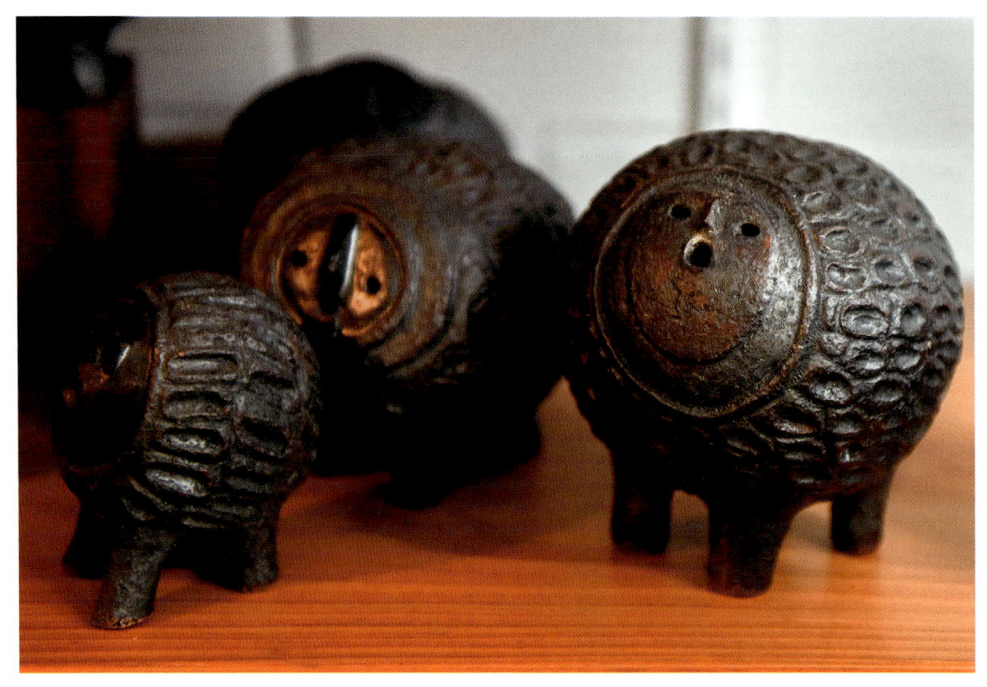

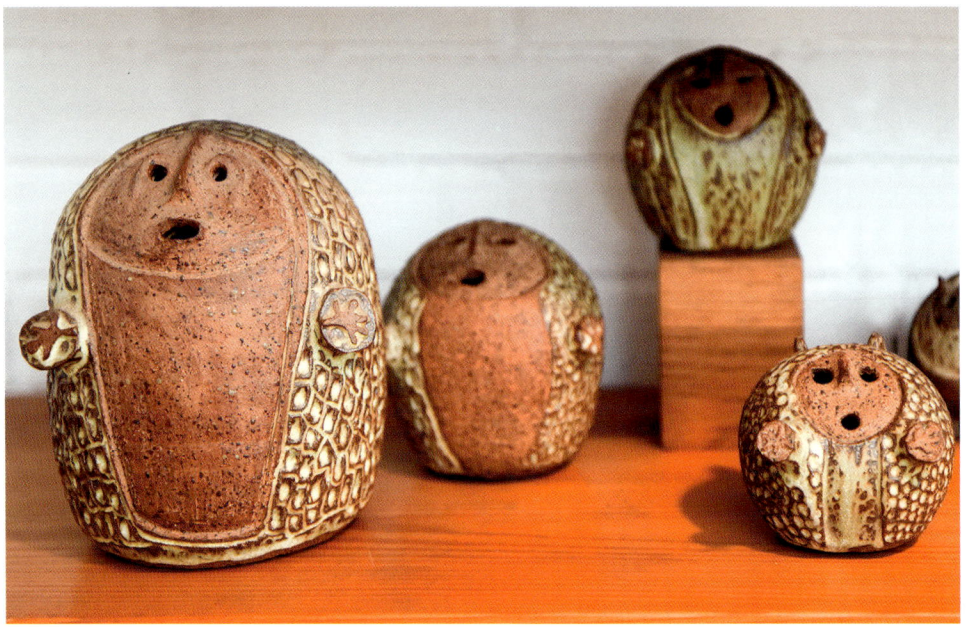

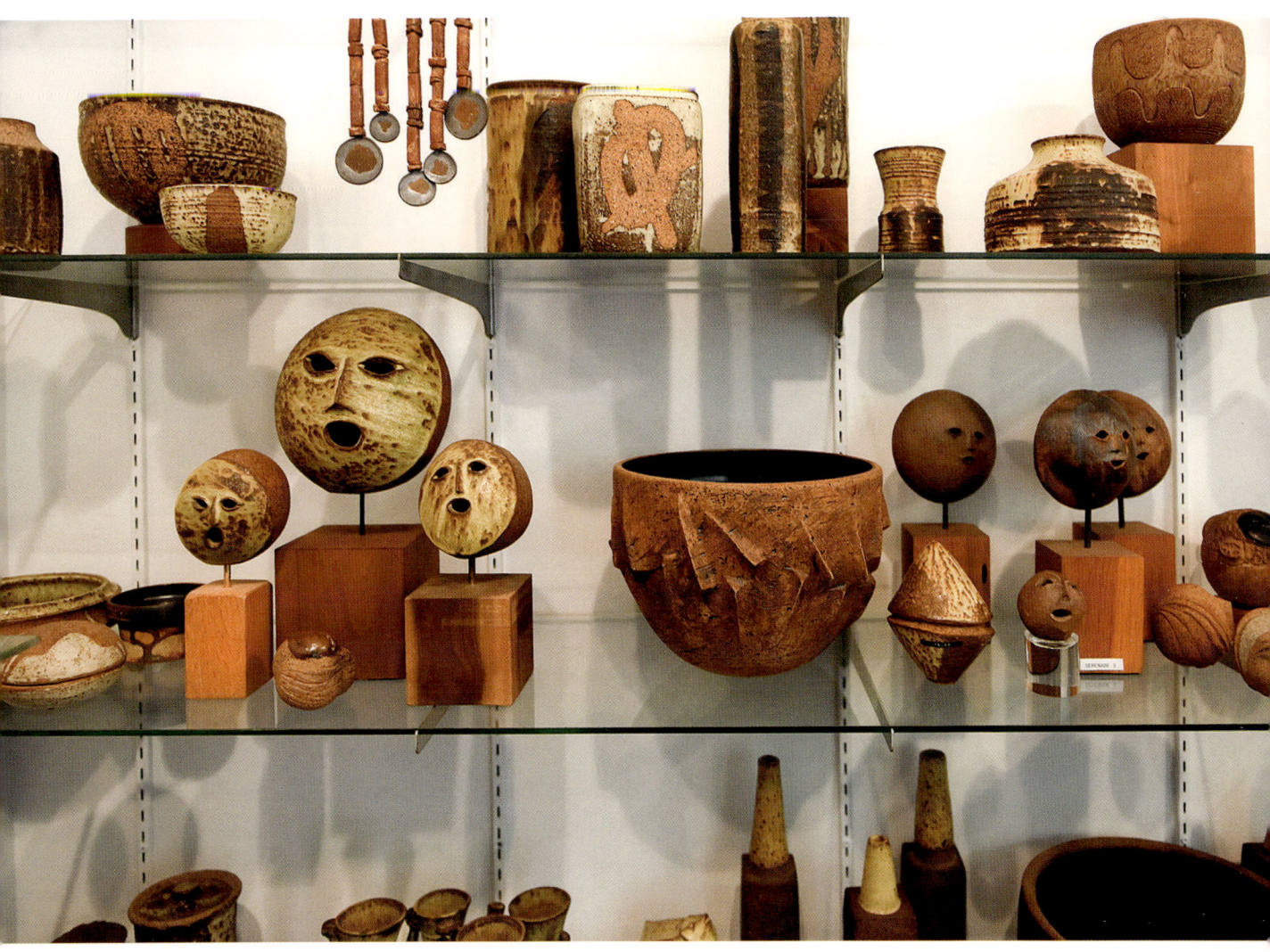

Black's stoneware heads almost seem to sing among his many vessels.

———

(opposite) Oanderson's playful ceramic animals tend to occur in distinct herds differentiated by their colors and patterns.

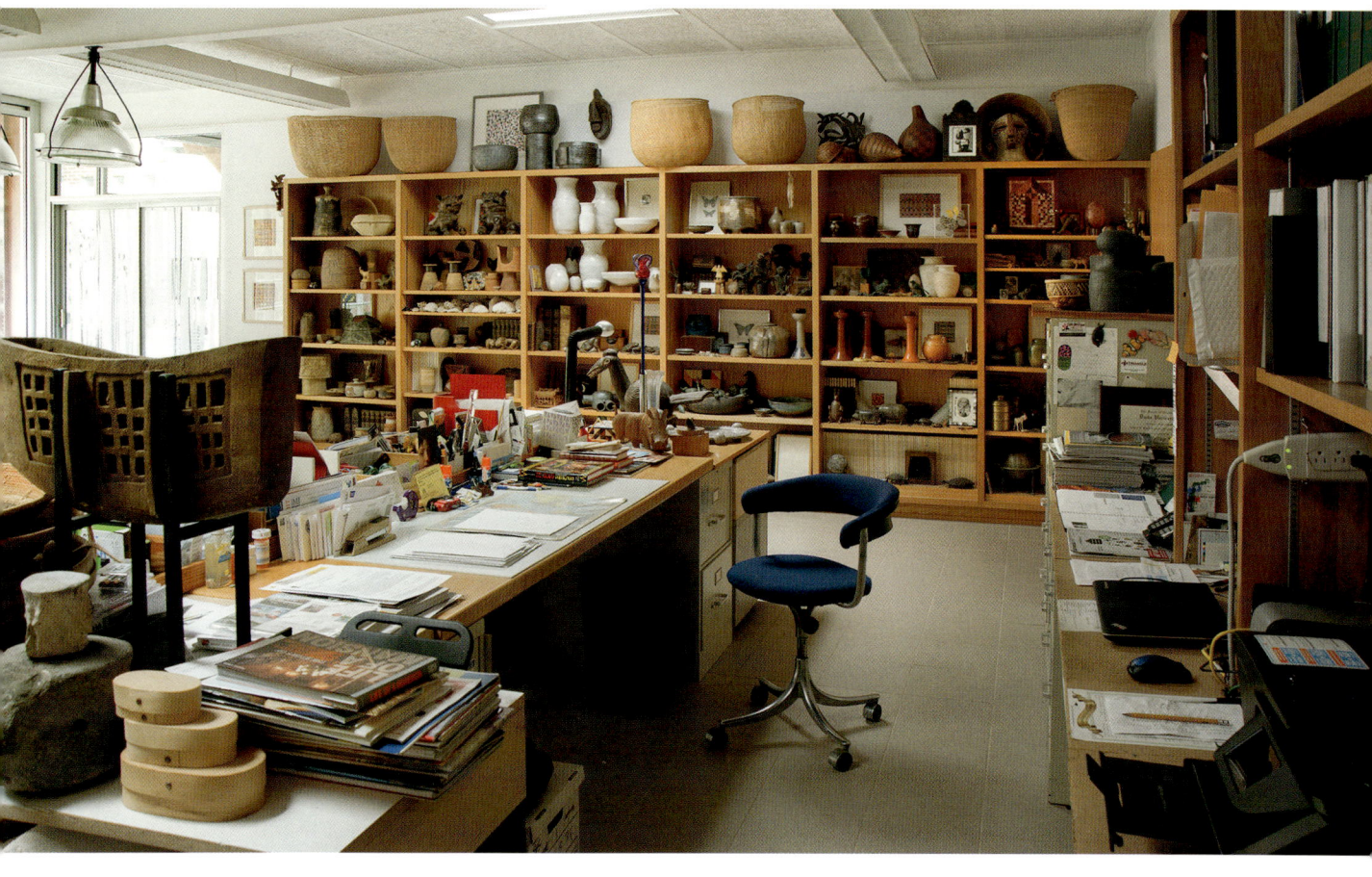

Shelves crammed with baskets, ceramics, masks, and other ethnographic artifacts line three of the four walls in the former classroom that now serves as the house office. White-glazed vessels on the far wall are part of the couple's extensive Jugtown Pottery collection.

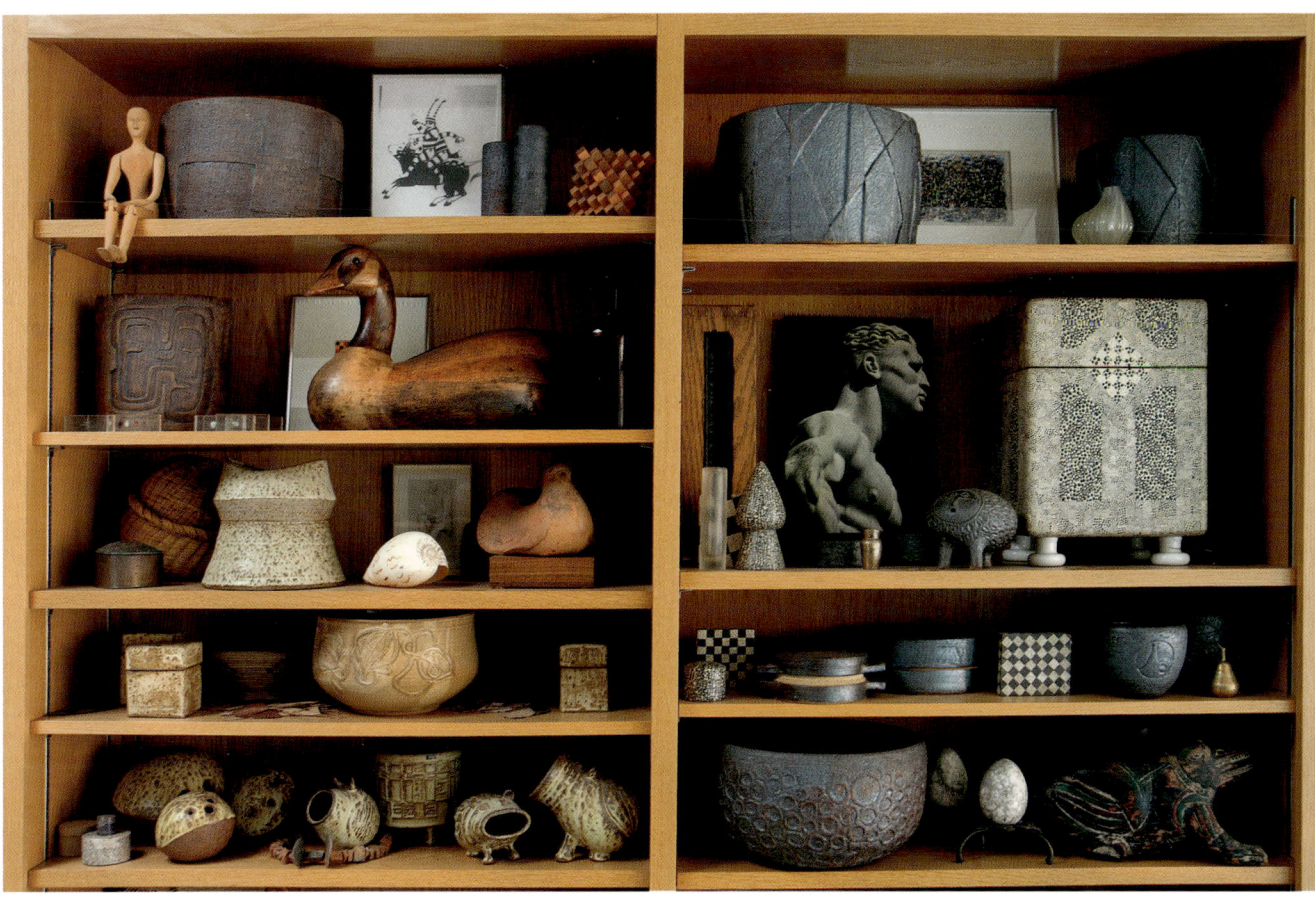

Black and Sanderson often collaborated on ceramics, with Black creating the basic forms and Sanderson then carving surface patterns and decorative details into the unfired clay.

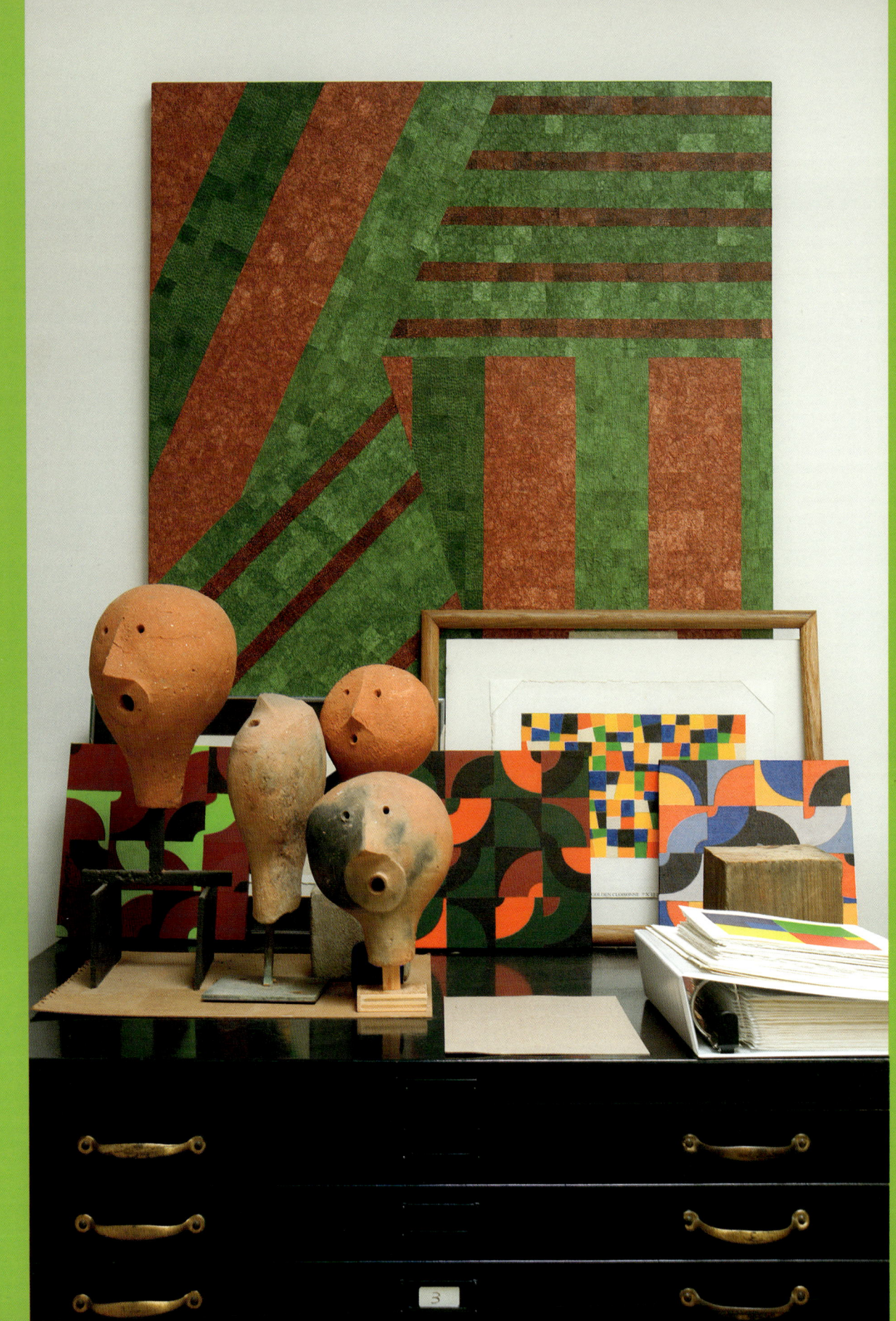

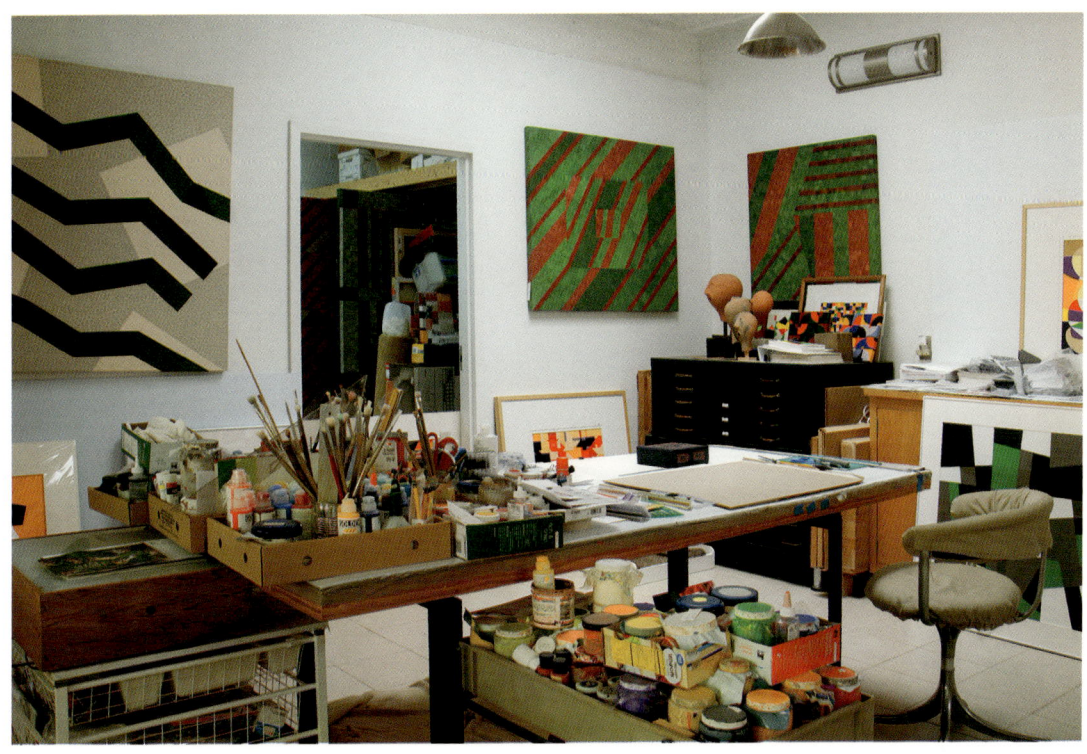

Skylights let natural light into the painting studio, where *Momentum #2*, *Pulsation*, and *Oblique* (all 1985) hang near a doorway into the painting storage room.

———

(*opposite*) On top of a flat file, several of Black's ceramic heads seem to be whistling in front of his acrylic over paper on canvas collage, *Oblique* (1985, 34½" x 34½").

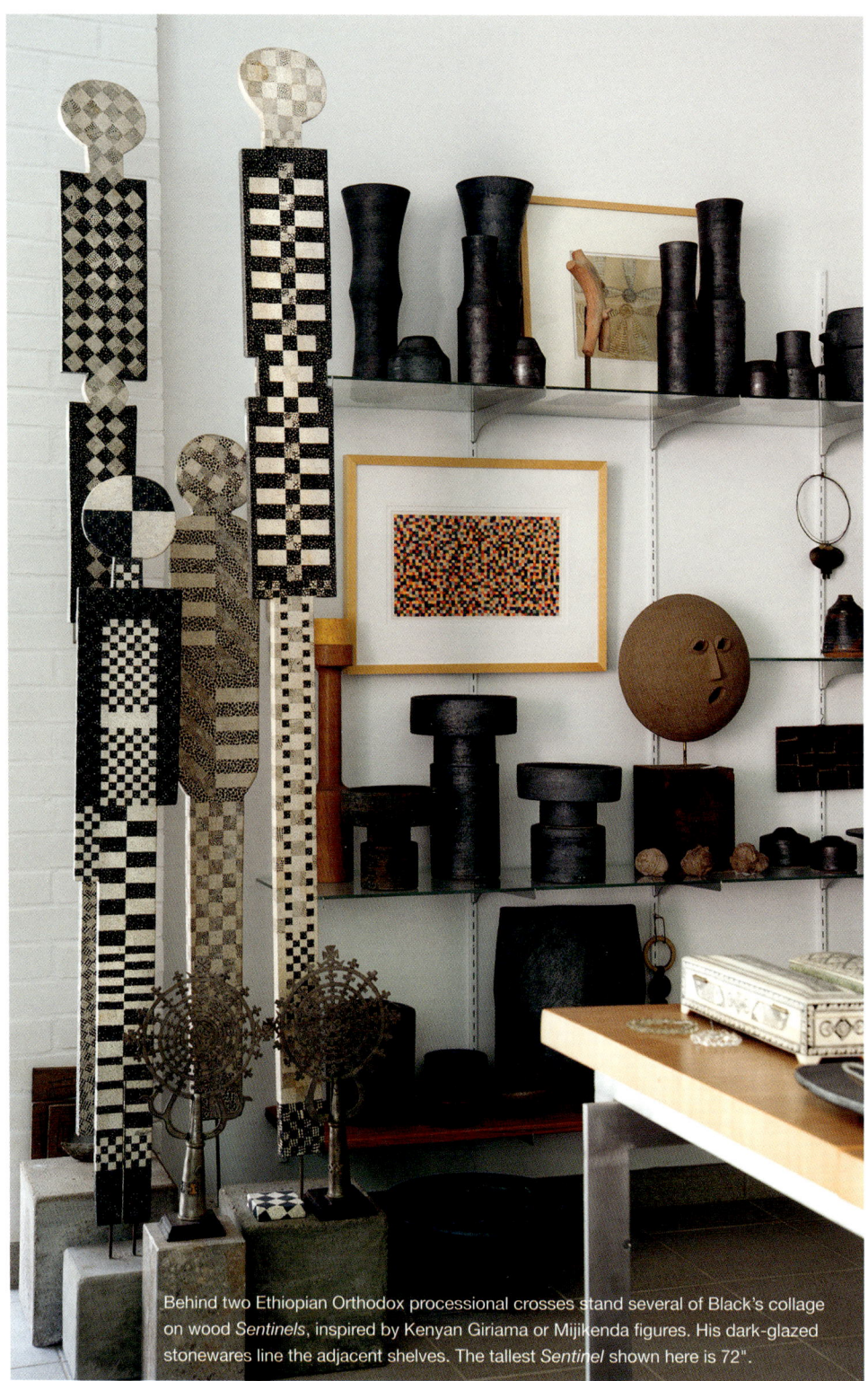

Behind two Ethiopian Orthodox processional crosses stand several of Black's collage on wood *Sentinels*, inspired by Kenyan Giriama or Mijikenda figures. His dark-glazed stonewares line the adjacent shelves. The tallest *Sentinel* shown here is 72".

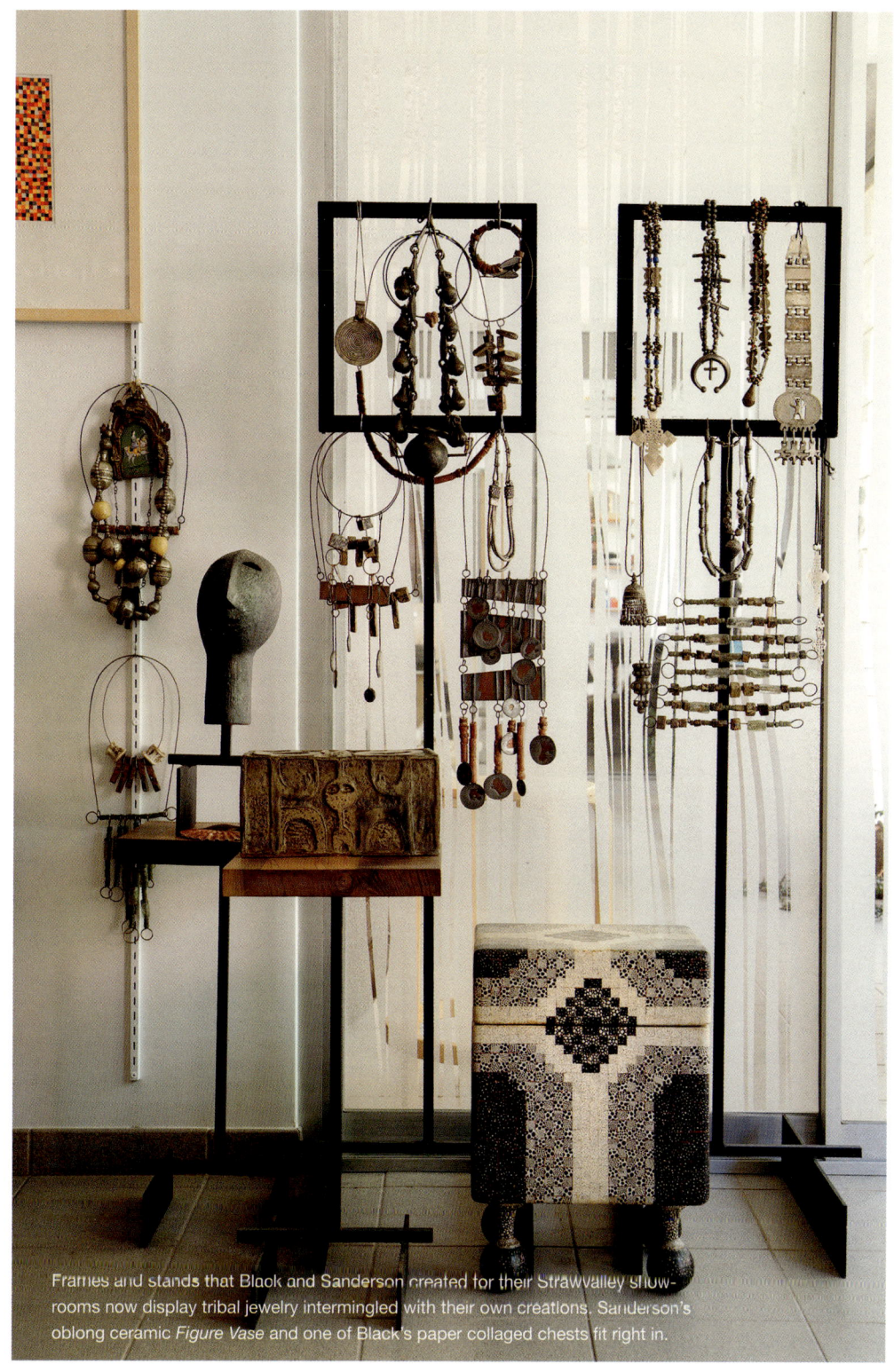

Frames and stands that Black and Sanderson created for their Strawvalley show-rooms now display tribal jewelry intermingled with their own creations. Sanderson's oblong ceramic *Figure Vase* and one of Black's paper collaged chests fit right in.

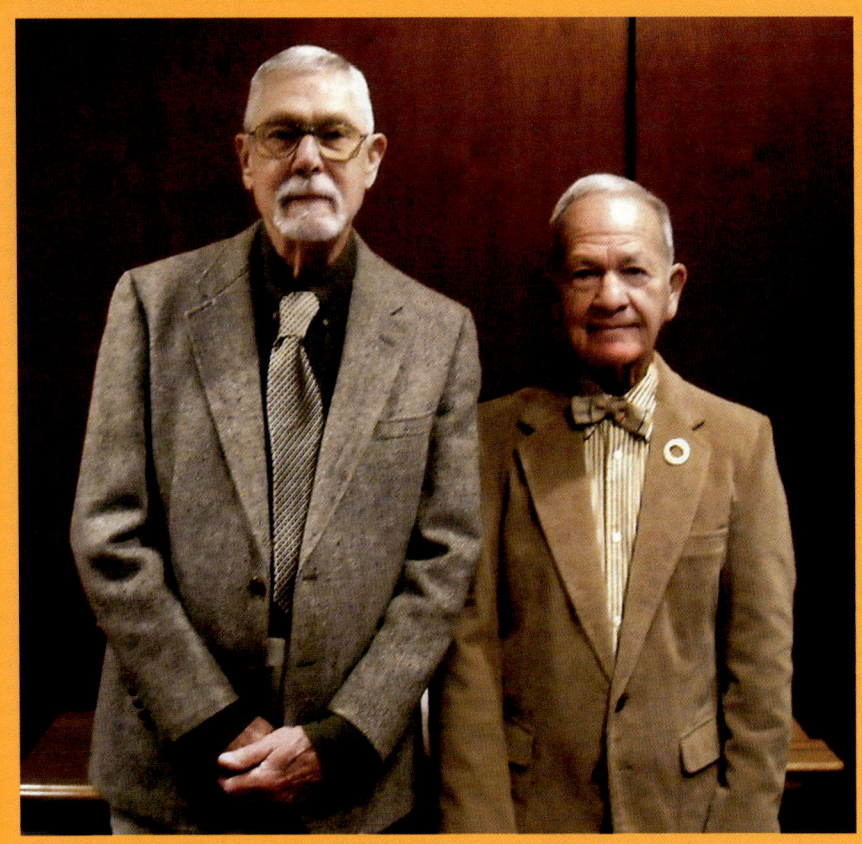

Black and Sanderson on their wedding day in Rockville, Maryland, November 5, 2013.

Curriculum Vitae of the Artists

Robert Keith Black

(b. 1929, Wake Forest NC)

American Craftsmen's Council annual exhibition, 1963.

North Carolina Museum of Art, 26th Annual Arts Association Show, 1963.

Rich's Gallery, Atlanta, "Designer-Craftsmen of Southern Appalachians" exhibition, 1964.

Mint Museum of Art, Charlotte NC, 1964.

Syracuse (NY) Pottery Annual, 1965.

Piedmont Crafts Fair, Winston-Salem, NC, 1965, featured artist-demonstrator.

North Carolina Museum of Art, "Craftsmen Southeast" exhibition, 1966.

North Carolina Museum of Art, "North Carolina Craftsmen" exhibition, 1971. Stoneware jar awarded Best of Show and Purchase Award; tall stoneware vase awarded Honorable Mention.

Lee Hansley Gallery, Raleigh, 1998.

Gallery of Art & Design, NC State University, "20/20 Visions" exhibition, 2004. *Stoneware Globe*, *Tripod Figural Vase* and two smaller stoneware vases purchased for permanent collection.

J. Ormond Sanderson, Jr.

(b. 1928, Raleigh NC)

Everson Museum of Art, Syracuse NY, 1962. Awarded Thomas C. Thompson prize for enamels: *Forest*.

Atlanta Art Association, "Craftsmen of Southeastern States" exhibition, 1963. Award winner for *Sunseed and Galls*, *Martyr*, *The Cell*.

Mint Museum of Art, Charlotte NC, 1964. Best in Show for *Madrigal*, *Cells*, *Microcosmos*.

Rich's Gallery, Atlanta, "Designer-Craftsmen of Southern Appalachians" exhibition, 1964.

Everson Museum of Art, Syracuse NY, 1964.

American Pavilion, Worlds Fair, Queens, New York, 1964. Featured artist.

North Carolina Museum of Art, "Craftsmen Southeast" exhibition, 1966. National Merit Award for *Sunbird*.

Smithsonian Institution, Washington, "Objects: USA" exhibition, 1969. Featured in book by Lee Nordness by the same title.

Scripps College Invitational, San Francisco, 1970.

North Carolina Museum of Art, "North Carolina Craftsmen" exhibition, 1971.

Gallery of Art & Design, NC State University, "20/20 Visions" exhibition, 2004.

Enamel boxes by Sanderson were given by the American Craftsmen's Council to founder Aileen Osborn Webb (Mrs. Vanderbilt Webb), and by the North Carolina Arts Council to Princess Grace of Monaco.

TOM PATTERSON began writing about contemporary art in the early 1980s for *Art Papers* and *Brown's Guide to Georgia*, and his essays and exhibition reviews have subsequently appeared in *afterimage*, *American Ceramics*, *American Craft*, *Aperture*, *ARTnews*, *BOMB*, *Folk Art*, the *Charlotte Observer* and *Winston-Salem Journal*. He has served as editor of *Arts Journal* and *ARTVU*, US editor of *Raw Vision* (the international journal of outsider art) and as executive director of the Jargon Society, an independent publishing house founded by poet Jonathan Williams. Patterson's books include *Contemporary Folk Art: Treasures from the Smithsonian American Art Museum*, *Howard Finster: Stranger from Another World*, and *St. EOM in The Land of Pasaquan*, recently reissued by University of Georgia Press. He has curated exhibitions for the American Visionary Art Museum, the Terra Museum of American Art, the Southeastern Center for Contemporary Art, Virginia Commonwealth University's Anderson Gallery, the Halsey Institute for Contemporary Art, the Center on Contemporary Art (Seattle) and the Gregg Museum of Art & Design. He lives in Winston-Salem, North Carolina.

JOHN MARK HALL grew up in eastern North Carolina, earned a degree in architecture at NC State, and attended the North Carolina School of the Arts. A scholarship to the American Ballet Theater brought him to New York City, where he trained in ballet and worked for architect Paul Rudolph before moving to Europe to work as a fashion model and pursue photography. His photographs have been featured in *The New York Times*, *The Wall Street Journal*, *Architectural Digest*, *Elle Décor*, and *Veranda*, while his books include *Biedermeier*, *Greek Revival America*, *Private Gardens of Connecticut*, *Gardens in the Spirit of Place*, *Living with Art*, *Fresh Cuts*, *Adventures with Old Houses,* and *Sacred Spaces: The Home of Anne Spencer*. His photographs are in the collections of the Metropolitan Museum of Art, the Parrish Museum, and the Cleveland Museum of Art, as well as numerous private and corporate collections.

ROGER MANLEY has served as director and curator of NC State's Gregg Museum of Art & Design since 2010. Before that, he worked as a folklorist, writer, photographer, and filmmaker. His photographs are in more than two dozen corporate and institutional collections, including the Amon Carter and High Museums, the Library of Congress, National Portrait Gallery, Pitt-Rivers Collection, and Princeton University, while his books range from *Home Made* (with text by Reynolds Price), *Plankhouse* (with text by

North Carolina Poet Laureate Shelby Stephenson), and *The End is Near!* (with texts by Steven Jay Gould and the Dalai Lama), to *Signs and Wonders: Outsider Art Inside North Carolina*, *Self-Made Worlds*, and several books in the *Weird US* series.

BECKY KIRKLAND, NC State University Communications photographer, took the images that appear on pages 47, 73, 78, 79, 101, 104, and 105.

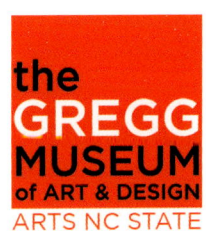
the
**GREGG
MUSEUM
of ART & DESIGN**
ARTS NC STATE

The Gregg Museum of Art & Design is the collecting art museum of North Carolina State University, and one of six arts programs that together comprise Arts NC State. Each year the museum presents a series of changing exhibitions of the finest regional, national, and international visual arts in its galleries, accompanied by relevant programs that are open to the public. The Gregg's holdings reflect the curricula of the university's many colleges, and are as diverse as the course offerings. Providing materials for teaching, study, and research, the objects suggest opportunities for inspiring new and innovative designs, and help explain the art-making process. The Gregg is a place where objects spark ideas.

MISSION STATEMENT

As part of a research-extensive land-grant university, the Gregg Museum of Art & Design inspires creativity, innovation, and the expression of ideas. The Gregg Museum makes its collections and activities freely accessible to the university, the community, and the public. In fulfilling its mission, the Gregg Museum

- Acquires and preserves a collection of art, craft, and design relevant to the university, the community, and the state;
- Encourages the use of the collection for teaching, learning, research, and enjoyment;
- Illuminates the human experience through thought-provoking exhibitions and publications; and
- Facilitates critical and creative thinking, lifelong learning, and a passion for discovery through instruction and programs.

MUSEUM STAFF

Jordan Brothers Cao, *assistant registrar*
Mona Fitzpatrick, *associate director of arts development*
Matt Gay, *art preparator*
Mary Hauser, *registrar and associate director*
Janine LeBlanc, *collections assistant*
Hilary Leggette, *museum operations manager*
Roger Manley, *director*
Jeannifer Sandoval, *visitor services and security coordinator*
Zoe Starling, *curator of education*
Tamar Harris Warren, *events and facilities coordinator*

FRIENDS OF THE GREGG BOARD
2017–2018

Shawn Brewster, *President*
Linda Dallas
Jaye Day-Trotter
Dan Ellison, *Past President*
Anna Ball Hodge
Bernard J. Hyman
Justin LeBlanc
John Millhauser
Anne Pace
Charles Phaneuf, *Secretary/Treasurer*
Dana Raymond
Kathleen Rieder
Angela Salamanca
Roby Sawyers
George Wallace
Grace Li Wang
Susan Woodson